Praise for Charles Carrin's
Spirit-Empowered Theology

"An amazing book that can be used as a Protestant catechism and teaching instrument regarding the Christian faith. It contains a vast amount of knowledge that is needed by contemporary Christians. I especially recommend it to those who are beginning their journey into the theological realm of 'Word and Spirit' truth. This book belongs in your library."

Randy Clark, D.Min., Th.D., overseer, Apostolic Network of Global Awakening; founder, Global Awakening; author, *There Is More!*, *The Healing Breakthrough* and more

"Millions of people today are searching for a reliable voice of authority. Papa Charles Carrin has provided us with a foundation of what we need to know in order to live a supernatural life in a natural way. *Spirit-Empowered Theology* is the inheritance given to all of us who long to live a life that honors the past in order to bring heaven to earth. This book is a treasure trove, allowing access to wisdom for anyone who wants to burn brightly without burning out. I consider it an honor to have been invited to review and comment on such an inspired life work. I encourage you to read it and receive new levels of power, love and wisdom for a supernatural lifestyle!"

Leif Hetland, founder and president, Global Mission Awareness; author, *Seeing Through Heaven's Eyes* and *Healing the Orphan Spirit*

"Theology, however good and sound it is, is lifeless unless it is Spirit-empowered. In his book *Spirit-Empowered Theology*, Pastor Charles Carrin sets forth in three hundred questions not only sound, but empowered theology—that is, both biblically sound doctrine as well as an overview of Christian history, thereby empowering readers to better understand both their identity in Christ and their rich Christian heritage. A perusal of the book, obviously, will greatly reward its reader with a wealth of knowledge."

Michael Peterson, ordained Pentecostal pastor; lifelong Bible researcher; former administrator, School of Social Work, University of Pittsburgh

"*Spirit-Empowered Theology* is a valuable treatise that helps all of us to more clearly understand the value and power of our faith in these tumultuous times."

R. A. Beisner, pastor, The Father's Paradigm Ministry, Hyde Park, New York; retired justice, New York State Supreme Court

"Charles Carrin is a prince of preachers, a sound theologian and an absolute lover and practitioner of the presence and power of the Holy Spirit. In *Spirit-Empowered Theology*, Charles has undertaken perhaps the most comprehensive work of his life. He leaves us with a treasure trove of pertinent questions and answers that are the product of his many years of ministry experience and study. All have been reviewed, edited and annotated by a distinguished group of present-day revival leaders who likewise have many years of study and practical experience. This book is a golden resource, now available to up-and-coming leaders who will be needing answers regarding issues, situations and circumstances arising from the soon-coming mighty wave of revival that is about to break upon the entire globe."

John and Carol Arnott, founding pastors, Catch the Fire Ministries; overseers, Partners in Harvest, Toronto, Canada

"The immense wisdom of a life lived passionately pursuing God and His Kingdom resonates throughout this book. These are questions we wrestle with, and I don't personally know of many who are as theologically and experientially qualified as Charles Carrin to biblically answer them."

David McQueen, lead pastor, Beltway Park Church, Abilene, Texas

SPIRIT-
EMPOWERED
THEOLOGY

SPIRIT-EMPOWERED THEOLOGY

· A CONCISE ONE-VOLUME GUIDE ·

Charles Carrin

Chosen

a division of Baker Publishing Group
Minneapolis, Minnesota

© 2017 by Charles Carrin

Published by Chosen Books
11400 Hampshire Avenue South
Bloomington, Minnesota 55438
www.chosenbooks.com

Chosen Books is a division of
Baker Publishing Group, Grand Rapids, Michigan

Printed in the United States of America

Library of Congress Cataloging-in-Publication Data is on file at the Library of Congress, Washington, DC.

ISBN 978-0-8007-9817-8

Cover design by Darren Welch Design

17 18 19 20 21 22 23   7 6 5 4 3 2 1

Death and condemnation to a church that is not yearning after the Spirit, crying and groaning until the Spirit has wrought mightily in her midst. He is here! He has never gone back since He descended at Pentecost. . . . If we do not have the Spirit of God, it were better to shut the churches, nail up the doors, put on a black cross and say, "God have mercy on us!" If you ministers have not the Spirit of God, you better not preach and you people had better stay at home. I think I speak not too strong when I say that a church without the Spirit of God is rather a curse than a blessing. "This is the solemn word: 'The Holy Spirit or nothing and worse than nothing!'"

Charles Spurgeon (1834–1892),
Metropolitan Tabernacle, London

To those brave believers everywhere who are willing to defend the full New Testament message without apology or fear (2 Timothy 3:16), who uphold Scripture's integrity, embrace its faith "once delivered to the saints" (Jude 3), and who "fully preach the gospel of Christ" with signs and wonders confirming the Word (Romans 15:19)

Contents

Contents

10

Contents

11

Part 15: Who Were Significant People in Church History? 267

Contents

15

Contents

16

Foreword

More and more of those who confess Christ value the Scriptures less and less. Not that they don't believe the Bible as the Word of God. They just don't seem to apply it to the practical part of their lifestyle and decision-making. Instead they allow the opinions presented on social media and by their cultural heroes to shape their values. Truth, then, becomes whatever the latest fad dictates. It almost seems as though they add Jesus to this mix to make things nice.

Of equal concern is another extreme: those who study Scripture but do not demonstrate the kind of lifestyle Jesus lived. For some reason they fail to notice that Jesus trained His disciples to do what He did and then told them to train their disciples in the same way. So they mark their Bibles from cover to cover but exhibit little life, joy or power in their lives. The Holy Spirit has little influence on day-to-day living.

We must address both of these issues of lack—whether lack of hunger for God's Word or lack of value for the Person of the Holy Spirit—to fully realize the purpose of the Lord for our day.

Spirit-Empowered Theology is part of the answer. It is a wonderful book for many reasons. It is alive!—and as such, it makes every reader an instant student of the Scriptures. Not a know-it-all; we have enough of those. Rather, the author provides access to answers that would otherwise be hard to find. This book does a great job igniting readers with real-life questions so the answers find a place in their hearts.

One of the most fascinating things about the Bible is that revelation knowledge from what is written creates hunger for more of the Bible. In the natural realm, we get hungry by *not* eating. But in the Kingdom of God, we get hungry by *eating.* Discovering answers to everyday dilemmas and questions about God, His will, our lives and the world around us creates an appetite for more of what God says and thinks. I pray that this book stirs great hunger for God and His Word in the hearts of countless numbers of people.

As a young man, I had interest in the Bible but little real passion. One book, *The Normal Christian Life* by Watchman Nee, awakened my heart to the value of God's Word. Nee's insight into the Scriptures provoked a hunger in me that has never subsided—and it has been 46 years. I expect the same to happen with those blessed enough to get *Spirit-Empowered Theology* and take it to another level. This book will engender students of God's Word.

Charles Carrin is a wonderful man with great credibility throughout the Body of Christ. It does not take long to realize what he values most—his relationship with the Holy Spirit. But as you will see in this amazing book, his value for the Holy Spirit is rooted in his love for God's Word. In fact, he models the answer for our present dilemma—poverty of biblical knowledge or disregard for the Holy Spirit—with a richness in both that should inspire us all. His equal passion for the Scriptures and for the Holy Spirit makes a beautiful rainbow.

I absolutely love this book!

Bill Johnson, senior leader, Bethel Church, Redding, California;
author, *When Heaven Invades Earth* and *The Essential Guide to Healing* (with Randy Clark)

Acknowledgment of Consulting Editors

Every sincere Christian writer hopes that his or her words are effective to promote the Gospel and honor the name of the Master. Further, I hope the words in this book are expressed clearly and will reach the reader's heart with truth and power.

It is my great honor to thank the following individuals who served as consulting editors for this work, individuals who reviewed designated portions of the manuscript for accuracy, clarity and faithfulness to Scripture.

John and Carol Arnott	Bill Johnson
Stephen Chitty	R. T. Kendall
Randy Clark	Michael Peterson
Leif Hetland	Jack Taylor

Each of you is not only a dear friend, but also a joyful sharer of the Gospel with the Holy Spirit's "signs and wonders" the world over. I am grateful to you.

Introduction

Why This Study?

"None are more hopelessly enslaved than those who falsely believe they are free."

So wrote Goethe. It is in that awareness, I share the following study as an aid to bringing greater spiritual freedom to all of us. God's liberty releases authority and power. Jesus said, "If the Son makes you free, you shall be free indeed" (John 8:36). His final message to the disciples on the day of Ascension was that they would "receive power" when the Holy Spirit came upon them (Acts 1:8).

As disciples of Christ, our goal is to experience His freedom, receive His empowering and "come to the unity of the faith and of the knowledge of the Son of God" (Ephesians 4:13). The only written resource for that is the Bible, and it alone carries the seal of divine authority. All other opinions, no matter how long established, widely respected or historically endorsed, are but human speculation and must bow to the superiority of the Word. Scripture is our final authority. Of itself, it boldly says, "All Scripture is given by inspiration of God" (2 Timothy 3:16).

The Bible commands each of us to "be diligent to present yourself approved to God, a worker who does not need to be ashamed, rightly dividing the word of truth" (2 Timothy 2:15). We are not commanded to divide error from truth in Scripture, but to divide and analyze its pure truth. Readers who approach the Bible thinking parts are invalid are hopelessly crippled before they start. In trusting all of it we become better equipped to "contend earnestly for the faith which was once for all [time] delivered to the saints" (Jude 3). It is "the faith"—the inalterable, life-changing Bible message—that brings freedom. Readers who find themselves embraced in divine assurance that the words of Scripture are God-inspired soon discover they are being transformed to the image of Christ. That transformation opens them to greater anointing and impartation of the Holy Spirit; the Spirit's power operates most freely in those who accept the totality of the divine Word.

For that reason, this study is intended specifically for those who believe in the plenary and permanent inspiration of the Bible—Old and New Testaments. It is not enough to believe Scripture was inspired but to believe it still is. While much of today's Scripture-attack centers on the Holy Spirit's charismata—or miraculous gifts—and those who defend them, the real issue is whether or not Scripture itself is reliable. Can we believe it or can we not? If Paul's instructions in 1 Corinthians 12–14 are no longer valid how can we trust the rest of his writings? Is our faith resting falsely on other Bible promises that are no longer true? Does Scripture warn us about this dangerous failing in itself?

The fact is this: Moses sanctified the book of the Old Covenant by sprinkling it with the blood of bulls and goats; Jesus sanctified the book of the New Covenant by sprinkling it with His own blood (see Hebrews 9:11–23; 12:24). As such, each covenant is inalterable, cannot be added to or taken from, and of which no part has lost the Divine Seal. As the Holy Spirit's inspired volume, the Bible is to be loved, believed, protected and promoted. Those who have experienced the Holy Spirit's miraculous power have no choice but to believe the Scriptures, love them and promote them. It was this sealing of the Holy Spirit that Jesus promised on the day of the Ascension when He said, "John truly baptized with water, but you shall be baptized with the Holy Spirit not many days from now. . . . You shall receive power when the Holy Spirit has come upon you" (Acts 1:5, 8). This was said to disciples who had already received the Holy Spirit's regenerating work on the day of the resurrection (see John 20:21–22).

I have included certain non-theological topics I feel are vital to the Church today. I hope that this combination will inform you in Scripture, empower you in the Spirit and promote unity among those who accept the Holy Spirit's baptism and those who do not. I have tried to present facts of science, history, medicine, etc. from authoritative sources. But be aware, secular resources do not always agree among themselves. And in answering questions, there has been some unavoidable repetition of Scriptures.

Where I have succeeded, be thankful; where I have failed, be gracious. Above all, be blessed! Live in the glory!

Charles Carrin

PART 1

Who Is God?

1. What Is God's Nature and Being?

First of all, it is impossible to identify God. We have neither the conceptual ability to comprehend Him nor the vocabulary to describe Him. He is, and exists in, a dimension we have never seen. Our sources of information are threefold: His sovereign choice to reveal Himself to us, Scripture and the revelation of nature (see Matthew 11:27; Romans 1:19–20; 1 Corinthians 2:10; 2 Timothy 3:16).

What we know is this: God Almighty is the Original Cause, Creator, only deity, eternal and First Being of all things; He alone is sovereign. He is the initial source and personification of perfect love, perfect purity, perfect purpose and perfect power. All energy, all intelligence comes from Him. Only He had the choice of saying or not saying, "Let there be light." He so chose, light came, darkness vanished and creation had begun. Intelligent design and order were instantly and universally established by His Word (see Colossians 1:17; Hebrews 11:3).

As Sovereign, possessing all power and free range, it is His uncontested privilege to be what He chooses. He is not restrained in any capacity. By His own choice, God the Almighty exists in singularity and multiplicity. He alone has the capacity to transcend time, space and all the limitations that exist within—and without—our cosmos. He created it. It is subject to Him. He is independent of everything, dependent on nothing. Of His Being, we have no capacity to describe Him. Atheists have no capacity to deny Him.

2. How Do We Know That God Is Trinitarian?

While maintaining absolute unity within Himself, God sovereignly manifests His Being in three divine Personages: Father, Son and Holy Spirit (see Genesis 1:26; John 1:1–14; 2 Corinthians 13:14).

In reference to Himself in Genesis 1:1, God used a plural subject, *elohim*, but a singular verb, *bara'*: "In the beginning God created. . . ." This unusual model of His oneness in plurality established a pattern that is followed consistently in the Genesis account of Creation—even though it is in violation of basic Hebrew grammar, which insists that nouns and verbs agree in number. It is equally significant that when Genesis speaks of pagan gods—elohim—it reverts to its original format of noun/verb agreement. God's introduction of Himself immediately challenges us with His plurality.

In the opening pages of Scripture, God the Almighty revealed His Trinitarian nature to Abraham in bodily form. Abraham is the father of faith both to Jews and Christians. The Jews acknowledge Him in His singularity; Christians acknowledge Him in His plurality. Both are correct.

The language of Scripture reveals this:

Genesis 18:1: "The LORD appeared to" Abraham in the form of
Genesis 18:2: "three men . . . standing by him."
Genesis 18:21: The LORD said, "I will go down [to Sodom]."
Genesis 18:22: "Then the men . . . went toward Sodom" but
Genesis 18:22: "Abraham still stood before the LORD."
Genesis 19:1: "Now the two angels [the Lord] came to Sodom in the evening."

In this setting, the Lord appeared to a man as a man: He stood before Abraham in human form. At the same time He (note the wording: "I" will go down to Sodom) appeared in Sodom as two angels. This Trinitarian display of Himself is obvious and unmistakably clear.

Two distinctly different but vitally important announcements were being made at this moment: The promise of Isaac as the royal seed through whom the Redeemer would come, and, simultaneously, God's vengeance on the sinfulness that would cause the Redeemer's death. In our present three-dimensional realm, this display of plurality and singularity at the same time is not possible. God's realm puts no restraint on Him.

3. How Is God Both Singular and Plural?

Scripture's opening lines introduce us to God's plurality and singularity: "God said, 'Let Us make man in Our image, according to Our likeness" (Genesis 1:26).

From the beginning of Creation, God's ultimate plan was that mankind would someday rule and reign with Him (see Revelation 5:10; 20:6; 22:5). His giving Adam dominion over the earth and every living thing was the introduction of that plan. This was done in spite of humanity's foreknown rebellion and fall into sin. Against that setting of rebellion, God would display His grace as superior to mankind's disgrace.

To qualify humanity for this role, God planned further to impart His own nature into mankind. This is "Christ in you, the hope of glory" (Colossians 1:27; see also 1 Corinthians 6:19; 1 Peter 1:23). The bestowing of the seed and nature of Christ in us can only happen because of God's allowing divisibility and repetition within Himself (see Romans 8:10; Colossians 1:27; 1 John 3:9). He could not impart Himself into mankind had He been an indissoluble, solitary Being.

At the same time, "the Lord is One." Difficult to understand? Yes. But true. His dimension exists without the limitations of ours. In Christ, God became human that humans might become godlike: "He called them gods, to whom the Word of God came" (John 10:35; see also Exodus 4:16; 7:1). This is the same Word that became flesh: "In the beginning was the Word, and the Word was with God, and the Word

28

was God. . . . And the Word became flesh and dwelt among us, and we beheld His glory, the glory as of the only begotten of the Father, full of grace and truth" (John 1:1, 14–15).

4. What Are the Three Great Attributes of God?

First, God is omniscient. Not only does He know everything, having perfect foreknowledge of all events universe-wide (see 1 John 3:20), but Isaiah wrote that He "[declared] the end from the beginning, and from ancient times things that are not yet done" (Isaiah 46:10). Jesus taught that even a sparrow cannot fall to the earth apart from the Father's knowledge. The hairs of our heads are numbered (see Matthew 10:29–30). There is not an unspoken word in our tongues that God does not already know (see Psalm 139:4). He even saw us in the womb (see Psalm 139:15–16).

Solomon expressed this truth perfectly when he said, "You alone know the hearts of all the sons of men" (1 Kings 8:39). "There is no creature hidden from His sight, but all things are naked and open to the eyes of Him to whom we must give account" (Hebrews 4:13). God is incapable of ignorance.

Second, God is omnipotent. He is all powerful. As Creator, He is unlimited in sovereignty and strength. He said, "Let there be light," and light came! (Genesis 1:3). No other power could resist Him. The universe also needs His power and strength to sustain it. Job said, "I know that You can do everything, and that no purpose of Yours can be withheld from You" (Job 42:2). "The Lord said to Moses, 'Has the LORD's arm been shortened?'" (Numbers 11:23). Nowhere is God's omnipotence seen more clearly than in the act of Creation. "By the word of the LORD the heavens were made, and all the host of them by the breath of His mouth" (Psalm 33:6). Jesus declared, "All authority has been given to Me in heaven and on earth" (Matthew 28:18–19).

29

Third, God is omnipresent. He is everywhere. It is impossible for Him to be absent anywhere. David said, "If I ascend into heaven, You are there; if I make my bed in hell, behold, You are there. If I take the wings of the morning, and dwell in the uttermost parts of the sea, even there Your hand shall lead me" (Psalm 139:8–10). While the Father occupies the throne of heaven, Jesus at His right hand, His Spirit permeates the universe and all regions beyond.

5. What Is the Sovereignty of God?

Three attributes of God bring the unavoidable realization that He is sovereign.

He is omniscient. God knows everything.

He is omnipotent. God is all powerful. As Creator, He is unlimited in strength.

He is omnipresent. God is everywhere. It is impossible for Him to be absent anywhere.

His will, authority, power are irresistible. God Almighty is answerable only to Himself. There is none other to whom He can or should give account. Creation came into being because He alone willed it to be so. The world will end when He chooses. Of Himself He said, "I am God, and there is no other; I am God, and there is none like Me, declaring the end from the beginning, and from ancient times things that are not yet done, saying, 'My counsel shall stand, and I will do all My pleasure'" (Isaiah 46:9–10). "No one can restrain His hand or say to Him, 'What have You done?'" (Daniel 4:35).

But God's nature is love; His sovereignty is only an aspect of His nature. It does not exist independently of His love. Even though God has all power and is independent of every control, He will not violate his own covenant of grace. He loves us and will not change.

This is a foundational truth: God has sovereignly given every human being a will that is free to make the choice of love. As individuals, we are under God's providential and secret care—like an umbrella over our lives that guides and protects us—but from which we may voluntarily leave.

Freedom provides the only environment in which love can exist. A sovereignly controlled robot is incapable of love. The reality of our free choice—displayed in the framework of God's sovereignty—is demonstrated in the opening pages of Scripture. After Adam's first disobedience, God, knowing mankind's propensity for continuing rebellion, acted "'lest [Adam] put out his hand and take also of the tree of life, and eat, and live forever'—therefore the LORD God sent him out of the garden of Eden" (Genesis 3:22). At this point God's sovereignty responded protectively to the danger in the man's free will; He protected him from greater harm.

From the rim of the universe to the core of every atom, God's love maintains creation in the same perfection for which it was originally designed. The Hebrew writer explains Jesus' role in that perfect creation: "Through whom also He made the worlds; who being the brightness of His glory and the express image of His person, and upholding all things by the word of His power, when He had by Himself purged our sins, sat down at the right hand of the Majesty on high" (Hebrews 1:2–3). Next, that same love blankets the lives of every individual on the planet. In speaking to the disciples on this topic, Jesus asked them, "Are not two sparrows sold for a copper coin? And not one of them falls to the ground apart from your Father's will. . . . Do not fear therefore; you are of more value than many sparrows" (Matthew 10:29–31).

Since we are created in God's image He wants our choices also to be love-motivated. Identically, there could be no honor to Him if our worship were forced and involuntarily given.

Is God sovereign? Yes. Are humans free to obey or disobey? Absolutely. God's sovereignty does not negate our responsibility.

6. What Are Some of the Old Testament Names of God?

YHWH: This name is reverenced by Jews as being too holy to speak. For that reason it contains no vowels, thus making it unpronounceable. Many Jews today spell it *G_D*. God's identity was revealed to Moses as I Am at the burning bush. It identifies Him in His timeless, eternal state—the One who has always been, is, will always be. He is the One who is without beginning or end. Often identified with vowels as *Yahweh*, this was the name for God that Jesus used in His preaching.

Jehovah Jireh: Usually translated as "The Lord Will Provide," this name of God appears in Genesis 22 when He rescued Isaac from the altar and provided a wild ram to die in his place. Abraham called the place *Jehovah Jireh*, meaning, "in the Mount of the Lord it shall be provided" (Genesis 22:8).

Elohim: Genesis 1:1 introduces us to the name *elohim* and provides our first knowledge about God's plurality and His being all powerful. The word means that He is "mighty, strong, famous." In English we generally put an *s* at the end of a word to change it from singular to plural. To pluralize a singular Hebrew word, the letters *im* are added to the end—like *cherub* and *cherubim*. The word *eloha* becomes *elohim*; thus, the very first sentence in Genesis reveals God's plurality: "In the beginning God. . . ." Psalm 19:1 says, "The heavens declare the glory of elohim."

El Shaddai: *El* translates as "God," and *Shaddai* comes from the Hebrew word for *mountain*. In the Old Testament the word *mountain* implies "nations," meaning a big expanse. Combined, we have the name of Almighty God—God of the nations. Theologically, this widens the concept from a Hebrew tribal God to His being God of all the earth. His reign is not local but universal. In Genesis 17 when God promised that Abraham and Sarah would have a son, He called Himself "I [am] El Shaddai." The word *am* is implied, not written, but can legitimately be understood as present.

Jehovah Sabaoth: God is called "The Lord of Hosts" more than 285 times in Scripture. It means literally that He is the God of armies of angels. We see a small part of the hosts displayed when the Syrian army surrounded the prophet Elisha and his servant. The young man was stricken with fear: "And Elisha prayed, and said, 'Lord, I pray, open his eyes that he may see.' Then the Lord opened the eyes of the young man, and he saw. And behold, the mountain was full of horses and chariots of fire all around Elisha" (2 Kings 6:17–18). Such unseen protection surrounds us many times today.

Jehovah Shalom: The story of Gideon in the Bible opens with his hiding his meager food supply from the enemy behind the winepress. It ends with his having obeyed the Lord and brought deliverance to his people. It was he who called the Lord the "God of Peace"—Jehovah Shalom.

Jehovah Rapha: "I am Jehovah Rapha who heals you," God told Israel (Exodus 15:26). He introduced Himself as Israel's healer at the same time they were experiencing their worst crisis. Excited and rejoicing, they had just left Egypt, heading to the Promised Land. But their circumstances did not go well. After crossing the Red Sea, they traveled three days without water; finally they came to an oasis only to find its waters poisonous. God showed them a tree, which, cut down and put into the water, would remove all the poison. The tree typified Christ and His ability to sweeten life's greatest crisis. It was in this setting that the Lord revealed Himself as "The Lord, Your Healer"—or "Restorer." The word *rapha* can be translated either way. He healed in the ancient day and He is still healing in ours.

7. Why Does God's Character Seem Different in the Old and New Testaments?

What appears to be differences in God's character in the two Testaments is this: The Old Testament events are a visible dramatization—acting out—of New Testament doctrine and truth. In effect, the Old Testament is a staged presentation of New Testament theology.

Take this example. Israel warred against actual physical enemies on the battlefield; the Jews experienced both success and failure. In the New Testament, Christians war against powers, principalities, etc. in the heavenlies. Israel engaged in actual physical battles; in the New Testament we are engaged solely in "spiritual warfare." We learn how to battle spiritually by observing Israel's techniques on the field. But in both covenants, "The wrath of God is revealed from heaven against all ungodliness and unrighteousness" (Romans 1:18).

There is no change in the character and nature of God from one Testament to the other. Paul explains, "For since the creation of the world His invisible attributes are clearly seen" (Romans 1:20). Throughout history, God has remained consistently the same. Paul mentions this very point: "Whatever things were written before [in the Old Testament] were written for our learning, that we through the patience and comfort of the Scriptures might have hope" (Romans 15:4).

God is the same in both covenants.

8. What Is God's Nature as Father?

The most identifying feature in the nature of God is fatherhood. His fatherhood is the fountainhead of all universal love and order. As gravity grips, bonds, holds the physical universe together, so love, originating in the fatherhood of God, grips, bonds, holds together the total created dimension—physical and spiritual. This includes the redeemed Body of Christ and all the realms of nature. God does not want an organization of people; He wants a family. Paul attempts to explain this when he writes: "For this reason I bow my knees to the Father of our Lord Jesus Christ, from whom the whole family in heaven and earth is named" (Ephesians 3:14–15). Note that it is the "whole family" that bears the Father's name. This identifies us as blood relatives, carriers of His uniqueness and nature.

Theologically, He is referred to as the first Person of the Godhead. His fatherhood was revealed through Jesus who said, "O righteous Father! The world has not known You, but I have known You; and these have known that You sent Me. And I have declared to them Your name [Father], and will declare it, that the love with which You loved Me may be in them, and I in them" (John 17:25–26). It was the appearance of the Son that disclosed the identity of the Father. Both Father/Son identities were rejected angrily by the Jews: "Therefore the Jews sought all the more to kill [Jesus], because He not only broke the Sabbath, but also said that God was His Father" (John 5:18). It is only in knowing the fatherhood of God that we experience the fullness of His love in ourselves.

9. What Is God's Nature as Son?

In Jesus "dwells the fullness of the Godhead bodily" (Colossians 2:9). He is "King of kings and Lord of lords" (1 Timothy 6:15). It is He by whom "the worlds were framed" (Hebrews 11:3). "All things were made through Him, and without Him nothing was made that was made" (John 1:3).

> [Jesus] is the image of the invisible God, the firstborn over all creation. For by Him all things were created that are in heaven and that are on earth, visible and invisible, whether thrones or dominions or principalities or powers. All things were created through Him and for Him. And He is before all things, and in Him all things consist. And He is the head of the body, the church, who is the beginning, the firstborn from the dead, that in all things He may have the preeminence.
>
> Colossians 1:15–19

The love and compassion of Jesus is seen in the grace He offers mankind: "Come to Me, all you who labor and are heavy laden, and I will give you rest" (Matthew 11:28). Theologically, Jesus is identified as the second Person of the Godhead, existing co-equally with the Father and Spirit before time began and prior to His birth at Bethlehem. It was His human body through which he could experience mortality and die. Scripturally, Paul compares Adam and Jesus this way: "'The first man Adam became a living being.' The last Adam became a life-giving spirit" (1 Corinthians 15:45).

10. What Is God's Nature as Spirit?

The Spirit of God is His active, creative being. God's power is revealed through His Spirit: "In the beginning God created the heavens and the earth. The earth was without form, and void; and darkness was on the face of the deep. And the Spirit of God was hovering over the face of the waters." The Father "breathed into [the man's] nostrils the breath of life [the Holy Spirit]; and man became a living soul" (Genesis 2:7 KJV). *Breath*, *ruwach* in Hebrew, is the word for "wind, spirit." In the New Testament Greek, the word for "wind, spirit, breath" is *pneuma*.

The meaning is the same in both Testaments. The Spirit's power-release was true in original Creation and is true today in a believer's regeneration. The prophet Samuel told King Saul, "The Spirit of the LORD will come upon you, and you will prophesy with them and be turned into another man" (1 Samuel 10:6).

The word *spirit* is neither male nor female; it identifies God in a non-physical, sexless role (see Genesis 1:1–2). The names *Father* and *Son* portray masculinity. *Spirit* does not. The Holy Spirit is referred to as the third Person of the Godhead.

All four gospels record the Holy Spirit's appearance as a dove—though not becoming a literal dove—at the baptism of Jesus (see Matthew 3:16; Mark 1:10; Luke 3:22; John 1:32). The dove is a gentle bird that avoids clamor and discord. At the baptism of Jesus when the dove descended and the Father spoke, "This is My Beloved Son in whom I am well pleased," we have the only instance in Scripture when the Trinity is manifestly present as Father, Son, Spirit at the same time (Matthew 3:17).

Jesus' ministry did not begin until the Holy Spirit came upon Him. At His first sermon in Nazareth He explained: "The Spirit of the LORD is upon Me, because He has anointed Me to preach the gospel" (Luke 4:18). Every gift and fruit of the Holy Spirit was present in Jesus without measure (see John 3:34).

11. How Did the Holy Spirit Work in Jesus?

Jesus experienced two specific and different works by the Holy Spirit: conception and anointing. Conception occurred in the womb of the Virgin Mary and anointing occurred during His baptism in the Jordan River. One without the other would have left Him and His ministry incomplete.

The Holy Spirit's first work in Jesus: conception. Jesus was conceived in the womb of the virgin by the Spirit. In answer to Mary's question of how her pregnancy would occur, the angel said to her, "The Holy Spirit will come upon you, and the power of the Highest will overshadow you; therefore, also, that Holy One who is to be born will be called the Son of God" (Luke 1:35). Jesus, who preexisted eternally as God, was transferred to the womb of the virgin by the Spirit and became man: "A body You have prepared for Me'" (Hebrews 10:5); "He took not on him the nature of angels; but he took on him the seed of Abraham" (Hebrews 2:16 KJV).

The Holy Spirit's second work in Jesus: anointing. During His baptism in the Jordan, Jesus was anointed by the Holy Spirit. John bore witness, saying, "I saw the Spirit descending from heaven like a dove, and He remained upon Him. I did not know Him, but He who sent me to baptize with water said to me, 'Upon whom you see the Spirit descending, and remaining on Him, this is He who baptizes with the Holy Spirit'" (John 1:32–33). Prior to His anointing by the Spirit, Jesus healed no sickness, cast out no demon, performed no miracle. That changed immediately with the Spirit's descent upon Him.

Jesus' conception by the Spirit was for the purpose of His redemption of mankind. His anointing at baptism by the Spirit provided His earthly ministry with the Spirit's miraculous power.

It is probable that Jesus' cry from the cross, "My God! My God! why have You forsaken Me?," came because the anointing of the Spirit lifted from Him. The Spirit's internal work of conception remained; the anointing did not. That part of Jesus' ministry was now finished; complete. Had the Comforter remained it is probable that He could not have died. As the ultimate scapegoat, He had to be abandoned by God for death to claim Him.

12. What Does Relationship with the Holy Spirit Mean?

There can be no converted life begun or maintained except by the continual presence of the Holy Spirit. Religion can function without Him; true spirituality cannot. It is He, the Holy Spirit, who hovered over the formless mass of the earth and brought light and order to its primeval darkness (see Genesis 1:1–2). From the beginning of recorded history, the Holy Spirit is identified with action and vitality. Whether working in the vastness of the universe or a human's microscopic conception, and later in that same person's adult soul, it is He, the Holy Spirit, whose ultimate goal is to bring us into comradeship with God. He will then sustain that union into eternal life.

The Holy Spirit is the only true God on the earth. There is no other. He is the only source of life for the Church and is the indispensable origin for all the good that exists. It is He who raised Jesus from the dead and offers to indwell and motivate us (see Romans 8:11). If we grieve the Holy Spirit, He may become silent, imperceptible to us, and we will find ourselves seemingly abandoned to a frustrated and unspiritual state. It was in the apparent fear of this condition that David cried out, "Do not take your Holy Spirit from me" (Psalm 51:11). There is no substitute for the Spirit's authentic relationship, which He establishes between us and the Father.

13. How Does the Holy Spirit Speak Today?

Scripture identifies several ways the Spirit speaks to believers today.

The Holy Spirit bears witness directly to our spirits and leads us internally. We know by the inner witness of the Holy Spirit to our spirits that we are children of God, and that God has given us eternal life in His Son (see Romans 8:16; 1 John 5:6–11).

The Holy Spirit leads us externally. Paul and his fellow travelers attempted to go to Asia and Bithynia, but the Holy Spirit did not permit them (see Acts 16:6–7; see also Genesis 24:27; 1 Samuel 10:6; Galatians 5:16–19).

The Holy Spirit speaks in words and sentences. One of the servants of the Ethiopian queen, a eunuch of great authority, had gone to Jerusalem to worship and was returning home. He was riding in his chariot reading the book of Isaiah when Philip heard the Holy Spirit speak: "Go near and overtake this chariot'" (Acts 8:29). When Philip explained the Scriptures, the eunuch received salvation and was baptized.

The Holy Spirit speaks prophetically through others. A prophet named Agabus spoke to a gathering in Antioch predicting a great famine—which occurred under the reign of Claudius Caesar (see Acts 11:27–28; see also Acts 21:9–11).

The Holy Spirit gives direct revelation knowledge. First Corinthians 2:9–10 explains that God reveals to us through His Spirit the things He has prepared for those who love Him. Paul writes further that mysteries were made known to him through revelation (see Ephesians 3:1–6).

The Holy Spirit speaks through the written words of Scripture. Peter makes clear that we must pay attention to Scripture, since its prophetic words are not of human origin but inspired by the Holy Spirit (see 2 Peter 1:19–21).

The Holy Spirit speaks through visions and dreams. Several verses confirm the fact that God speaks to us, waking or sleeping, as He wills (see Joel 2:28; see also Matthew 2:13; Matthew 27:19; Acts 9:10–12; 16:9; 2 Corinthians 12:1–2).

The Holy Spirit speaks through creation. Creation is a visible revelation of God to all mankind, showing clearly His "invisible attributes"— including His "eternal power and Godhead"—through all that He has made. Because God has shown these things clearly, His wrath is directed toward those who deny or suppress the truth (see Romans 1:20). David states in a psalm: "The heavens declare the glory of God; and the firmament shows His handiwork. Day unto day utters speech, and night unto night reveals knowledge. There is no speech nor language where their voice is not heard" (Psalm 19:1–3; 50:6; 97:6).

PART 2

Who Are We?

14. How Are Human Beings the Pinnacle of God's Creation?

"Man"—referring in these verses to male and female alike—is the only created being made in the image and likeness of God: "God said, 'Let Us make man in Our image, according to Our likeness. . . . So God created man in His own image; in the image of God He created him; male and female He created them" (Genesis 1:26–27).

It was through Christ, who in the beginning was the Word, that "all things were made . . . and without him nothing was made that has been made. In Him was life, and the life was the light of men" (John 1:3–4). In Christ, the Word that became flesh, dwells "all the fullness of the Godhead bodily; and [we] are complete in Him" (Colossians 2:9–10). All wisdom originates with Him: "Christ [is] the power of God and the wisdom of God" (1 Corinthians 1:24). The Lord God is the ultimate designer of the universe, the creator of its various laws, the eternal One who spoke artistic beauty and order into the vastness of space and directed the celestial choir as He laid the earth's foundations. He endows our hearts with wisdom and gives understanding to our minds (see Job 38:4–7, 33, 36).

Luke 3:38 speaks of Adam as the "son of God." Mankind as the pinnacle of God's creation was thus created as God's son.

Two purposes are inherent in our being made in the image and likeness of the Creator: to be creative and to rule over the earth. Man was given the mandate to rule and reign over the earth. Genesis 2:15 says that God "took the man and put him in the garden of Eden to tend and keep it."

And all of us carry part of His creativity, shown in what we call talents. Whether it be through music, biology, poetry, mechanics or astronomy, the manifestation of special abilities in us is God re-expressing His creativity through us. These are natural gifts, mental gifts, not spiritual gifts. They can be enhanced in us as we seek His increase of them. The wise person spends time with Jesus seeking the enlargement of any natural senses and talents. The potential of God's creativity in the children He loves is endless.

15. What Is Our Three-Part Design?

God's specific purpose in creating us in His own image and likeness was that we would have dominion over the earth and everything in it (see Genesis 1:26). As such, we would also be capable of having fellowship and camaraderie with God.

To achieve this, God gave us a "tripartite" design, a transportable temple of the Holy Spirit, equipping us to "rule and reign" with God. The apostle Paul explained: "Do you not know that your body is the temple of the Holy Spirit who is in you, whom you have from God, and you are not your own? For you were bought at a price; therefore glorify God in your body and in your spirit, which are God's" (1 Corinthians 6:19). As humans, we portray Israel's three-part Temple in this way: The outer court represents the body; the Holy Place represents the soul; and the Most Holy Place represents the spirit. Paul referred to this unique construction again when he wrote, "May your whole spirit, soul, and body be preserved blameless at the coming of our Lord Jesus Christ" (1 Thessalonians 5:23).

God is Spirit; our greatest likeness to God is that, though we live in bodies, we, too, are spirit: "There is a spirit in man, and the breath of the Almighty gives him understanding" (Job 32:8). The Bible makes a careful distinction between the spirit and the soul. While there is much we do not know, we are assured that each spirit originated from God, draws its nature from the eternal realm, and is therefore indestructible. "Spirit" is the first, original form of life existing in God before creation.

Like God, the human spirit is eternal. Even in hell one's spirit cannot be destroyed; it survives forever.

Since we are spirit, it is with the heart—not the mind—that one believes unto salvation. Paul explained this: "If you confess with your mouth the Lord Jesus and believe in your heart that God has raised Him from the dead, you will be saved. For with the heart one believes unto righteousness, and with the mouth confession is made unto salvation" (Romans 10:8–10). It is possible to believe in Jesus with the mind only—as a historical figure—but this does not produce saving faith or a regenerate spirit.

Scripture also explains the miraculous origin of the soul: "The LORD God formed man of the dust of the ground, and breathed into his nostrils the breath of life; and man became a living being" (Genesis 2:7–8). Adam's living soul, *nephesh*, was created when the Spirit of God "breathed into" the form made of earthen clay. In that incredible "union" of Spirit and soil, a soul came into being. The soul or psyche is the mind, functioning in the brain and expressing itself as intelligence, will, emotions.

In the origination of humanity it seems that the spirit was imparted but the soul was created. As such, the soul, like the Holy Place in the Temple, stands as intermediary between the spirit and the body. The body, the outer court of worldly commerce, touches earth; the spirit, the Most Holy Place, touches heaven. The soul touches both body and spirit, earth and heaven.

The body is a marvel of engineering brilliance. After attaching to the uterus wall, the impregnated ovum remains motionless for some minutes, absolutely still, as if in reverential silence—then it explodes into activity, engineering body parts with lightning-fast velocity. Bones, brain, blood, organs, skin, personality, intellect, talents, voice tones, attitudes, memory and all other life components begin organizing (see Ecclesiastes 11:5; 1 Corinthians 12:18). We have nothing with which to compare such massive and flawless organization of functioning physicality. Did you realize, for instance, that one million optic nerves grow separately from eye to brain, brain to eye, and join their counterparts perfectly in the middle?

Awesome!

16. What Is the Spiritual Function of the Human Heart?

The physical heart, which beats about 100,000 times a day, is a miraculous organ. Only the size of a fist and weighing about ten ounces, it generates the largest electromagnetic field in the body. In fact, the electrical field of the heart, as measured in amplitude by an electrocardiogram (ECG), is about sixty times greater than the electrical field of the brain, as recorded in an electroencephalogram (EEG). A brain weighs about three pounds. These two generators operate near each other but do not compete or counter the other's effectiveness.

Is this an accident? No, we are created in the image and likeness of God and wonderfully made! We are God-designed to have fellowship with the Creator. In this regard, the spiritual function of the heart is as vital as its physical function.

The heart is the seat of conscience, desire, longing, dreams, intention, thoughts and more. This capacity of the heart is a spiritual function—and vital in our walk with God. We remember the Lord's words to Samuel when He had sent the great judge and prophet to the house of Jesse to anoint the next king: "The LORD does not see as man sees; for man looks at the outward appearance, but the LORD looks at the heart" (1 Samuel 16:7). Just as the mind is the agent for our believing intellectually, so the heart is the agent for our believing spiritually. The mind initiates; the spirit consummates. "With the heart one believes unto righteousness, and with the mouth confession is made unto salvation" (Romans 10:10). Jesus said, "If you do not believe that I am He, you will die in your sins" (John 8:24). He was speaking of our spirits.

Since we are fully redeemed when we believe in Jesus—the spirit by regeneration, the mind by renewal, the body by resurrection at His return—the work of the Holy Spirit in us is twofold. For the experience to be complete, we must make the mental decision to confess with our physical mouths and also believe in our spiritual hearts that Christ has been resurrected from the dead. In so doing, we instantly become born again and a sharer in His resurrection. Only in heart-belief is there spiritual change.

In this distinction we find the difference between being religious and being truly spiritual. Salvation does not result from mental cooperation. The heart must believe. This experience is personal between the believer and God. It has absolutely nothing to do with religious identities.

17. Where Is a Human Being's Innermost Depth?

"In the last day, that great day of the feast, Jesus stood and cried, saying, If any man thirst, let him come unto me and drink. He that believeth on me, as the scripture hath said, out of his belly shall flow rivers of living water" (John 7:37–38 KJV). The Greek word for *belly* is *koilia*. Ancient Greeks used this word to describe the concave arch of heaven and what they assumed was its bowl-like planetary sky. They then applied that same word to the human torso below the rib cage where they imagined there was something "heaven-shaped." Instead of translating the word as "bosom" or "belly," some translations wrongly interpret it as "heart." This causes confusion. The word for heart is *cardia*—not *koilia*.

Koilia is the body area in which we sometimes experience deep spiritual/physical yearning (see Song of Solomon 5:4; Jeremiah 4:19). In Philemon 7, Paul wrote, "The bowels of the saints are refreshed by thee, brother" (KJV). The entire human body comprises the Temple of the Holy Spirit, and in some capacity each part possesses a spiritual significance. Jesus made reference to eyes, ears, hands, feet and face, in this way (see Matthew 13:15). Our five physical senses can be exercised to discern good and evil (see Hebrews 5:14).

People who experience authentic intercessory prayer find frequently that it comes from the *koilia* part of the body in the form of intense groaning. Paul explained this when he wrote, "Likewise the Spirit also helps in our weaknesses. For we do not know what we should pray for as we ought, but the Spirit Himself makes intercession for us with groanings which cannot be uttered" (Romans 8:26). It is probable that when Elijah was praying on Mount Carmel with his head between his knees he experienced this *koilia* type of intercession (1 Kings 18:42).

Scripture does not identify any joint functions of our *cardia* and *koilia*. We only know that both exist and that we are being "fitted together," growing into a "holy temple in the Lord" for a "dwelling place of God in the Spirit" (Ephesians 2:19–22).

18. Was Adam Super-Intelligent?

In Adam's innocent state he conversed intelligently with God, his mind possessing wisdom that went far beyond our comprehension today. Genesis 2:19, for example, says that "God formed every beast of the field and every bird of the air, and brought them to Adam to see what he would call them. And whatever Adam called each living creature, that was its name." What an extraordinary display of intellectual ability and creativity! Some believe that this extreme intellect was not lost but merely locked away and is still present in all of us.

Studies of "savant" personalities give us much to consider. *Savant* (Latin, *sapere*) means to "to be wise" and is used to identify scholars and those highly knowledgeable about a particular subject. In this regard, the word is also used to describe individuals generally with mental disabilities or brain injuries who exhibit brilliance in some particular field, such as mathematics or music. From birth Leslie Lemke could not walk, eat or speak, but at age thirteen he heard Tchaikovsky's twenty-minute-long Piano Concerto No. 1 on television one time and, with no musical training, played the entire concerto from memory.

Some cognitive-neuroscientists estimate that even Einstein operated on less than a tenth of the brain's actual prowess. If true, this leaves us to wonder what Adam would have been like with the full use of his intellectual potential.

47

19. Why Are Our Natural Abilities Inferior to Those of the Animals?

The mind has only five natural sources of information. It receives knowledge through hearing, seeing, touching, tasting and smelling—all marvelous senses with which God has equipped the mind and body to function together. But we recognize that animals have senses that are vastly superior to mankind's. Some species of sharks can detect electromagnetism from a flashlight battery a thousand miles away. The common housefly has eyesight vastly superior to ours. If we had "fast vision" like a hawk, we could read print on a whirling airplane blade.

Obviously, we are not as well equipped environmentally as are animals. Why is that so? How can it be that we who are created in the image and likeness of God, who can send rockets into outer space, are still less capably equipped than wild creatures?

The fact is that we are not less equipped: We are generally not using the equipment God gave us! Apparently, He designed us with inferior natural abilities because He endowed us with far greater spiritual powers (see 1 Corinthians 12–14). The human being has the potential for great things by virtue of our superior spiritual gifting.

The apostle Paul wrote more of the New Testament, participated in more signs and wonders, experienced more visions and dreams, and broke through more obstacles than anyone else we know. Sounding almost boastful he said, "I thank my God I speak with tongues more than you all" (1 Corinthians 14:18). What does this tell us? Mankind has the potential for direct communication with God (see Jude 20–21). It is this that sets us apart from the rest of the animal kingdom.

20. Where Is the Battleground for the Christian?

Salvation, which is instantly complete in our spirits, means renewal, restoration to life and a joining to God in sinless perfection. What is instantaneous for the spirit is a process for the soul. Since the soul—the mind, will and emotions—touches both the spiritual and natural dimensions, its relationship can be with either realm and it can be influenced by either. The soul, thus, becomes the battleground between God and powers of darkness. During that struggle, if the soul fails to "grow in grace," it may become attracted again to the world and forget that it was purged from its old sin (see 2 Peter 3:17–18; see 1:9). In that state the mind might be taken captive by worldliness, and the person might return to his old life of sin and carnality.

This loss of relationship with the Lord is sometimes called backsliding or apostatizing. Backsliding is a state of recoverable separation from the Christian faith, while apostasy is usually regarded as a final denial of God and His Word. Apostasy, from the Greek *apostasia*, involves complete defection from and renouncing of God and His Word. The backslider may still love God, realize he is in a fallen state, repent and find restoration. The apostate, however, denies the reality of grace and salvation.

In death, the regenerate spirit and the renewed soul apparently unite, escape the body and, as one inseparable being, are taken consciously into the presence of God. The body returns to the earth, awaiting its resurrection and reunion with the soul and spirit.

21. How Is the Mind Made New?

The new birth not only opens the door of heaven to us but also opens the door to a "more abundant life" here on earth (see John 10:10). Part of this opportunity is achieved as we are "transformed by the renewing" of our minds (see Romans 12:2). Accomplishing this renewal is a process that Scripture explains generously. It is God's will that having been born again, we "grow in the grace and knowledge of our Lord and Savior Jesus Christ" (2 Peter 3:18).

Sadly, many born-again Christians do not avail themselves of this wonderful opportunity and continue suffering much needless grief. For such people, their habits remain the same, their conversations remain the same, and their handicapped outlooks on life remain unchanged. Faith cannot grow in such a negative mindset. Renewal of our minds is the answer. We are created in the image and likeness of God who is the original Creator (see Genesis 1:26; 5:1). Because of that, we all have creative talents, abilities and attributes that can be released only through the renewal of our minds. God is the original engineer, artist, choreographer, etc. For the one desiring success in a particular area of interest, renewal of the mind is the answer.

But even more, we cannot "enter into life" without obedience to God and His mental cleansing and restoration (see Matthew 19:17). How is it achieved? Religious performance will not produce it. Ultimately it is the revelation of the Word that brings the illumination to and renewing of the mind. The inner working in one's spirit needs to be paired with the illumination that only God's Word can give. Psalm 119:130, 133 explains: "The entrance of Your words gives light; it gives understanding to the simple. . . . Direct my steps by Your word."

Walking in the disciplines of the faith enhances this process of mind renewal. Heartfelt repentance, prayer, private worship, meditation, fellowship with other genuine believers—these disciplines all help to bring transformation. Quiet time with God is vital.

Further, being filled with the Holy Spirit imparts spiritual gifts that open a new relationship with the Father and empower us for greater Christian witness. How does this affect our minds? Mentally, we are stabilized, calmed and renewed. From that comes an intensified love for Jesus, a greater assurance of faith and genuine desire for relationship with Him. Many experience an enhanced love for other believers, deeper tranquility in times of stress, deepened spirituality and freedom from religiosity. Many Scriptures speak about mind renewal but the following ones are primary: John 8:32; Romans 12:1–2; 2 Corinthians 4:16; 10:4–5; Ephesians 4:23; Philippians 4:6–7; Colossians 3:2, 16.

22. How Can We Stay Free from Mental Bondage?

Scripture amply supplies us with the tools of rescue and self-defense to avoid captivity of the soul. First of all, a repentant lifestyle that is strong in faith, devoted to God, consistently involved in public and private worship, devoted to Scripture and active in Christian service is the best protection from being captured. The one who grows in grace, guards against immaturity and maintains fellowship with other mature Christians will escape this mental snare.

The prophet Hosea declared that God's people were "destroyed for lack of knowledge" (Hosea 4:6). The apostle Paul exhorted us not to "be children in understanding" but to be mature (1 Corinthians 14:20). Perhaps one of the most poignant warnings came from Paul, who explained, "If our gospel is veiled, it is veiled to those who are perishing, whose minds the god of this age has blinded [hooded], who do not believe, lest the light of the gospel of the glory of Christ, who is the image of God, should shine on them" (2 Corinthians 4:3–4).

For those who are weary, heavy laden and cannot find rest, Jesus calls, encouraging them to come to Him. His promise is: "You will find rest for your souls. For My yoke is easy and My burden is light" (Matthew 11:29–30). Once in that rest, victims discover they can live free from the yoke of bondage (see Galatians 5:1–5; 2 Timothy 2:24–26).

23. How Do We Discern Good and Evil?

Many Spirit-filled people fail to realize the importance of having their spiritual gifting work in harmony with their natural discernment. There is a spiritual gift of "discerning of spirits," and believers also have a human capacity to exercise their senses to discern right from wrong.

Why is it important to know this? An authentic message in tongues or a prophetic word may be given to someone in the middle of the pastor's sermon or the soloist's presentation. Without the receiver's senses being properly exercised, he or she might feel authorized to interrupt.

Not so. Gifts of the Spirit are not to function apart from good judgment. The writer to the Hebrews said that our minds must be exercised to discern good and evil, right and wrong: "For everyone who partakes only of milk is unskilled in the word of righteousness, for he is a babe. But solid food belongs to those who are of full age, that is, those who by reason of use have their senses exercised to discern both good and evil" (Hebrews 5:13–14). It is the responsibility of those receiving spiritual gifts to exercise them with propriety. It was this very point that prompted the apostle Paul to write, "Desire earnestly to prophesy, and do not forbid to speak with tongues. Let all things be done decently and in order" (1 Corinthians 14:39–40).

Not only the gifts of the Holy Spirit, then, but also the fruit of the Spirit help bring discernment.

And finally, we discern good and evil through the Bible. Hebrews 4:12 says that "The word of God is living and powerful, and sharper than any two-edged sword" and that it "is a discerner of the thoughts and intents of the heart."

24. How Are Believers the Bride of Christ?

Jesus often illustrated His teaching by using the example of marriage. His first miracle was done at a wedding in Cana of Galilee when He turned water into wine (see John 2:1–11). One of His most significant parables is the story of the ten virgin-bridesmaids who were invited to a wedding but at which five were shut out (see Matthew 25:1–10). In another parable, He told about the king who gave a marriage feast for his son (see Matthew 22:2–14). The purpose of the wedding in Jesus' teaching was to emphasize intimacy in its most intense and pure way. The concept is climaxed in Scripture when the apostle John hears in his revelation the announcement of the Marriage Supper of the Lamb, when the redeemed become the "Bride of Christ" (see Revelation 19:6–9). Our "Bride" relationship with Jesus will be a completely new revelation and a departure from concepts we have known on earth.

Yet, during His ministry Jesus emphasized that in heaven the redeemed "neither marry nor are given in marriage, but are like angels of God" (Matthew 22:30; Mark 12:25; Luke 20:34–35). This seems contrary to His emphasis on marriage. The question, then, is, How can we be married to Christ? How can we be "one" with Him?

To understand this awesome relationship, we have to get beyond our present concept of the physical world. The day of Jesus' resurrection, when the disciples were hiding behind locked doors, He appeared suddenly in the room with them. The walls surrounding them had not kept Him out. They were terrified, thinking He was a ghost. He calmed them quickly, saying, "Behold My hands and My feet, that it is I Myself. Handle Me and see, for a spirit does not have flesh and bones as you see I have" (Luke 24:36–39). They touched Him, aghast at His duality: He was both physical and spiritual, separately distinct in each, but real in both dimensions.

Since Jesus passed through the wall, could He have also passed through their physical bodies? Could He have been inside of them? Yes. If they had been in spiritual bodies could they have done the same with Him? Yes. This is a distinction of the spirit world. It is at this point we are forced to stop. We are on very hallowed ground—a place where we tread no further. But the point is this: It may be that the "Bride and Groom" intimacy we share with Christ will be the revelation of Christ in us— physically and spiritually—as the hope of glory (see Colossians 1:27).

25. Who Takes the Initiative in Our Coming to God?

When Jesus told His listeners the parable of the Prodigal Son, we were given a beautiful lens through which to see the restorative heart of God the Father. Luke 15:20 describes how the father saw the prodigal first—even when the weary youth was a long way off. The father had compassion, ran to this one who had sinned against him and embraced him. Even immediately after the Fall it was the Father who was looking for Adam. The question "Where are you?" was not a geographic question but a question of the heart.

Jesus said: "No one can come to Me unless the Father who sent Me draws him; and I will raise him up at the last day" (John 6:44). He repeated that message: "Therefore I have said to you that no one can come to Me unless it has been granted to him by My Father" (John 6:65). This shows us further that, even when we respond to His welcoming embrace, even in this regard, salvation can never be claimed as a human achievement: "We love Him because He first loved us" (1 John 4:19). Of ourselves, we cannot see God or approach God. The initiative belongs to God and He offers Himself freely to mankind.

The unsaved person who rejects God's call to salvation, expecting to respond later in life, may discover that that opportunity never returns. Paul warned the church in Rome about a certain generation whom God finally rejected—people who chose to follow the lusts of their hearts, serving their own bodies rather than God. In their decision not to "retain God in their knowledge, God gave them over to a debased mind"—not prohibiting their choices of unrighteousness, sexual immorality, envy, murder, pride, unforgiveness, disobedience to parents and much more (see Romans 1:24–32).

As to humanity's ability to approach God by individual choice, Scripture says: "You cannot see My face, for no man shall see Me, and live" (Exodus 33:20); "No one has seen God at any time. The only begotten Son, who is in the bosom of the Father, He has declared Him" (John 1:18); "Not that anyone has seen the Father, except He who is from God; He has seen the Father" (John 6:46); God "who alone has immortality, dwelling in unapproachable light, whom no man has seen or can see" (1 Timothy 6:16); God is "not willing that any should perish but that all should come to repentance" (2 Peter 3:9).

This can give believers hope as we keep praying for and reaching out to the lost. Paul wrote to young Timothy that the Lord's servants must be about the business of gently instructing those who need to repent, so that they "may come to their senses and escape the snare of the devil, having been taken captive by him to do his will" (2 Timothy 2:25–26).

PART 3

What Is the Bible?

26. What Is the Bible's Message?

The Bible is God's written revelation. In it, God provides one consistent theme of His love and provision for mankind. It is a written account of Creation, the revelation of Himself to mankind and His presence in the history of human events. It is the work of the Holy Spirit: He dictated to more than forty authors over a period of sixteen hundred years. There are 66 books in the Old and the New Testaments.

The Law of Moses—the first Covenant—was sprinkled with the blood of animals (see Hebrews 9:18–19). The second Covenant was sanctified by the Messiah, sprinkling it with His own blood (see Hebrews 9:11–25; 12:24). As such, each covenant is inalterable, cannot be added to or taken from, and of which no part has lost the Divine Seal. Revelation 22:19 levies a severe warning against anyone changing Scripture. As to its permanency, Jesus said, "The Scripture cannot be broken" (John 10:35).

The Old Testament's history deals primarily with God's revelation of Himself to the Jews; the New Testament centers upon the life and ministry of Jesus Christ, recording the early history of the Church, and the establishment of Christianity. St. Augustine is credited as saying, "The old is in the new concealed; the new is in the old revealed." Each Testament was written under the inspiration of the Holy Spirit and to be understood must be read with His enlightenment. While Scripture remains unchanging, a specific illumination may appear according to an individual's particular need. This miraculous potential of its life-imparting power remains part of its great legacy.

The Bible is the most read book in the world. At least one book of the Bible has been translated into 2,454 of humanity's 6,900 languages. The entire Bible is available in 438 languages. Either the Old or New

Testament is available in 1,168 languages, and portions of the Bible are available in 848 languages.

No other book in history competes with the Bible. It speaks to every generation, circumstance and person with truths relevant to every age and situation. Jungle savages, college professors, small children, world leaders, sports figures—people from every culture and walk of life are impacted and changed by its holy truth.

27. How Could Both God and Men Write the Bible?

Men wrote the Bible—by divine inspiration.

Divine inspiration refers to the writers of the Bible being miraculously gifted by the Holy Spirit to follow His specific direction as they wrote. Referring to prophetic words of Scripture that were fulfilled about Jesus and witnessed by the disciples, the apostle Peter explained:

> We did not follow cunningly devised fables when we made known to you the power and coming of our Lord Jesus Christ, but were eyewitnesses of His majesty. For He received from God the Father honor and glory when such a voice came to Him from the Excellent Glory: "This is My beloved Son, in whom I am well pleased." And we heard this voice which came from heaven when we were with Him on the holy mountain. And so we have the prophetic word confirmed, which you do well to heed as a light that shines in a dark place, until the day dawns and the morning star rises in your hearts; knowing this first, that no prophecy of Scripture is of any private interpretation, for prophecy never came by the will of man, but holy men of God spoke as they were moved by the Holy Spirit.
>
> 2 Peter 1:16–21

Jesus told the disciples, "When He, the Spirit of truth, has come, He will guide you into all truth" (John 16:13). Those who would later write the New Testament would not have to rely on memory or history to record the details of His presence and work. When the Holy Spirit came upon Jesus' followers, He would both reveal and dictate the Gospel message: "The Helper, the Holy Spirit, whom the Father will send in my name, He will teach you all things, and bring to your remembrance all things that I said to you" (John 14:26). As the Holy Spirit spoke through them, they wrote without error. He dictated; they transcribed. He inspired; they recorded.

$28.$ How Does the Holy Spirit Speak through the Bible Today?

As the Holy Spirit guided the writers of Scripture through divine inspiration, so *divine revelation* allows the reader of the Bible to see beyond the surface message of the words and understand their spiritual meaning. Every believer needs this but especially those who preach the Gospel. The apostle Paul explained: "God . . . made us sufficient as ministers of the new covenant, not of the letter but of the Spirit; for the letter kills, but the Spirit gives life" (2 Corinthians 3:5–6). It is possible to study the Scripture as literature, apart from the Holy Spirit's guidance, and experience none of its enlightenment. Jesus explained, "When He, the Spirit of truth, has come, He will guide you into all truth . . . and He will tell you things to come" (John 16:13). We must have the Holy Spirit's illumination to understand Scripture properly.

"All Scripture is given by inspiration of God" (2 Timothy 3:16). Everyone who reads, believes and applies Scripture "rightly [divides] the word of truth" and becomes "complete, thoroughly equipped for every good work" (2 Timothy 2:15; 3:17). The discovery of this awesome truth transforms lives. As modern Christians, it is our duty to believe all New Testament Scripture with equal devotion and commitment. There are no defunct parts. The Holy Scripture is the divinely inspired Word of God and the Church's only rule of faith and practice (see John 6:63;

14:26–27; 2 Timothy 3:16; 2 Peter 1:20–21). Without the Holy Spirit's specific revelation it is impossible to understand Scripture.

29. Why Four Gospels?

The Law of Moses required at least two witnesses in a trial. Three was better. "One witness shall not rise against a man concerning any iniquity or any sin that he commits; by the mouth of two or three witnesses the matter shall be established" (Deuteronomy 19:15). The gospels go beyond the demand of the Law and provide four witnesses to the life and ministry of Jesus Christ. These four give us an opportunity to see Him from four different directions. All writers tell about the same subject—but as if looking into a room through different windows.

30. What Are Synoptic Gospels?

The gospels of Matthew, Mark and Luke are called *synoptic* because they are similar and record many of the same events in Jesus' life and ministry. Approximately 90 percent of Mark's record is found in Matthew and about 50 percent appears in Luke. Much of Luke, chapters 10–20, is unique to him. *Synoptic* actually means "together-sight." The parables, for instance, are found only in the synoptic gospels.

Matthew addresses his message to a Jewish audience and quotes extensively from the Old Testament. He is the only one who uses the phrase *Kingdom of heaven*, which appears 32 times, and establishes Jesus' kingship. He assures his readers that Jesus is Messiah and ruler of the Kingdom of heaven. Many of the Jews remembered Matthew as Levi—the despised tax collector who had betrayed his own people by serving Rome. After encountering Jesus, Levi's life was radically changed. He became known far and wide as an honest man and lover of Jesus. His gospel is the longest of the four, being presented in 28 chapters and giving a full portrayal of the life and ministry of Jesus.

Mark, also believed to be John Mark, introduces Jesus by telling of His baptism and empowering by the Holy Spirit. Mark then proceeds to relate the preaching of the Gospel to the Kingdom of God and the living presence of His Spirit. Without hesitation, Mark tells the people that their entrance into this new Kingdom is through the doorway of repentance. Significantly, Mark was not one of Jesus' original twelve disciples, but his gospel was the first to be written and was widely circulated before the other three were composed. He is believed to have been closely associated with Peter. Mark writes primarily to the Gentile Christians in Rome and emphasizes Jesus' role as God's servant who died at the hands of Roman authorities. He provides significant information about Jesus' crucifixion and resurrection.

Luke, Gentile, beloved physician and companion of Paul, begins his gospel by focusing on the family identity of Jesus and those around Him. Great detail is given to the birth of John the Baptist, his elderly parents, and their physical and emotional circumstances. The same pattern of careful detail to the family follows with Joseph, Mary and the birth of Jesus. Luke gives more emphasis to Jesus' compassion for Samaritans and Gentiles, showing His willingness to risk His own safety by reaching out to those who were despised and rejected by the Jews. Jesus had already announced that He had come to "set captives free." This theme continues throughout the gospel of Luke as its primary message. Like Mark, Luke was not an original disciple during the public ministry of Jesus. Even so, he provides a thoroughly historical description of Jesus' life and ministry among the Jews. His introduction of John the Baptist is thorough, including John's announcement, "I indeed baptize you with water; but One mightier than I is coming, whose sandal strap I am not worthy to loose. He will baptize you with the Holy Spirit and fire" (Luke 3:16).

The gospel of John, written by the disciple "whom Jesus loved" (John 13:23), is unique among the four gospels. Composed several decades after the others, it bears little resemblance to them. The writings of Matthew, Mark and Luke were widely known and believed by thousands; repeating what they had said years before would have been pointless for John. By the time of John's writing, AD 70, the Church had been fully established, the city of Jerusalem destroyed by Roman General Titus, and the stones of its magnificent Temple demolished as Jesus had predicted (see Matthew 24:2). For such reasons, John's gospel was composed independently of the others. The primary reason for its differences, however, is as Peter explained: "Holy men of God spoke as they were moved by the Holy Spirit" (2 Peter 1:21). John, like the others, did not choose his own message; it was given to him by God.

31. What about "Conflicting Doctrines" in Scripture?

The apostle Peter said this of Paul's writings: "Paul, according to the wisdom given to him, has written to you . . . in which [letters] are some things hard to understand, which untaught and unstable people twist to their own destruction, as they do also the rest of the Scriptures" (2 Peter 3:15–16).

Students of the Bible have found deliberate tension in the Scriptures—tension that challenges us by appearing to suggest conflicting doctrines. All the while, the Bible does not acknowledge the tension is there. Our task is to accept both sides as true, pursue the Holy Spirit's enlightenment, and discover the point of reconciliation in what seem to be conflicting truths. As an example we can view the centuries-long debate between Reformed theologians and Arminian theologians who challenge each other with equally valid amounts of Scripture. Instead of accepting the tension, they oppose it, embracing one pole at the expense of the other.

"Rabbi" John Duncan (1796–1870), the Scottish theologian famous for his devotion to the Jews, said, "Preach the antinomy of truth and carry each out as far as it is possible to carry it but do not attempt to reconcile them." He illustrated this with the placement of stones in an arch: By pressing against each other, the stones exert the strength necessary to preserve the whole arch. The tension between truths exists only in the natural realm, not in the spiritual.

32. What about "Conflicting Accounts" in Scripture?

What about events described in Scripture that seem to be irreconcilable? Consider the controversy swirling around Judas Iscariot by what appears to be conflicting accounts of his death. One Scripture says he hanged himself. Another records how he purchased a field with the money he received for betraying Jesus. In it, he fell and all his bowels gushed out. (See Matthew 27:3–5; Acts 1:16–19.)

First of all, why the detail about his belly bursting open? We find the answer in at least two illustrations of Scripture. When God cursed the serpent for his betrayal of mankind, he said, "On your belly you shall go . . . all the days of your life" (Genesis 3:14). The ultimate disgrace God could put upon him was the dragging of his belly through the dirt. Why was contempt focused on his belly?

We find the answer the day Jesus cried out in the Temple, "He that believeth on me, as the scripture hath said, out of his belly shall flow rivers of living water" (John 7:38 KJV). The quote is purposely given here from the King James Version, which correctly translates the Greek word *koilia* as "belly"—not as heart. The difference is important. The word *koilia* refers to that part of the body directly under the rib cage. In Greek thought, this space typified the concave arch of heaven that they believed God had redesigned in humanity. What part of Judas burst open? The same part for which God had showed contempt in Satan—and that Jesus had declared could produce "rivers of living water."

It is not accidental that the Bible details the death of Judas as it does. He could not have merely stumbled while running across a field, fallen, and burst open. The apostle Paul explained that our bodies are Temples of the Holy Spirit (1 Corinthians 6:19). Judas showed ultimate contempt for this honor and both accounts of his death are true. As with the serpent, Judas' *koilia* ended in disgrace. His Temple was splattered on the rocks. How did it happen? In the process of hanging himself, he plunged into a ravine and burst open on the dirt below.

Human logic and reason must give way to the Holy Spirit's divine challenge and submit humbly to His wisdom, for "all Scripture is given by inspiration of God, and is profitable for doctrine" (2 Timothy 3:16).

33. Do Early Copies of the Bible Exist and Why Is That Important?

The overwhelming demand for a written account about Jesus in the first century had no precedent in world history.

The message of Jesus hit the ancient world with such cataclysmic force that an almost-frantic copying of New Testament books was undertaken. Thirty years after the death of Jesus, Christians in the city of Rome were so numerous that when the city was severely damaged by fire, Emperor Nero blamed the disciples for the tragedy. In the frenzy that followed, thousands of believers were slaughtered in heinous ways. Christians were desperate for copies of New Testament books, and after the fire they flooded into Rome. Scribes copied the Scriptures painstakingly, treating the written Word with reverence.

As a result of ongoing hunger for Scripture, the number of New Testaments—the body of work having been completed by the end of the first century—eclipsed all the combined works of Plato, Herodotus, Euripides, Aristotle, Homer and other ancient writers. Today research reveals that 5,686 ancient Greek New Testament manuscripts survive. In contrast, only 7 copies of Plato survive, 8 of Herodotus, 9 of Euripides,

49 of Aristotle, 643 of Homer—and all of these were copied at least a thousand years after the original. This is not true of the New Testament. Portions of the gospels exist that date to the first century, including a fragment of the book of John that was written about 29 years after the apostle wrote the original. No secular book can make such a claim. Besides Greek copies, there are some 19,000 ancient New Testament transcripts in Syriac, Latin, Coptic and Aramaic languages.

This support-base of 24,000 historic New Testament manuscripts penned by scribes gives scholars the opportunity to compare them for accuracy. The result: These books are about 99.5 percent textually pure. Not only so, but these copies are better preserved than any other document from the past.

When the original New Testament letters were written, numerous people were still alive who had heard Jesus personally and would have protested loudly had the writing been inaccurate. No such complaints exist. None of Plato's or Aristotle's hearers was present to edit the copies authorities now accept as valid. The New Testament is deserving of that same justice.

34. What Are the Dead Sea Scrolls?

In 1946 a young shepherd named Juma was tending his flock in the wilderness outside Jerusalem, a little over a mile northwest of the Dead Sea, and passing the time by throwing rocks into the opening of a cave. One of the stones landed in the cave with the sound of breaking pottery. He went to tell his two cousins who were close by, returned with one of them and went in. There they saw dozens of clay jars filled with ancient scrolls—but disappointedly—found no gold.

Even so, word of the discovery spread quickly. Scrolls were brought out and the leading archeologist of the day, William Albright, after examining them, announced that some were books from the Hebrew Bible a thousand years older than anything the Jews then possessed.

This led to the discovery of ten other caves in the area containing more ancient artifacts, all of which were named the "the Dead Sea Scrolls."

In an eleven-year period—from 1945 to 1956—some 981 scrolls or fragments were retrieved from caves in the area, representing all of the books of the Bible except Esther. One was the complete book of Isaiah and today is on display in Jerusalem. Most of the writing is in Hebrew; some is in Aramaic, Greek and a small portion Nabataean. The majority are parchment; others are papyrus and one copper.

It is believed the caves were the storage place for a religious Jewish group, the Essenes, whose commune was close by. Forty percent of the materials found are the earliest known copies of books from the Hebrew Bible. Thirty percent are from the era of the Second Temple (516 BC to AD 70), after the Old Testament canon had closed. Many of these were penned within the lifetime of Jesus, others within a century or two before. Not all can be read. The fragile condition of many prevents their being opened. Among them are the non-biblical books of Enoch, Tobit, the Wisdom of Sirach and Jubilees; Psalms 152–155 have also been identified. The rest, approximately 30 percent, are non-religious and valuable for providing information of that day.

35. Who Determined the New Testament Canon of Scripture?

The word *canon* as applied to the New Testament comes from an interesting Hebrew and Greek origin. It is derived from a concept meaning a "reed or cane"—apparently referring to the plant Cyperus papyrus, which was abundant in the Middle East. The reeds of this plant were uniformly straight, sometimes reaching a height of sixteen feet, and were used widely as measuring rods. Spiritually, it could symbolize the importance of daily measurement of one's faith, morals, attitudes.

Equally important, the soft, pulpy interior of the plant was the source for making paper. Much ancient writing, including copies of the Bible, was done on papyrus. Scrolls of it exist today. It was an easy transition to refer to Scripture as the "canon"—whether the "reed" by which one kept one's faith straight with truth or the paper on which that truth was written. Writings were determined to have canonical authority only if they were spiritually straight and reliable rules of faith and practice.

In the year AD 367, Athanasius, Archbishop of Alexandria (Egypt), a premier theologian, published in his "Easter Letter" a list of 27 approved books that he classified as canonical. This is considered to be the first authoritative listing of New Testament books; until then, most of the books had circulated separately among churches. He also listed the Old Testament books, which were already established as authoritative. The bishop, with the sanction of other godly scholars, simply recognized which documents bore the Holy Spirit's endorsement and which did not (see Hebrews 9:11–23; 12:24). Canonizing did not authorize Scripture; it merely acknowledged which books were authorized and anointed by the Holy Spirit. Athanasius explained: "These [books] are fountains of salvation that they who thirst may be satisfied with the living words they contain. In these alone is proclaimed the doctrine of godliness." The first council to accept this canon might have been the Synod of Hippo in North Africa (AD 393). It was also accepted by the Council of Carthage (AD 397).

36. What Is the Septuagint Translation?

The Septuagint is a Greek translation of the Hebrew Old Testament and other Jewish writings that was begun in Alexandria, Egypt, in 275 BC. The city contained the Royal Library of Alexandria, the world's greatest library at that time—believed to have housed some 400,000 scrolls, including works of Plato, Socrates, Aristotle and other significant writers—but did not hold a copy of the Hebrew Bible. Ptolemy II reputedly made the request of Eleazar, the Jewish High Priest in Jerusalem, for a copy of the Hebrew Scriptures in the Koine Greek language. In response, seventy top Jewish scholars were sent from Jerusalem to the Library to make the translation.

Gathering on an island called Pharos, the scholars completed the translation of the Torah or Pentateuch, the first five books of the Bible, in 72 days. This was followed in time by the rest of the Old Testament. The translation of the Hebrew Bible and the Apocrypha came to be called the *Septuagint*, which means "translation of the seventy." The Dead Sea Scrolls, discovered in 1946, give credence to the Septuagint.

Following Egypt's conquest by Alexander the Great in 332 BC, Greek became the official language for culture and commerce. By the time the seventy Jewish scholars began the translation some decades later, the city of Alexandria was home to a huge colony of Greek-speaking Jews. This, then, was the version of the Old Testament that they used. It was also the version of the Hebrew Scriptures that Jesus and the apostles quoted. In addition, the New Testament was joined to this version of the Old Testament to stand as the Bible used by the Church. What about this? Consider Paul's explanation: God "made us sufficient as ministers of the new covenant, not of the letter but of the Spirit; for the letter kills, but the Spirit gives life" (2 Corinthians 3:5–6). Regardless of the Bible version we use, without the anointing of the Holy Spirit to give revelation and empower our message, we will bring forth a faulty, insufficient Gospel. Authentic preaching is not from the "letter" of Scripture but its revelation.

Regarding the Library itself, the structure was built in elegant Egyptian style and consisted of gardens with a peripatos walkway similar to the one approaching the Acropolis in Athens, Greece. There was a large dining room, reading room, meeting rooms, lecture halls and residences for a hundred scholars who worked there full time. Book topics consisted of astronomy, mathematics, natural sciences, religion, physics and other subjects vital to the day.

37. What Is the Historical Significance of the King James Version of the Bible?

The King James Bible, commonly known as the Authorized Version, is an English translation begun in 1604 and completed in 1611. Immediate upon his ascension to the throne of England, King James VI ordered a new English translation of Scripture. Puritans demanded it; leaders in his own Church of England opposed it. Strangely, the King sided with the Puritans. Forty-seven scholars were assembled at the Hampton Court Conference, near London, where a new English version was begun. The New Testament was translated from the original Greek, the Old Testament translated from ancient Hebrew and Aramaic.

More than any other book in human history, the King James Bible has been the instrument for civilizing many remote sites of mankind. When the evangelical Foreign Mission movement began in the late 1700s and early 1800s, Christian missionaries carried the King James Bible to many places around the world. Jungle villages, lonely desert outposts and frozen tundra of the far north heard Scripture from the King James Bible. Wherever the missionaries went, churches, hospitals, schools and universities sprang up. Its message brought stability to family life and laid the foundation for good government. Everyone benefitted. The "KJV" has critics as well as admirers, but no one has defended it more than Catholic scholar Alexander Geddes. In 1786 he said, "If accuracy and strictest attention to the letter of the text be supposed to constitute an excellent version, this is of all versions the most excellent."

38. What Are Other Historic English Bibles?

Prior to the publication of the King James Bible in 1611, six English translations appeared in the previous century. They were: *Wycliffe's Bible*, hand-printed in about 1382; the *Tyndale Bible*, the New Testament being published in 1526 and Old Testament portions by 1536; the *Coverdale Bible*, 1535; the *Matthew Bible*, 1537; the *Great Bible*, 1539; the *Geneva Bible*, 1559; the *Douay Bible*, 1582; and the *Bishops' Bible*, 1568.

When the first English settlers arrived in 1607 to establish the Jamestown colony, as part of King James' Virginia Company, it was most likely the Geneva Bible that they brought ashore. When the Pilgrims landed at Plymouth in 1620 they, too, brought the Geneva Bible with them. Interestingly, the Pilgrims, dissenters from the Church of England, did not bring the newly published King James "Authorized Version" of 1611. That may have been prejudice against the king who had "driven them out of the land"; he was not their friend.

39. What Are the Apocrypha?

The Apocrypha are a collection of ancient Greek, Latin and Semitic writings that predate Christianity and are inserted into some Bibles between the Old and New Testaments. Historically, they were endorsed by the Roman Catholic Church at the Council of Trent, 1545–1563, and are included in Catholic Bibles today.

Why are the Apocrypha omitted from most Protestant Bibles? Principally because none of the apocryphal writers claimed divine inspiration. Jewish rabbis never acknowledged the apocryphal books as sacred Scriptures. After the overthrow of Jerusalem in AD 70, the Jews destroyed all the apocryphal writings available. The books were not accepted as sacred during the first four centuries of the Church; nor were they included by Archbishop Athanasius when he set the canon of Scripture in AD 367. The first of the four books of Maccabees is the only one regarded as a reliable historical source.

The Apocrypha also contain doctrines that conflict with the Old and New Testaments, doctrines like prayers for the dead, silver being used to pay for a soul's redemption from hell, and fallen man's sinless perfection.

In part, it was Roman Catholic teaching originating in the Apocrypha that enraged Martin Luther and began the Protestant Reformation.

40. Why Is the Book of Enoch Not Included in Our Bible?

The book of Enoch is an ancient Hebrew-Aramaic text believed by many to be an authentic work by the great-grandfather of Noah. The apostle Jude refers to Enoch in his New Testament letter: "Now Enoch, the seventh from Adam, prophesied about these men also" (Jude 14) and quotes his prophecy of the Lord's judgment against "ungodly acts" and "harsh words." Jewish rabbis argued against Enoch's authorship of the book bearing his name; modern scholars have dated the manuscript as having been written between 100 and 300 BC.

The writing, which reads in the sense of Scripture, deals heavily with the theme of fallen angels and their sexual encounters with human women. The book was cherished by the early Essene sect; when the Dead Sea Scrolls were discovered in 1946, copies of Enoch were among them.

The Jews did not include the book of Enoch when forming their biblical canon, even though many of that day held it in high esteem. Some Jewish rabbis argued against Enoch's message of fallen angels incarnating into human bodies and fathering children by earthly women, actions referred to in Genesis 6:1–4. Justin Martyr, when stating that evil came from demons who were the spirits of offspring of angels and human women, was quoting Enoch. Many other church fathers including Irenaeus (122–c. 202), Tertullian (c. 160–c. 220) and Origen (c. 185–c. 254) endorsed the book of Enoch. Even so, enough reliable opposition arose against the book by learned Jewish scholars that it was not included in the Bible. Along with the book of Enoch, the Apocrypha, books of Wisdom, of Sirach, Jubilees and other ancient writings were not included.

These decisions were made with much prayer and deliberation. We are safe in trusting the guidance of the Holy Spirit as ancient rabbis canonized the Old Testament and those working with Archbishop Athanasius the New.

41. What Does the Power of the Gospel Look Like?

In 1959, nineteen-year-old Minnesotan Bruce Olson, over the protests of family and friends, flew alone to South America to become a missionary to the stone-age Motilone Indian tribe. No white man had ever entered Motilone territory and survived. Olson traveled alone hundreds of miles into the interior—and was welcomed into Motilone territory by being shot with an arrow, taken to a village and tied to a post. But amazingly he survived. At that point, he could hardly have imagined that for the next forty years he would live as a Motilone, learning their ways, speaking their language, translating the New Testament for them, and slowly bringing them to a life-changing encounter with Jesus Christ. In one generation after encountering Jesus Christ, the Motilone tribe has evangelized eighteen other jungle tribes. Today scores of Motilone health centers and medical stations, along with scores more schools and agricultural centers serve the tribe. The tribe has produced missionaries, lawyers and business administrators. Natives are achieving political status and have represented South America's Indian tribes in a world conference.

Such is the power of the Gospel of Jesus Christ.

PART 4

What Is the Significance of Jesus' Death and Resurrection?

42. How Many Old Testament Prophecies Are about Jesus?

It is estimated that Jesus fulfilled more than 350 Old Testament prophecies involving every aspect of His life and ministry. Here are twelve major prophecies fulfilled in Him:

He would be born of a virgin (Isaiah 7:14; Matthew 1:22–23).

His lineage would come through King David (Isaiah 9:7; Luke 1:32).

Bethlehem would be the place of His birth (Micah 5:2; Matthew 2:1).

His birth and kingship would be announced by a star (Numbers 24:17; Matthew 2:1–2).

A massacre of children would occur at Bethlehem (Jeremiah 31:15; Matthew 2:16–18).

God would call His Son out of Egypt (Hosea 11:1; Matthew 2:14–15).

He would be betrayed for thirty pieces of silver (Zechariah 11:12–13; Matthew 26:14–16).

He would be marred (Isaiah 52:14; Matthew 27:27–30).

His hands and feet would be pierced (Psalm 22:16; John 20:24–27).

Like Moses' serpent, He would be lifted up (Numbers 21:9; John 3:14).

Not one of His bones would be broken (Psalm 34:20; John 19:33–36).

He would be raised from the dead (Psalm 16:10; Mark 16:6).

43. What Is the Most Complete Prophecy of Jesus in the Old Testament?

The fullest prophecy of Jesus is given in Isaiah 53:1–12. The prophet who lived from 740–681 BC describes the Messiah as a man who was rejected and whom God punished on our behalf. He was a man of sorrows. He was despised, and yet He carried our griefs and sorrows. He was bruised for our sins and sicknesses. We who sinned have peace because He suffered. He died, like a lamb to the slaughter, on our behalf. He was cut off from the land of the living and buried in a rich man's tomb. But when He could see at last the results of His sacrifice, He would be satisfied. God would allot Him a portion with the great. Now as the pleasure of the Lord prospers in His hand, He lives to make intercession for us.

44. What Is the Significance of 39 Lashes on Jesus?

Jewish and Roman law both required forty lashes for someone being put to death and 39 lashes for someone with a lesser crime. Deuteronomy 25:3 details the Jewish instruction: "Forty blows he may give him and no more." Roman law was fiercer and required that if the executioner failed to put the victim to death with forty lashes that the executioner was put to death. This guaranteed that a flogger would not be merciful to the victim. When death was not intended, the Romans felt that 39 lashes would bring a person to the point of death without killing him.

Christ carried the death sentence but His death was reserved for the cross. According to prophecy, He had to be "lifted up," suspended between heaven and earth. This portrayed His making reconciliation between earth's sin and heaven's holiness. Jesus foretold His own execution: "As Moses lifted up the serpent in the wilderness, even so must the Son of Man be lifted up" (John 3:14; see Numbers 21:9). Additionally,

Jesus had to be "numbered with the transgressors"—i.e., the two thieves who were crucified with Him (Mark 15:28). That meant He could not die with His body touching the ground or alone at the whipping post. In authentic typology, the flogger represents us who put our sins upon him.

Roman scourging, called *verberatio*, according to Sempronian (123 BC) and Porcian (248 BC) laws, was the most vicious inflicted by any ancient culture. The whip was made with three belts of leather, each three feet long, and attached to a wooden handle. A sharp piece of metal, glass or bone was embedded in the lash that would cut the victim's flesh in long, open wounds. Victims usually bled to death. Roman citizens were exempt from flagellation and the punishment was reserved for slaves or non-Romans (see Acts 16:37). Romans always made scourging a public spectacle. Jews usually administered floggings at the synagogue.

It was during the beating of Jesus that Isaiah's prophecy was fulfilled: "He was wounded for our transgressions, He was bruised for our iniquities; the chastisement for our peace was upon Him, and by His stripes we are healed" (Isaiah 53:5; see Matthew 8:17; 20:18–19). Numerous medical resources claim there are 39 different categories of disease. If that be so, then it could well apply that each lash Jesus received transferred one of those 39 from us to Him. It was at this specific time that the Father "made Him who knew no sin to be sin for us, that we might become the righteousness of God in Him" (2 Corinthians 5:21).

45. What Happened to the Two Thieves?

Jesus, as the divine Redeemer, was suspended on the cross, His head skyward, feet not touching the ground, lifted between heaven and hell, portraying the final separation of the two realms. Two thieves, representing both spheres, hung on crosses on either side. One thief was saved in his dying moments.

Seven hundred years before the birth of Christ the prophet Isaiah wrote, "He poured out His soul unto death, and He was numbered with the transgressors, and He bore the sin of many, and made intercession for the transgressors" (Isaiah 53:12). King David, a thousand years before Jesus' birth, described the crucifixion scene. Speaking for Jesus, he said, "All those who see Me ridicule Me; they shoot out the lip, they shake the head, saying, 'He trusted in the LORD, let Him rescue Him; let Him deliver Him, since He delights in Him!'" (Psalm 22:7–8). At the time of the crucifixion these prophecies were fulfilled in this way:

> Likewise the chief priests also, mocking with the scribes and elders, said, . . . "If He is the King of Israel, let Him now come down from the cross, and we will believe Him. He trusted in God; let Him deliver Him now if He will have Him; for He said, 'I am the Son of God.'" Even the robbers who were crucified with Him reviled Him with the same thing.
>
> Matthew 27:41–44

Then, as Luke describes, one of the criminals appeared to have a change of heart and rebuked the other criminal for his blasphemy, saying that their punishment was justly given but that "this Man" has done nothing wrong. When the criminal asked to be remembered by Jesus when He came into His Kingdom, Jesus replied, "Assuredly, I say to you, today you will be with Me in Paradise" (Luke 23:44).

The cross atop every Russian and Eastern Orthodox Church portrays all three crosses. Above the big bar of Jesus' cross is another small bar representing the repentant thief. Jesus is between him and hell, protectively lifting him toward heaven. Beneath the feet of Jesus is another broken cross with the bar pointing downward toward hell. This represents the cross of the unrepentant thief.

46. What Is the Significance of Jesus' Bones Not Being Broken?

Part of Roman execution was to break the victims' legs and make suffering as violent as possible. Usually, this hastened the victim's death.

At the crucifixion of Jesus there was another important factor: His body was still on the cross, sundown was approaching and the Jewish Passover would begin. The priests wanted the three bodies removed from the crosses before the celebration began. The soldiers returned to the site, broke the legs of the two thieves, but finding Jesus was already dead they left His bones intact (see John 19:31–33).

Why was Jesus spared this brutality that the other two suffered? In Scripture, bone symbolizes a bride. When God created Eve, He removed a rib from Adam's body from which she was created. Seeing her, Adam said she is "bone of my bones and flesh of my flesh" (Genesis 2:23). The night of the first Passover in Egypt, Moses commanded the Jews not to break any bone of the paschal lamb (see Exodus 12:46). Unknown to them, the bone had deep prophetic meaning about their future Messiah. One of their ancestors, Joseph, who had rescued his family from famine and death, also forecast an authentic picture of Christ. Knowing this, Moses exhumed Joseph's centuries-old bones in Egypt and had them reburied in the land of Israel (see Exodus 13:19). Speaking prophetically of Jesus, King David foretold of the Father guarding His bones and keeping them from being broken (see Psalm 34:20). Centuries later, the apostle John wrote that not one of Jesus' bones was broken (see John 19:32–33). John later described the Bride of Christ in her unbroken state and dressed in fine linen, clean, bright, and beautiful (see Revelation 19:6–9). You, I, all saved people as part of His Bride were in Christ at the cross but were spared the pain of being broken.

47. Why Was Jesus Forsaken at the Cross?

At Jesus' baptism, the Holy Spirit—in the form of a dove; not a literal dove—anointed and remained on Him (see John 1:33). From that moment on, it was the Spirit who performed the will of the Father and did all the miraculous works accomplished through Jesus. Immediately after baptism, in His first sermon in Nazareth, Jesus explained this: "The

Spirit of the LORD is upon Me, because He has anointed Me to preach the gospel to the poor; He has sent Me to heal the brokenhearted, to proclaim liberty to the captives and recovery of sight to the blind, to set at liberty those who are oppressed; to proclaim the acceptable year of the LORD" (Luke 4:18–19).

At the cross, the joint working of Jesus and the Spirit being complete, the Spirit lifted from Him. Note: It was not the Spirit's work of incarnation that departed; it was the anointing only. This apparently was unanticipated by Jesus. When the Comforter lifted He screamed, "My God, My God, why have You forsaken me?" The Comforter was all He had. If the anointing of the Comforter had remained on Him at the cross, it is possible Jesus might not have died. Abandonment was necessary. Jesus' desertion had been forecast centuries before by the example of the scapegoat. Leviticus 16:8–10 explains: "Then Aaron shall cast lots for the two goats: one lot for the LORD and the other lot for the scapegoat." The sins of Israel were confessed upon the head of the scapegoat; it was then led away to the backside of the desert and abandoned to die of loneliness and thirst. This was the forecast for Jesus; it meant He faced death as a sin-cursed man and with universal iniquity upon Him.

Of this moment He had earlier said, "My Father loves Me, because I lay down My life that I may take it again. No one takes it from Me, but I lay it down of Myself. I have power to lay it down, and I have power to take it again. This command I have received from My Father" (John 10:17–18).

48. Why Did Blood and Water Come from the Body of Jesus?

A corpse does not bleed. Once the heart stops and blood pressure drops to zero, there is nothing inside the body to force the blood out. It can no longer flow. In the case of Jesus, this was not so. Scripture explains that "when they came to Jesus and saw that He was already dead . . . one of the soldiers pierced His side with a spear, and immediately blood and water came out" (John 19:33–34).

Jesus had earlier offered this special water to the woman at the well when He offered her living water that would become "a fountain of water springing up into everlasting life" (John 4:14). Again, on one of the feast days in Jerusalem, Jesus stood and cried out to the crowds, "If anyone thirsts, let him come to Me and drink. He who believes in Me, as the Scripture has said, out of his heart will flow rivers of living water'" (John 7:37–38). By this He was speaking of the giving of the Holy Spirit at the soon-coming Pentecost when all the disciples would be filled—baptized—with the Holy Spirit.

The Roman spear that opened the body of Jesus for the release of blood and water had an earlier parallel in the ministry of Moses. During Israel's flight from Egypt and their finding no water in the desert, God spoke to Moses, saying, "Behold, I will stand before you there on the rock in Horeb; and you shall strike the rock, and water will come out of it, that the people may drink" (Exodus 17:5–6). While Israel was blessed to have water, the experience was also prophetic of the coming of Christ.

Paul gave deeper insight to Israel's experience in the wilderness when he wrote that the children of Israel "all were baptized into Moses in the cloud and in the sea, all ate the same spiritual food, and all drank the same spiritual drink. For they drank of that spiritual Rock that followed them, and that Rock was Christ" (1 Corinthians 10:2–5).

49. Does the Blood of Jesus Have Power?

Had Jesus been killed at age two, as Herod attempted, or 31 years later as the Romans achieved, His blood would have had the same redemptive power. As a babe, conceived by the Holy Spirit, He was fully the Son of God when Mary gave birth to Him; whether He died by Herod's spear or the Roman cross would have made no difference.

But a second work of the Holy Spirit was necessary before the benefit of His blood could be applied to mankind. As with Moses in Egypt, killing the Passover Lamb and putting its blood in the basin did not save Israel. The blood had to be applied to the doorpost of each person being saved. Without the application of the blood, the Israelites' firstborns would have perished with the Egyptians'. Identically for us, the blood of Jesus must be applied personally to each one being saved (see Romans 3:23–25).

This fact, that the blood must be applied, necessitated the Holy Spirit's second work in Jesus: anointing. This occurred during Jesus' baptism in the Jordan when the dove of the Spirit came upon Him, empowering Him to proclaim the Gospel message. Prior to the Holy Spirit's descent that day, Jesus healed no one, performed no miracle, preached no "Gospel of the Kingdom." That changed abruptly when the Holy Spirit anointed Him (see Luke 4:18).

So also today, the Holy Spirit's anointing is our necessary empowering for effective ministry. Jesus' specific instruction was that the disciples wait in Jerusalem until they had been endued with "power from on high" (Luke 24:49). Paul equated his "fully" preaching the gospel of Christ with the "mighty signs and wonders" done by the Holy Spirit (Romans 15:19). Seminary degrees and ordination ceremonies can be impressive, but without the anointing of the Holy Spirit they are woefully insufficient. Such are artificial substitutes. They can impart prestige but no power. The Church has suffered severely because of the absence of spiritually empowered preaching and its replacement with religious lecturing.

What is the power of the blood? Scripture explains: "The life of the flesh is in the blood, and I have given it to you upon the altar to make atonement for your souls; for it is the blood that makes atonement for the soul" (Leviticus 17:11). Paul tells us that Christ died for us, justifying us and saving us from wrath through His blood (see Romans 5:7–10; see also Revelation 7:14).

The miraculous life of Jesus is in His blood: It has power to save. Without the application of the blood to each one personally there is no salvation. Similarly, there is no authority, no power.

50. Why Was the Temple Veil Torn?

The gospel accounts tell us that in the final three hours of Jesus' suffering on the cross, darkness covered the land. At midafternoon, "Jesus cried out again with a loud voice, and yielded up His spirit. Then, behold, the veil of the temple was torn in two from top to bottom" (Matthew 27:50–51).

Historians say this beautiful veil of blue, purple and scarlet, made of fine twisted linen, was approximately four inches thick and sixty feet high. Dimensions in Herod's Temple, standing at the time of Jesus, were much greater than Moses' Tabernacle. The height and thickness of the veil made its destruction more astonishing. (See Exodus 26:31–33.)

On the Day of Atonement each year the High Priest would go into the Holy of Holies behind the veil and sprinkle blood of sacrificial animals on the Ark of the Covenant. This did not remove Israel's sin but held back the wrath of God. The destruction of that veil and the exposure of Israel's Most Holy Place announced that God would never again accept such sacrifices. The final, most awesome and eternal sacrifice had been made on a cross a short distance away. The one about whom John the Baptist had declared, "Behold! The Lamb of God who takes away the sin of the world," had made the supreme and ultimate sacrifice (John 1:29).

The priests must have been speechless. Nothing could have been more shocking to them than the exposure of the Most Holy Place to human eyes. In that moment God was saying, "I am finished with the sacrifice and death of animals. The Lamb of God has ended it forever!"

In typology only, the tearing of the veil may also mean that the Shekinah glory, once hidden behind thick folds, was now free to invade the world. This happened later at Pentecost when the Holy Spirit rushed upon the disciples.

51. When Did Jesus Actually Take Our Sin upon Himself?

Jesus was born sinless and lived without sin, but the Father "made Him who knew no sin to be sin for us, that we might become the righteousness of God in Him" (2 Corinthians 5:21). At what point did this occur?

Scripture explains that Jesus "was in all points tempted as we are, yet without sin" (Hebrews 4:15). But when He went to the cross He was already carrying the full weight of mankind's sin and guilt upon Himself. The "divine exchange," the time when He lost His innocence and became the sin-bearer for mankind, took place at the whipping post. With each lash, humanity's sin, disease, guilt was transferred to Him.

Isaiah's prophetic passage describing the "Suffering Servant" explains that Jesus has "borne our griefs and carried our sorrows." He was "smitten by God"—wounded for our transgressions, bruised for our iniquities, chastised for our peace, brutally whipped for our healing (Isaiah 53:4). In the physical realm His body was being beaten to the point of death; in the spiritual realm an exchange was taking place. With the final lash Jesus, "who knew no sin," had assumed the full burden of our sin. The transfer was complete. He carried it to the cross, died and entered Sheol bearing it. When He rose from the dead, victorious over death, He left all sin behind. Jesus bore our sin to the grave without us.

Specifically, Jesus:

Was made sin with our sinfulness that we might be made the righteous of God in Him (see 2 Corinthians 5:21).

Became the scapegoat for us (see Leviticus 16:8–10; Mark 15:20).

Took our shame and gave us His glory (see Psalm 69:7; Romans 5:1–2).

Endured our poverty that we might share His riches (see 2 Corinthians 8:9).

Was wounded for us that we might be made whole (see Isaiah 53:4–5; 1 Peter 2:24).

Was punished that we might escape the wrath of God (see Isaiah 53:4–5; Romans 5:9).

Suffered our rejection that we might receive the Father's acceptance (see Matthew 27:45–46; Ephesians 1:3–4).

Became a curse for us that we might receive the blessing (see Galatians 3:13–14).

Jesus died our death so that we might share His life (see John 10:10; Romans 6:6–7; Galatians 2:20).

52. Who Was Responsible for Jesus' Death?

For many centuries after the crucifixion, the Jews suffered horribly, their villages destroyed and men, women, children, brutalized and murdered by so-called Christian mobs. The accusation was that Jews were "Christ-killers."

This was not true.

Nor did the Romans kill Jesus.

Jesus answered the question Himself when He said: "My Father loves Me, because I lay down My life that I may take it again. No one takes it from Me, but I lay it down of Myself. I have power to lay it down, and I have power to take it again. This command I have received from My Father" (John 10:17–18).

The beauty of Christ's death is in these words. He surrendered His life freely so that sinners could receive it freely. As God, He could not die; as man, He could not raise Himself from the dead. As the "God-man" He could do both. By choice, He released His own life: "Father! Into your hands I commit my spirit." But He also had power to "take it again."

Paul explains the purpose of His death: "All have sinned and fall short of the glory of God," but we are "justified freely by His grace through the redemption that is in Christ Jesus" (Romans 3:23–25). It is by Jesus' sacrifice and the atonement of His blood that we are saved from hell, born again, filled with the Holy Spirit and destined for heaven.

53. What Is Meant by Jesus' Descending into Hell?

Certain Bible words have the potential for conflicting interpretations. This is true particularly of *sheol* (Hebrew) and *hades* (Greek), which mean "the grave, hell or simply place of the departed dead—good or bad." When Jacob was told that his son Joseph was dead, the old man broke into tears saying, "I shall go down into the grave [sheol] to my son in mourning" (Genesis 37:35). Jacob was not referring to sheol as a place of torment, nor even as Joseph's grave, since he believed his son's bones were scattered unburied in the desert. Instead, to Jacob, sheol was a place of happy reunion. In this concept, sheol later became known as "Abraham's bosom" (Luke 16:22). The King James Version translates the word *sheol* 31 times as "the grave" and another 31 times as "hell." Three times it is translated as "pit." The context determined how the translators interpreted it, and in some cases we are left without a definitive meaning. Hebrew also uses the word *queber* (*kever*) in reference to "a grave, sepulcher, tomb, crypt, etc." This word has no reference to anything more than the place of burial.

While hell is eternal and very real, the idea that Jesus suffered its literal fire for three days is alien to sound biblical theology. Jesus told the repentant thief on the cross, "Today, you will be with Me in Paradise" (Luke 23:43). Secondly, when Paul spoke of Jesus descending into the "lower parts of the earth," he meant that Jesus' body went downward to the grave (Ephesians 4:9). Thirdly, according to significant biblical scholars, the statement that Jesus preached to the "spirits in prison" (1 Peter 3:19) refers to the pre-incarnate Jesus—the living Word of God—preaching by the Holy Spirit through Noah to the people of his day. This claim is very affirmable with the rest of Scripture. The New Testament speaks of propitiation—the turning away of the Lord's wrath—only in regard to Jesus shedding His blood on the cross. Nothing else added to that work of redemption. His shout from the cross, "It is finished!," was the universe-wide proclamation that redemption was complete, final, total.

54. What Do the Names *Christ* and *Messiah* Mean?

Messiah in Hebrew and *Christ* in Greek are exact equivalents. Both mean "Anointed One." This is a reference to the Holy Spirit's descent on Jesus during His baptism in the Jordan River. When the Holy Spirit came upon Him, Jesus officially became the Messiah. That was the moment of His anointing.

The anointing of the Spirit is not to be confused with Jesus' conception by the Spirit—which was a totally different work. Conception by the Spirit prepared Him for the redemptive work of the cross. That event united God and man into one human being, equipping Him with both natures: one for death as man and the other for resurrection as God. Anointing by the Spirit prepared Him for Gospel ministry, specifically the miraculous works such as healing, miracles, raising the dead, etc. He explained this in the synagogue of Nazareth when He said, "The Spirit of the LORD is upon Me, because He has anointed Me" (see Luke 4:18).

God had promised Israel a deliverer. Jesus was the fulfillment of that promise.

55. Why Is the Resurrection Vital?

The resurrection of Jesus was much more than the mere raising of His corpse into life. His resurrection was the absolute, utter, total defeat of the death principle and its power in the universe. The ancient struggle between life and death, light and darkness, good and evil came to an abrupt and final end.

Jesus had earlier explained that He had the power not only to lay His life down but also to raise it up again (see John 10:17). After that triumph, He appeared to the disciples and said, "All authority has been given to Me in heaven and on earth" (Matthew 28:18). Paul explained this authority when he wrote that Jesus was the creator of all things "in heaven and that are on earth, visible and invisible" (Colossians 1:16). In addition, the authority means that "in Him all things hold together" (Colossians 1:17 NASB; see Hebrews 11:3).

If Christ had not been raised, then our faith would be futile. If Christ had not been raised, we would still be lost in our sins (see 1 Corinthians 15:14, 17). In fact, had the resurrection of Christ failed, the entire universe would have imploded into chaos and darkness. The announcement of the angels—"He is not here! He is risen! Come see the place where the Lord lay!"—was the declaration for which creation waited.

Paul shares the glorious news that by opening our hearts to Jesus' redemptive work we are no longer slaves to sin. We died with Christ; we also "shall be in the likeness of His resurrection" (Romans 6:5). Because Jesus rose from the dead, we also are "alive to God in Christ Jesus our Lord" (Romans 6:11).

PART 5

What Is the Kingdom of God?

56. Is the Kingdom Now or Later?

The Kingdom of God was the core subject of the ministry of Jesus. He spoke the word *church* only three times in the gospels (see Matthew 16:18; 18:17) but talked about the Kingdom some 130 times. He "loved the church and gave Himself for her" (Ephesians 5:25), but His focus was on the Kingdom. If we are to be like Him our focus will be the same: First on the Kingdom, then on the Church.

In its widest scope, the Kingdom is the rule of God over every aspect of creation—from the core of every atom to the rim of the universe and beyond. This includes the visible and invisible dimensions of all that is, everything that has been, will ever be. Nothing is exempt from the Kingdom's reign. This remains true even though Satan has come against the accessible parts of the Kingdom: "From the days of John the Baptist until now the kingdom of heaven suffers violence [such as the beheading of John], and the violent take it by force" (Matthew 11:12). Violence reaches only that part of the Kingdom that has been committed to man; Satan cannot reach the Kingdom's heavenly source. Hence, Jesus' words to Pontius Pilate: "My kingdom is not of this world. If My kingdom were of this world, My servants would fight, so that I should not be delivered to the Jews; but now My kingdom is not from here" (John 18:36).

In other aspects, the Kingdom is in the process of expanding its rule now, and in heaven will reveal its total presence and purpose. The final display of Kingdom glory is foretold in Scripture: "Then comes the end, when He [Jesus] delivers the kingdom to God the Father, when He puts an end to all rule and all authority and power. For He must reign till He has put all enemies under His feet. The last enemy that will be destroyed is death" (1 Corinthians 15:24–26). Isaiah foretold the Kingdom's presence: "For unto us a Child is born, unto us a Son is given; and the government [Kingdom] will be upon His shoulder" (Isaiah 9:6).

The Kingdom is the medium through which God has extended spiritual authority for believers to rule and reign with Him (see Ephesians 1:18–20; 2:6; 3:10). In this capacity it is possible for one to be near the Kingdom but not in it, to be an heir of it but not exercise the power of it. Most tragically of all, it is possible for one to read about it in Scripture but not to have the personal revelation of it. To one young man Jesus said, "You are not far from the kingdom of God" (Mark 12:34).

57. Where Is the Kingdom?

Jesus spoke of the "Kingdom" about 130 times in the gospels; forty times He designated the "Kingdom of heaven" and 71 times the "Kingdom of God."

Observe the difference. He answered the Pharisees this way: "The kingdom of God does not come with observation; nor will they say, 'See here!' or 'See there!' For indeed, the kingdom of God is within you" (Luke 17:20–21). When Pontius Pilate quizzed Him about the Kingdom, He answered differently: "My kingdom is not of this world. If My kingdom were of this world, My servants would fight, so that I should not be delivered to the Jews: but now My kingdom is not from here" (John 18:36). In response to Pilate, Jesus was apparently speaking of His future earth-based Kingdom in the Millennial reign. Read the word *now* in the context of "no longer is My Kingdom from here."

On the Day of Ascension the disciples asked Him, "Lord, will You at this time restore the kingdom [an earthly kingdom] to Israel?"

He responded, "It is not for you to know times or seasons which the Father has put in His own authority" (Acts 1:6–7). The disciples were given "power and authority over all demons, and to cure diseases" and sent out "to preach the kingdom of God" (Luke 9:1–2). The future Kingdom of the Millennial reign on earth was not their concern.

Is this understanding correct? Perhaps yes, perhaps no. Scripture provides us with no clear distinction. John the Baptist told the people in his day, "Repent, for the kingdom of heaven is at hand!" (Matthew 3:2). That message of repentance must be the dominant Kingdom influence in our lives.

58. What Is the Difference between the Kingdom and the Church?

Matthew is the only gospel writer who records the word *church* and only three times (see Matthew 16:18; 18:17). The first mission of the Church—the Body of Christ—is to reveal the Kingdom and her glorious King. The modern Church has shifted that focus—to the local bodies of members. In so doing, the Church, which was birthed at Pentecost, has cut herself off from Kingdom authority and power. Herein lies the failure of modern Christianity and its lack of New Testament superiority. The current Church has friendly persuasion—but nothing more. Her gospel is powerless; it has no impact on the masses.

The Church exists solely because the Kingdom came first. The Kingdom is infallible; the Church is subject to error. The Kingdom does not submit to the Church; the Church submits to the Kingdom. The Kingdom does not draw its power from the Church; the Church draws her power from the Kingdom. The Kingdom is free from humanity; the Church is dependent on it. The Kingdom of God is preexistent, preeminent, predominate; the Church is subservient to the Kingdom. The Kingdom is cosmic, universal, unlimited by distance or age; apart from the Kingdom, the Church is confined to time and space. The Kingdom is the shout; the Church is the echo. The Kingdom is the substance; the Church is the shadow.

Unfortunately, most of Christianity has reversed the order, placing all or most of its value upon the Church or denominational fragments of it. The Westminster Catechism, for example, composed by England's leading Divines in 1646, devotes a chapter to the Church but nothing to the Kingdom. The Kingdom and the Church, in their sequential order, are both revelations of the same rule and government of God. Kingdom rule is fixed and unchangeable; Church rule is not. Kingdom authority is as inalterable as gravity; Church rule is frequently under the administration of unreliable men and women. Kingdom power is sovereign, irresistible, eternal. It emanates from the nature and character of God; Church power is frequently a mere contest directed by circumstances. While the Kingdom reigns, the Church argues. The Kingdom is ruled by a King—the risen, glorified, reigning Christ; the Church is often ruled by religious politicians. Though God intends that the Church draw her power and authority from the all-sufficient Kingdom, the Church has determinedly drawn upon herself.

The result of ignoring the Kingdom is that churches corporately, and Christians personally, experience power failure. Power does not originate with the Church. Power comes only from the Holy Spirit through the Kingdom. Those who reject this are left with nothing. The Church receives the "anointing" and ministers it to the people. Without the Holy Spirit, churches have no life-source and become simply religious organizations.

Many historic denominations in America are dying for this reason: They reject the Scriptures teaching about the Holy Spirit's baptism and gifts and rely on their own strength. Many churches have abandoned the Bible and have opened their doors to "doctrines of demons." Paul expressed it this way: "Now the Spirit expressly says that in latter times some will depart from the faith, giving heed to deceiving spirits and doctrines of demons, speaking lies in hypocrisy, having their own conscience seared with a hot iron" (1 Timothy 4:1–2). The Holy Spirit is the only life-source for the Church. There is no other.

59. What Is Our Authority in the Kingdom?

The Kingdom is the rule of God in which He has also extended spiritual authority to believers to rule and reign with Him (see Matthew 19:28; Luke 22:30). He said, "Behold, I give you the authority . . . over all the power of the enemy, and nothing shall by any means hurt you" (Luke 10:19). The Gospel of the Kingdom, which presents the parables, the keys and other constituents of Kingdom power, is much, much more than a mere presentation of Bible facts (see Matthew 4:23; 24:14; Mark 1:14). Authentic Gospel is the vocal declaration of Jesus' atonement, accompanied by the Holy Spirit's anointing, which draws into one message all the spiritual and physical benefits of Kingdom authority.

Where the full Kingdom Gospel is preached it will be confirmed with "mighty signs and wonders" (Romans 15:19). Much of the modern Church rejects spiritual gifts, which contain Kingdom power. In that state, the Church is left with little more than religious argument. All the while, the Spirit is saying to the Church, "Come to the Kingdom!"

The Old Testament foretold the Kingdom: "And in the days of these kings the God of heaven will set up a kingdom which shall never be destroyed; and the kingdom shall not be left to other people; it shall break in pieces and consume all these kingdoms, and it shall stand forever" (Daniel 2:44). The New Testament affirms the Kingdom: "He will be great, and will be called the Son of the Highest; and the Lord God will give Him the throne of His father David. And He will reign over the house of Jacob forever, and of His kingdom there will be no end" (Luke 1:32–33).

60. How Is the Kingdom Demonstrated?

Only within the boundaries of the Kingdom of God is the Church presented. With that understanding, we can better embrace the following

Scriptural promises about the work the Church will do to demonstrate the Kingdom. The Church will:

Teach repentance (see Matthew 3:2)

Cast out demons (see Matthew 12:28)

Understand mysteries (see Matthew 13:11)

Use the Kingdom keys (see Matthew 16:19)

Preach the Gospel (see Matthew 24:14)

Receive an inheritance (see Matthew 25:34)

Baptize new believers (see Acts 8:12)

Teach about Jesus (see Acts 28:31)

Move in power (see 1 Corinthians 4:20)

Walk through the entrance into the everlasting Kingdom (see 2 Peter 1:11)

61. What Is the Gospel of the Kingdom?

The word *Gospel* means "Good News" and to be authentic must be presented with the original New Testament message and power intact. It should not be edited or compromised. Jesus said to the disciples, "Go therefore and make disciples of all the nations, baptizing them in the name of the Father and of the Son and of the Holy Spirit, teaching them to observe all things that I have commanded you; and lo, I am with you always, even to the end of the age" (Matthew 28:19–20). Jesus was emphatic. His instruction, "Teach them all things," referring specifically to the Church at the "end of the age" is unmistakably clear. He expects the modern Church to be taught "all things" that He commanded the first-century Church to observe. There is only "one Lord, one faith, one baptism" (Ephesians 4:5). The Church, through the final century, is to be taught the original "one faith" He taught the first-century Church. There is to be no change.

62. What Three Preaching Commissions Did Jesus Give?

On three different occasions, Jesus commissioned disciples to preach the Gospel publicly. The first two times, they were commanded to speak to the Jews only and not to the Samaritans. He said, "Go rather to the lost sheep of the house of Israel. And as you go, preach, saying, 'The kingdom of heaven is at hand'" (Matthew 10:5–7). The final commission, the "Great Commission," was given after the resurrection and at the time of Jesus' ascension. Taking the disciples to the Mount of Olives, He instructed them to go into all the world. Specifically, He said, "All authority has been given to Me in heaven and on earth. Go therefore and make disciples of all the nations, baptizing them in the name of the Father and of the Son and of the Holy Spirit, teaching them to observe all things that I have commanded you" (Matthew 28:18–20). Observe Jesus' language: "Teaching them to observe all things that I have commanded you." Jesus intended there to be no change in the belief and practice of the last-century Church from that of the first-century Church.

63. What Is the Abundant Life in the Holy Spirit?

American poet Henry David Thoreau (1817–1862) wrote, "The mass of men lead lives of quiet desperation." While this may be true for many, it is not the life Jesus intended for us—and placed within our reach. He desires that we experience the serene life available in the Holy Spirit (see John 16:33). Is such a life possible? Yes. We can enter into a state of life that is elevated above the mood swings of the world (see John 10:10). It is only here that we step into the "secret place" of the Most High (Psalm 27:5).

Paul assures us that the peace of God that surpasses all human understanding will protect both our hearts and minds through Christ (see

Philippians 4:7). We can turn to the wonderful example of Stephen who, while being stoned to death, saw heaven open and Jesus standing before him. Was this the first time Stephen had experienced such serenity? Not at all. It was serenity that enabled him to face this moment. When John Huss was being burned alive at the stake he burst into a joyous song. While religious frenzy gripped the crowd around him, John was bathed in the serenity of heaven. It is inward serenity in times of crisis that is the great achievement of the Christian life. This is what Scripture describes as the abundant life.

PART 6

What Is the Church?

64. When Was the Church Born?

The Holy Spirit's sudden appearance in the Upper Room at Pentecost exploded with the sound of a rushing mighty wind, cloven tongues of fire, miraculously spoken languages and anointing on everyone present (see Acts 2:1–4). Never in the history of the world had so much holy energy erupted in one small place at one time. Everyone present was radically filled and empowered. In this miraculous setting the Church was born.

Forty days before this event, the resurrected Jesus led the disciples to the Mount of Olives for their final visit. Before ascending into heaven from the mount, He told them to return to Jerusalem and wait to "receive power when the Holy Spirit has come upon you; and you shall be witnesses to Me in Jerusalem, and in all Judea and Samaria, and to the end of the earth" (Acts 1:8). Up to this time, He had commanded the disciples to preach only to the Jews and to those in the local towns where He would be ministering. That changed. On the day of Pentecost the Church, the "Body of Christ," was birthed, anointed and equipped for worldwide evangelism (see Matthew 28:18–20; Mark 16:15).

Next to the resurrection in importance, this event impacted the world. There is no way to overemphasize its place in world history and its role in the eternal plan of God. In that awesome moment in the Upper Room, the message of the resurrection burst forth. It was this event to which Jesus referred when He said, "All authority has been given to Me in heaven and on earth. Go therefore and make disciples of all the nations" (Matthew 28:18–19).

65. Who Is the Church Today?

The Church can be identified in three major dimensions:

One: the local gathering. The "lowercase-c" church is the local congregation of worshiping believers, meeting routinely in an assigned place, who sing, pray, study, preach, evangelize, serve the community, reveal the grace of God in their personal conduct and attempt to win their communities to Christ (see Matthew 18:17; Acts 11:26). Whenever possible, individual believers are encouraged to participate in a local assembly of saints (see Hebrews 10:25). Local congregations are subject to many external differences: Nationality, language, local practice and tradition all play an important part in its outward identity. Any church that promotes separation from all other believers is an affront to the One who "loved the church and gave Himself for it" (Ephesians 5:25). The local church draws its authority and success from the Kingdom; it succeeds or fails according to its operating in Kingdom authority and power. The local church may fail; the Kingdom cannot.

Two: the believers worldwide. This "capital-C" Church, refers to the whole body of believers on earth—the Body of Christ—consisting of all authentic, functioning congregations worldwide, hidden and public, without regard to denominational identities, composed of regenerate, born-again disciples (see Acts 2:47; 8:1). Included in this number are many believers who are not identified with a local body.

Three: the Bride of Christ. This is the Church in its fullest sense, composed of all saved people of every age—those presently on earth and those already in heaven. This aspect of the spiritual Body of Christ is the mystical family of redeemed saints of all ages. All ethnic, language, cultural and historical differences are within her but do not divide her. In heaven the complete family of believers will finally discover the perfect relationship they had on earth but never knew. Paul wrote: "For this reason I bow my knees to the Father of our Lord Jesus Christ, from whom the whole family in heaven and earth is named" (Ephesians 3:14–15). Ultimately, this Church universal, without regard to earthly circumstances, will be the Bride of Christ. She will be presented to Him

101

"without blemish," clothed in "fine linen" without "spot or wrinkle" (Ephesians 5:27; Revelation 19:8). Scripture refers to Jesus as the "last Adam" and the "second Man" (1 Corinthians 15:45, 47). The Church is the Bride of Christ as Eve was of Adam: "For as in Adam all die, even so in Christ all shall be made alive. But each one in his own order: Christ the firstfruits, afterward those who are Christ's at His coming" (1 Corinthians 15:22–23).

66. What Is the Mission of the Church?

The first function of the Church is to be an instrument of worship to Almighty God. In true worship, believers participate in the adoration taking place in heaven and draw the anointing of the Holy Spirit upon themselves. This is gained through the Church's identity as the Body of Christ and position within the Kingdom of God. Please know that the visible Body of Christ on earth is still being anointed (see Luke 7:38; John 19:39). In our case, it is the Church in worship—prayer or preaching—that receives the unction. This is an unchanging principle. When that anointed state is achieved, the Holy Spirit releases His presence to do signs and wonders, and powerfully calls the unsaved to Christ. Paul describes such a condition when a stranger witnesses that holy Presence and "falling down on his face, he will worship God and report that God is truly among you" (1 Corinthians 14:25).

Unfortunately today, much of the Church is afflicted with performance, seeking to make a good presentation. A large measure of her attention is focused on this—how the service looks, how it sounds, the outward impression it makes. The Holy Spirit is grieved and "signs, wonders, mighty deeds" are missing. Even more tragically, in most modern churches the visible manifestations of the Holy Spirit are not welcome. This need not be so. The Holy Spirit is still available in all His original power for those who will receive Him. At this point most of the Church is deficient in anointed power. But this is going to change. An end-time revival will usher in massive, unstoppable waves of the Holy Spirit, sweeping through the Church and across the land (see Matthew 24:14; Revelation 5:9–10; 7:9–14). It is important to remember that when Scripture speaks of the "last days" it refers to the entire Church age (see Isaiah 40:5; Joel 2:28) in the sense that it began with the ascension of Jesus, plus Pentecost, and will end with His return at the Rapture. The last days have a starting point and they have an ending point.

The second function of the Church is to reveal the Kingdom and its glorious King. Unless the Church touches the glory of heaven first, this second function cannot fully take place. Such blessing is achieved only through the Holy Spirit's anointing on a congregation. In that blissful state, the Spirit is free to act, "confirming the word through the accompanying signs" (Mark 16:20). The true ministry of the Church is spiritual and cannot be achieved by mere intellectualism and physical activity. Paul explained this when he said, "By the power of the Spirit of God . . . I have fully preached the gospel of Christ" (Romans 15:19). To the Corinthians he said, "My speech and my preaching were not with persuasive words of human wisdom, but in demonstration of the Spirit and of power" (1 Corinthians 2:4).

Some 85 percent of all Christian conversions worldwide are taking place because of Spirit-filled believers, particularly as they hold to the orthodoxy of Scripture. Look at this example of the power of the Gospel. In the year 1900 there were approximately nine million Christians in the continent of Africa. In 2000 there were approximately 360 million believers—more than a third of the continent's total population.

67. What Are House Churches?

Following the spiritual explosion of Pentecost when the disciples were empowered by the Holy Spirit, thousands of new converts joined the young Church. In the beginning they met "daily in the temple, and in every house" for worship (Acts 5:42). This quickly created new problems. The religious power structure was endangered and persecution followed. Many believers left the nation of Israel, becoming missionaries, while others went underground. Acts 8:4 tells us that "those who were scattered went everywhere preaching the word." These early disciples had no church buildings and adapted to meeting in homes for worship. The New Testament details some fifteen instances where disciples gathered in the members' houses. Until the time of Emperor Constantine, when Christianity was legalized in Rome, all churches met secretly, usually in private homes. Once able to meet publicly, they began gathering in larger buildings, which established much of the form we maintain.

Worldwide today more Christians probably gather for worship in private homes than in public buildings. Many are disillusioned with the absence of spirituality in denominational churches and are searching elsewhere. House churches frequently answer that need. Some churches practice both congregational meetings on Sunday morning and home-meetings during the week. In many cases this has proved very successful. Home meetings promote direct fellowship among members and provide learning opportunities that are relaxed and informal.

Not only are house churches known to proliferate in nations where Christians are persecuted, but the Church generally grows. In China, for instance, after the People's Republic of China was established in 1949, the Communist Party killed thousands of Christians, expelled missionaries and destroyed church buildings. The few believers who survived went underground and began meeting secretly in private homes. Persecution became more severe but the government found it impossible to stamp out the Church. Secret house-church meetings saved believers from extinction. Today it is estimated that there are as many as one hundred million Christians in China, and that by the year 2030 China will have more professing Christians than the U.S. In America, where the government is becoming increasingly unfavorable toward Christianity, the forecast is that the Church here will also go underground and choose to meet in homes.

68. What about Growing Numbers of Christians Who Don't Go to Church?

Worldwide, a growing number of historic Protestant denominations are disappearing into spiritual darkness. Some have turned their backs on Paul's command to "Preach the word!" and have joined the ranks of those they were sent to convert (2 Timothy 4:2). Many have endorsed behaviors that Scripture warns against and have abandoned the authority of God's Word. The apostle Paul forewarned about a time of apostasy when he wrote of a great "falling away" (2 Thessalonians 2:3).

Caught in this confusion are sincere believers who hold to biblical principles but are abandoning the traditional denominations in great numbers. While many stop attending services, having lost hope for the Church, others find happiness in home churches where the Holy Spirit is fully accepted and free to work.

The Southern Baptist Convention is just one example of this. In years past, Southern Baptists have set the bar for outreach through missions and evangelism. Yet it is estimated, at the current rate, that half of the Baptist churches in America will close their doors by the year 2030. Tragically, the death rate among members of this denomination now exceeds the number of conversions and baptisms. Additionally, a number of Baptist pastors are returning to hardline Calvinistic theology, which has always witnessed a decline in evangelism and conversions. But even as large numbers of Baptists lose hope and leave their churches, many of their members, as with other denominations, are among those appearing in home meetings and being filled with the Holy Spirit.

69. Why Is Sunday the Christian's Day of Worship?

It can be justly argued that any seventh day—theoretically—may be a Sabbath. God "rested on the seventh day." Jesus faced the greatest antagonism from the Jews because of His refusal to keep the Sabbath as they did. Many of His miracles were done on the Sabbath—seemingly to annoy their religiosity. He stressed two points: "The Sabbath was made for man, and not man for the Sabbath," and "the Son of Man [He, Himself] is also Lord of the Sabbath" (Mark 2:27–28).

After the resurrection, on the first day of the week, Jesus appeared to Mary Magdalene, Cleopas and Peter (see Mark 16:9; Luke 24:18, 34). Then "the same day at evening, being the first day of the week," He appeared to the disciples, who were behind locked doors; Thomas was not with them (see John 20:19, 24). A week later He appeared to the disciples, including Thomas (see John 20:26). On the Day of Pentecost (the fiftieth day from Firstfruits and also the first day of the week), the Holy Spirit—as "a rushing mighty wind"—came upon the disciples in the Upper Room (Acts 2:1–2). Christians at Troas met on the first day to break bread, worship and minister the Word (see Acts 20:7). Paul instructed the churches of Corinth and Galatia to set aside a sum of money on the first day of the week to donate later (see 1 Corinthians 16:2).

In all these instances, the day of the event corresponds to our Sunday, but the message was this: The day of worship was no longer to be observed as a leftover from ceremonial Law but, rather, observed with the understanding that the "law of the Spirit of life in Christ Jesus" now governed them (Romans 8:2). We have been made "free from the law of sin and death" (Romans 8:2). Christians need to be very careful and not forget that "Christ is the end of the law for righteousness to everyone who believes" (Romans 10:4). We obey the Ten Commandments, which stand above the Levitical Law, but we do not surrender our freedom in Christ to Jewish observances.

70. What about the Pagan Origins of Christmas and Easter Celebrations?

Our modern names for days of the week—like many other words in acceptable use—are pagan in their origin. Saturday is named for the planet Saturn, Sunday for the sun, Monday for the moon, etc.—the days when ancients worshiped them. Thursday is named for Thor, god of war. Many names of months are also pagan.

Are we required to eliminate these words from our language? No. Epaphroditus and Apollos were men whom Paul called his fellow workers, fellow brothers, fellow soldiers, and yet their names are the male form of the name *Aphrodite*, the pagan goddess of love, and *Apollos*, the god of the sun. The Greek text even calls Epaphroditus an *apostolos*—i.e., apostle or "sent one" (Philippians 2:25). Paul did not require these men to change their names because they became Christians.

Hear this important point: Christianity is not required to bow and make changes in itself; instead, we change what is already made. Saturday, Sunday, Monday have been stripped of their paganism—as were the names Epaphroditus and Apollos. We are not the ones who retreat: "He who is in [us] is greater than he who is in the world" (1 John 4:4). Even in this regard, we overcome opposition "by the blood of the Lamb and by the word of [our] testimony" (Revelation 12:11). Paganism bows to Christ. Paul eased the issue of calendar names by writing: "One person esteems one day above another; another esteems every day alike. Let each be fully convinced in his own mind. He who observes the day, observes it to the Lord; and he who does not observe the day, to the Lord he does not observe it" (Romans 14:5–6).

It is not a point to be labored.

71. What Determines the Date for Easter?

Jesus' death and resurrection occurred on the same weekend as the Jewish Passover. Passover does not fall on a fixed calendar date but is determined by the full moon in spring. Early Christians were undecided whether to observe Easter on the first day of the week (Sunday) following the spring full moon or to choose a fixed calendar date, which would come on the weekend infrequently. In AD 325, the Council of Nicaea determined that Easter would be observed on the first Sunday after the first full moon on or after the vernal equinox, the equinox falling between March 20–22. Easter is delayed by one week if the full moon is on Sunday. This is the determination we use today. We happily accept the wisdom of the Council of Nicea by observing Easter on Sunday and not mid-week.

72. What Does It Mean to Be Baptized into Christ?

Being "baptized into Christ" refers to baptism in water as entrance into public discipleship in the Church. Our baptism into water in the name of the Father, Son and Holy Spirit, as Jesus instructed, is the announcement to hell, heaven, earth, angels, demons and humanity that we have "put on the Lord Jesus Christ" and are being resurrected to walk in newness of His life (Romans 13:14; see Matthew 28:19). Paul wrote,

> Do you not know that as many of us as were baptized into Christ Jesus were baptized into His death? Therefore we were buried [in water] with Him through baptism into death, that just as Christ was raised from the dead by the glory of the Father, even so we also should walk in newness of life.
>
> Romans 6:3–4

In submitting to water baptism and burial with Christ, a believer declares that he or she voluntarily chooses to die to self and become part of Jesus' visible Body, the Church. Paul explained further that, as sons and daughters of God through our faith in Jesus, we who "were baptized into Christ have put on Christ. . . . You are all one in Christ Jesus. And if you are Christ's, then you are Abraham's seed, and heirs according to the promise" (Galatians 3:27–29). In explaining the purpose of water baptism Peter wrote that baptism cleanses our consciences toward God (see 1 Peter 3:21).

Such a baptism should be attended with miraculous signs. Tertullian (c. 160–c. 220), the greatest Christian theologian of his day, instructed new believers to "rise from the water of baptism, praying and expecting the charismatic gifts of the Spirit" to come upon them. Cyril, Bishop of Jerusalem (c. 315–387), gave instructions to new Christians to expect to receive in water baptism the same miraculous gifts given to the first apostles. "If you believe," he wrote, "you will receive not just remission of sins, but also do things which pass man's power. And may you be worthy of the gift of prophecy also! . . . Prepare yourselves for the reception of the heavenly gifts."

73. What Is the Sealing of the Holy Spirit?

Anciently, the sealing of a document with the impression of the king's ring in wax gave the message absolute authority: It was to be obeyed. Pilate ordered such a Roman seal on Jesus' tomb to protect His body from thieves. In an equally powerful way, Paul included the concept of being "sealed" in connection with one of the Holy Spirit's great works.

The Spirit establishes us, anoints us, seals us and imparts Himself to us. Sealing is part of a current, progressive work of the Spirit in the believer. In view of this, we may wonder whether or not every believer has been sealed. The answer is no. Not necessarily. The Hebrew writer encourages us to "draw near with a true heart in full assurance of faith" (Hebrews 10:22). The expression "full assurance" goes far beyond mere mental agreement with the work of the Holy Spirit; unbelief has been overcome and in its place is unshakable confidence. How blessed is the one possessing it!

Most believers today who can identity a specific time of their spiritual baptism can also attest that it proved to be a definite "sealing" for them. How long does "sealing" last? Scripture tells us, "Do not grieve the Holy Spirit of God, by whom you were sealed for the day of redemption" (Ephesians 4:30). Once sealed, we remain so until "the day of redemption."

74. What Is the Purpose of Holy Communion?

In Holy Communion, we hold in our hands the only tangible object Jesus left us: Broken pieces of bread and a cup of wine. These simple elements are the memorial of His crucified body, blood and simplified life (see Luke 22:19). The elements do not portray Him in His glorified life and resurrected power but in the silence and darkness of death. What we hold is a wounded corpse, lacerated, pierced and dried. Isaiah describes Him this way: "There is no beauty that we should desire Him" (Isaiah 53:2).

What does it mean? In Communion, the broken body of Christ is put visibly into us (see Matthew 26:26). In baptism we are put visibly into the Body of Christ, the Church (see Romans 6:1–11). These two are companion experiences.

While the sacrament portrays Him exclusively in death and not in resurrection, it was done for us who will be resurrected "in glory" (1 Corinthians 15:43). He "who knew no sin [became] sin for us, that we might become the righteousness of God in him" (2 Corinthians 5:21). At that point, we were "without Christ, being aliens from the commonwealth of Israel and strangers from the covenants of promise, having no hope and without God in the world" (Ephesians 2:12–13). The writer to the Hebrews tells us there is no remission of sins without the shedding of blood (see Hebrews 9:22).

What happens when we eat the sacrament? It can be a moment releasing great spiritual blessing and power or one of terrible danger. Paul expresses grave precautions about participating wrongly in the Communion. He warns that if anyone eats the bread and drinks the wine in an unworthy manner, he will be guilty both of the body and the blood of the Lord (see 1 Corinthians 11:27). That is extremely frightening.

Yet, in many churches today the Communion is served as routinely as receiving the tithes and offerings. This was not so in the early centuries of the Church. Holy Communion was the high point of the worship and was forbidden to those whose un-repented sin was known.

Who determines one's worthiness to partake of "the Lord's table"? (1 Corinthians 10:21). Paul explains, "Let a man examine himself, and so let him eat of the bread and drink of the cup. For he who eats and drinks in an unworthy manner eats and drinks judgment to himself, not discerning the Lord's body. For this reason many are weak and sick among you, and many sleep" (1 Corinthians 11:28–30). The end result of the crucifixion, which is portrayed in Holy Communion, was expressed by William Tyndale: "Christ is in thee and thou in him, knit together inseparably. Thou cans't not be damned, except Christ be damned with thee; neither can Christ be saved [from the grave] except thou be saved with Him."

Because He lives, we "will live also" (John 14:19).

75. What Did Jesus Mean about Eating His Flesh, Drinking His Blood?

There was probably no one statement more offensive and angering to the Jews than when Jesus said, "Unless you eat the flesh of the Son of Man and drink His blood, you have no life in you" (John 6:53). The people were reviled. Jesus' full statement says:

"This is the bread which comes down from heaven, that one may eat of it and not die. I am the living bread which came down from heaven. If anyone eats of this bread, he will live forever; and the bread that I shall give is My flesh, which I shall give for the life of the world." The Jews therefore quarreled among themselves, saying, "How can this Man give us His flesh to eat?"

John 6:50–52

111

Later, in that same conversation, Jesus said, "Whoever eats My flesh and drinks My blood has eternal life, and I will raise him up at the last day" (verse 54). It was at this point that "many of His disciples went back and walked with Him no more" (John 6:66).

How does Jesus' statement involve the sacrament we observe today? The key is the phrase *This is the bread that comes down from heaven*. The bread of which Jesus spoke does not come from a bakery or earthly oven. It comes from heaven and ultimately returns to heaven. Christians eat this bread metaphorically in the sacrament through the Holy Spirit's anointing *on* the sacrament. When Paul spoke of the seriousness of Communion, he warned that whoever receives the elements "in an unworthy manner" is actually "guilty of the body and blood of the Lord" because that one "eats and drinks judgment to himself, not discerning the Lord's body. For this reason many are weak and sick among you, and many sleep" (1 Corinthians 11:27–30).

In many Communion services this warning is tragically ignored. It is rare for many believers to approach the Communion table with proper tears and fear, love and overwhelming devotion.

76. What Is the Relation between Water Baptism and Communion?

In baptism we are put into the visible Body of Christ—the Church (see Romans 6:3; Galatians 3:27). In Communion, the visible Body of Christ—the bread and wine—is put into us (see 1 Corinthians 11:26). Each action identifies us publicly as being disciples of Jesus, sharers in His covenant, children of God, heirs of heaven and joint-heirs with Christ. In a parallel way, when escaping from Egypt through the parted waters of the Red Sea, Israel was "baptized into Moses in the cloud and in the sea" (1 Corinthians 10:2). The sea symbolized burial in water with Christ; the cloud symbolized the anointing of the Holy Spirit. When Jesus was baptized in the Jordan River, the

Holy Spirit, as a dove, appeared from heaven and came upon Him (see Matthew 3:16).

Water baptism, vital as it is, does not remove filth of the flesh or cause one to be born again; it is the answer of a "good conscience" toward God of one already born again (1 Peter 3:21). This is why Peter said, "Repent, and let every one of you be baptized in the name of Jesus Christ for the remission of sins; and you shall receive the gift of the Holy Spirit" (Acts 2:38). In keeping with Peter's words, the early Church Fathers wrote about new converts rising from the waters of baptism with the gifts of the Spirit coming upon them. Without baptism there can be no good conscience. In fact, believers who refuse baptism are in rebellion.

But what about the thief on the cross who was not baptized? Paul answered that question when he wrote: "With the heart one believes unto righteousness, and with the mouth confession is made unto salvation" (Romans 10:1). The thief did both and in his dying breaths was born again. He was assured of Jesus' promise: "Today you will be with Me in Paradise" (Luke 23:43).

Whenever possible, every believer is commanded to be buried with Christ in baptism and be raised again to walk in newness of life. Ananias said to Saul of Tarsus, "Why are you waiting? Arise and be baptized, and wash away your sins, calling on the name of the Lord" (Acts 22:16).

77. What Does It Mean to Be Anointed?

Anointing is one of the great themes of Scripture. It is mentioned first when Jacob anointed his stone pillow where the angels appeared to him in a vision (see Genesis 31:13). When the prophet Samuel anointed young Saul as king over Israel, he kissed him, poured oil on his head and said, "Because the LORD has anointed you . . . the Spirit of the LORD will come upon you and you will prophesy . . . and be turned into another man" (1 Samuel 10:1, 6). In His first sermon in Nazareth Jesus said, "The Spirit of the LORD is upon Me, because He has anointed Me to preach the gospel to the poor" (Luke 4:18). In the beginning of the disciples' public ministry, Jesus commanded them to anoint the sick with oil and restore them to normalcy (see Mark 6:13). The apostle James instructed the elders of the Church to anoint the afflicted with oil and pray for them (see James 5:14).

Be aware that oil has no healing or miraculous power. It, like the water of baptism, is merely a visible tool by which the Holy Spirit may display His purpose and presence. The most powerful anointing we can receive today comes through the baptism with the Holy Spirit (see Acts 1:8). Following the anointing at Pentecost, the Church exploded with power. This incredible experience is available to everyone who will receive it. The Holy Spirit's presence can come upon an individual or a body of believers in worship, as well as upon their outreach ministries.

Could Paul's clothing be anointed? The answer is yes (see Acts 19:12). The proximity of Paul's garments to the Holy Spirit made them agents of power. Strange? Yes, but very true. Could Peter's shadow be anointed? Yes (see Acts 5:15). Can Holy Communion be anointed? Yes (see 1 Corinthians 11:27–30). Can oil be anointed? Yes (see Mark 6:13; James 5:14). Can a person be anointed? Yes (see 1 Samuel 10:1, 6). Can Gospel preaching be anointed? Yes (see Luke 24:32; Acts 2:37).

While "the gifts and callings of God are irrevocable" (Romans 11:29), anointing may lift. The Spirit's presence on a congregation or specific ministry does not come or remain automatically. The gift remains but the power to release it may be gone. Much depends on the worshipful respect of those receiving it. In a heaven-blessed Communion service, for instance, people should experience healing, deliverance, impartation as they receive the sacraments. The entire service—both people and sacrament—should experience the obvious presence of God. The word *sacrament* simply means "sacred element." Power appears or departs with the Holy Spirit. For this reason we are urged not to "grieve the Holy Spirit of God, by whom you were sealed for the day of redemption" (Ephesians 4:30).

78. What Is the Purpose of Signs and Wonders?

Signs and wonders can be loosely placed within two categories. The first is restorative miracles of mind or body, such as healing, deliverance and bodily resurrection from death. Signs and wonders of body and mind not only confirm the Gospel but attract many more to it. The second is celebration-miracles, such as occurred the day Jesus rode into Jerusalem on a donkey. His disciples became so uncontrollably happy—shouting, dancing, clapping their hands, throwing their coats on the ground before Him, waving palm branches they had stripped from the trees—that the Pharisees told Jesus to make His disciples be quiet.

When Philip preached in Samaria and the multitudes witnessed miraculous signs and wonders—the lame walking, demons shrieking—Scripture says that with "one accord" they obeyed the message they heard. There was great joy in that city (see Acts 8:5–8). In many places around the world today, untold numbers are being saved because they are attracted by the signs and wonders accompanying the Gospel—and they are expressing the joy of their salvation.

79. Why Is Unity in the Church Essential?

When Jesus conferred power upon the original disciples, He called all of them together and "gave them power and authority over all demons, and to cure diseases" (Luke 9:1). The key word is *together*. Jesus did not find each of them at separate places and confer power upon them individually. He required "oneness" of Spirit before conferring His anointing upon them and sending them out. Though they ministered in widely separated places, their anointing remained part of an original whole.

We see the importance of unity in the Old Testament as well. During Elijah's contest with the prophets of Baal on Mt. Carmel when the fire of God fell, the prophet made his offering at the "time of the evening sacrifice" (1 Kings 18:36). That refers to the sacrifice taking place on the great altar in Jerusalem eighty miles away. By observing the sunset, Elijah knew the moment when the priests at the Temple would be offering a lamb to God. Though outnumbered 850 to 1, Elijah was not alone. In a sense, he was participating in the corporate "binding and loosing" on earth (see Matthew 18:18). Anyone today who shares in the anointing and power of the Holy Spirit is partaking of precisely the same anointing that empowers all others. Those who fail to function in the Spirit's power need to examine their attitudes toward others in the Body of Christ.

80. What Healing Does Jesus Offer for Broken Relationships?

It is an axiom that where there is no respect there can be no love. No one can force another to love against his or her will. This is true not only of our relationship with God but also of the relationships we have with others. Parents soon find that discipline rising from a motive other than love is destructive and ruinous. Children who witness fighting and arguing often suffer from fear and insecurity. Abused and unloved children may produce those same qualities in their own offspring. Such patterns, once established in a family, can continue unhindered for many generations. This produces an ancestral line of damaged individuals who can't love because they don't know how. It was this very factor that Jesus offered to correct when He said, "Come to Me, all you who labor and are heavy laden, and I will give you rest" (Matthew 11:28). The heart of Jesus offers rest, peace, solace from the hurts inflicted on us—and the grief we bear from hurting others. In coming to Christ as the ultimate Savior, protector and healer, wounded people can recover from the damage done in hurtful relationships, and can learn truly to love.

81. On What Key Issues Does God Warn the Church about Ignorance?

The New Testament exhorts us seven times to "be not ignorant." Six of these admonitions are given by the apostle Paul, one by Peter. Seven is the number of completeness and all are of extreme importance. For the sake of uniformity, the Scriptures below use the King James Version. Do not be ignorant regarding:

1. Israel's rejection and restoration, and the fullness of the Gentiles: "For I would not, brethren, that ye should be ignorant of this mystery, lest ye should be wise in your own conceits; that blindness in part is happened to Israel, until the fullness of the Gentiles be come in" (Romans 11:25).

2. Israel's dual baptism of cloud and sea: "Moreover, brethren, I would not that ye should be ignorant, how that all our fathers were under the cloud, and all passed through the sea; and were all baptized unto Moses in the cloud and in the sea" (1 Corinthians 10:1–2). (In typology the cloud and sea symbolize both Spirit and water baptism.)

3. Opposition to the Gospel in Asia: "For we would not, brethren, have you ignorant of our trouble which came to us in Asia, that we were pressed out of measure, above strength, insomuch that we despaired even of life" (2 Corinthians 1:8).

4. Opposition to the Gospel in Europe: "Now I would not have you ignorant, brethren, that oftentimes I purposed to come unto you, (but was let hitherto,) that I might have some fruit among you also, even as among other Gentiles" (Romans 1:13).

5. The Holy Spirit's miraculous gifts to the Church: "Now concerning spiritual gifts, brethren, I would not have you ignorant" (1 Corinthians 12:1).

6. Jesus' Second Coming and those who have already died: "I would not have you to be ignorant, brethren, concerning them which are

asleep, that ye sorrow not, even as others which have no hope" (1 Thessalonians 4:13).

7. The day of the Lord coming "as a thief in the night": "But, beloved, be not ignorant of this one thing, that one day is with the Lord as a thousand years, and a thousand years as one day. . . . But the day of the Lord will come as a thief in the night" (2 Peter 3:8, 10).

Regarding topic number 5, Paul devotes 84 verses to spiritual gifts. Having begun the subject with the exhortation, "Concerning spiritual gifts I do not want you to be ignorant," he concludes with this stern rebuke: "But if anyone is ignorant, let him be ignorant!" (1 Corinthians 14:38). Paul had no patience for those who chose ignorance over his teachings about spiritual gifts or the Scriptures endorsing them.

82. What Is Scripture Telling Us about Renewal?

When Agabus warned the apostle Paul of persecution awaiting him in Jerusalem, he took Paul's belt, bound his own hands and feet, and said, "So shall the Jews at Jerusalem bind the man who owns this belt, and deliver him into the hands of the Gentiles" (Acts 21:11). The point is this: Prophecy often comes not only with words but also with demonstrations.

Scripture gives a powerful picture for the Church in the story of Eli the Priest and his young servant, Samuel. Scripture explains that when Eli was in physical and moral failure, God used the boy Samuel to close the old order and open a new one. At night, soon after bedtime, God called the boy three times. Each time Samuel arose, thinking it was Eli who spoke his name. Finally, the old man realized that God was speaking to the child, sent him back to bed with the instruction to say, "Speak, Lord, for your servant hears" (1 Samuel 3:10).

Eli represented the old order of religion in Israel. That order was God ordained, but by Eli's day it was surviving wholly on the revelation of its past; it had no fresh word from heaven and had replaced its "first love" with doctrine, formalism and ritual (see Revelation 2:4). Eli's spiritual eyes had dimmed with age; his most pressing concern was to be undisturbed and to rest in familiar surroundings of the past. He wanted things to remain as they were. That deception caused him to ignore God's warning about his sons and Israel's need for spiritual renewal. In seeing that circumstance, God said, "It is time to shut this system and begin a new era." That night, before Samuel was in the same sleep condition as Eli, God called the boy loudly, "Samuel! Get up! I am making changes!"

Samuel's youthfulness and vitality represent God's introduction of fresh life to Israel and the Church. As with renewal today, that life was radically different from the one God's people had known in the past. The new one was life-imparting, prophetic, challenging. With its arrival anciently, Israel's days of uninspired, liturgical worship were ended. The new prophetic era was confrontational, clashing, conflicting. Whether in Israel back then or Christianity today, times like that are stressful. Religious people fight back against such changes. Then or now, God is not moved by the people's complaints. He wants His Word obeyed.

Note that God did not speak to Eli. He had spoken to Eli earlier and had been refused. Identically, there are church boards and pastors today to whom God has spoken, been refused, and to whom He will not speak again. Instead, He is turning to those with vibrant and youthful hearts who are excited by the visions and promises His Spirit pours out on them, and who embrace the promise of ministering in power (see Acts 2:17). While Eli is in his chamber sleeping, Samuel is awake and hearing God. Through these men and women who listen with open hearts, the Kingdom will thrive.

83. How Soon after Death Are We with the Lord?

Two thieves were crucified with Christ; in his dying breaths one of them repented and said to Jesus, "'Lord, remember me when You come into Your kingdom.' And Jesus said to him, 'Assuredly, I say to you, today you will be with Me in Paradise'" (Luke 23:42–43). Fully alert and conscious, some minutes later, this man found himself out of his body, with Jesus and millions of others in the glory of Paradise.

Earlier, Jesus had told the story of a rich man and a beggar named Lazarus. Both died. The first was immediately in the pains of hell, the other in the glory of Abraham's bosom. There was no delay between their deaths and their destinations (see Luke 16:20–25). The apostle Paul said this about "a man in Christ": "Whether in the body I do not know, or whether out of the body I do not know, God knows—such a one was caught up to the third heaven. . . . He was caught up into Paradise and heard inexpressible words, which it is not lawful for a man to utter" (2 Corinthians 12:1–4).

People who die are immediately in the other dimension, fully alert and aware of their surroundings. For the saved, whether they are killed in terrible accidents or die slowly from long-term illness or fade away quietly in old age, the experience of death is an incredibly wonderful and beautiful event. The body may be in raging pain but the spirit departs to "be with Christ, which is far better" (Philippians 1:23)! These go to Paradise—a heavenly place of waiting—and remain there until resurrection, after which they simultaneously enter the fullness of heaven. This is what happened to Stephen, who was stoned to death. Scripture explains: "But he, being full of the Holy Spirit, gazed into heaven and saw the glory of God, and Jesus standing at the right hand of God, and said, 'Look! I see the heavens opened and the Son of Man standing at the right hand of God!'" (Acts 7:55–56).

Numerous people today who have authentic death experiences and return to this life give astonishing reports of the peace and beauty of the other realm. They meet loved ones who similarly died in the Lord (see Revelation 14:13). Many have given identical testimonies of seeing a beautiful light and being enveloped in heavenly glory.

84. What Negative Cycle Does the Church Often Repeat?

Historically, times of revival and failure have repeated in the Church and individual ministries in a specific, predictable pattern. The pattern is: (1) inspiration, (2) evangelization, (3) organization and (4) stagnation.

Every great move of God has begun with inspiration; it may start with one person or a small group praying for revival who experience an invasive inspiration of the Holy Spirit. John and Charles Wesley, Count Zinzendorf, Jonathan Edwards, George Whitefield and others led such revivals. What began as inspiration swept into powerful evangelization. In time, this necessitated organization. Eventually, organization required business sessions, board meetings and non-spiritual activity. Board meetings became "bored meetings." Stagnation suffocated inspiration. Technicality replaced spirituality. Prayer became formality.

Unless intense communion is maintained with God who brought inspiration, the movement will die in stagnation, or possibly continue as a business effort without inspiration. The key is this: While evangelization and organization continue to expand, the original inspiration must be maintained at all times. Every aspect of the revival must rely on its original inspiration. Only then can stagnation be prevented.

PART 7

What Are the Five-Fold Ministry Gifts?

85. What Are Offices within the Church?

Scripture explains that when Jesus "ascended on high, He led captivity captive, and gave gifts. . . . And He Himself gave some to be apostles, some prophets, some evangelists, and some pastors and teachers" (Ephesians 4:8, 11). Observe that this gifting was imparted at the time of Jesus' ascension and was intended for the future Church. This is not a reference to the special abilities of the twelve apostles or others who served alongside Him. Initially, Jesus' followers cast out demons and performed miracles because they functioned within their relationship to Him and the anointing that was upon Him; the personal empowering of those individuals took place at Pentecost after Jesus' death. Nor does this gifting refer to ordinary followers of Jesus through the ages who share the Good News. Every believer can be used in certain circumstances, as the Holy Spirit directs, to prophesy, evangelize, teach, etc. The gifting on those occasions is temporary, meant for a specific time and place. It is also distinct from unique characteristics or heart motivations with which an individual might operate—a gifting of mercy or helps, for instance.

These five gifts are unique. They were newly imparted as Jesus rose from the ground to heaven and were, in a sense, His "farewell" contributions to mankind. Unlike other gifts that the Holy Spirit might bestow, these five refer to individuals who hold active offices throughout the life of the Church. Taken together, the impartations are called the "five-fold ministry" gifts. No one is allowed to volunteer for any of the positions. Each individual is chosen by Christ and is identified by the anointing of the Holy Spirit upon his or her life and ministry (see John 15:16; Acts 2:22, 43; 5:12).

Jesus functioned in all five ministries and is our eternal example. These spiritual offices should never be severed from their corresponding ministry in Him. If such a breach occurs through egotism, pride, self-exaltation, the individual automatically disqualifies him or herself from Kingdom service and is answerable to God for the failure.

With the background of these facts, observe the five-fold presence of the enemy in this New Testament passage. Paul warns us to "put on the whole armor of God, that you may be able to stand against the wiles of [1] the devil. For we do not wrestle against flesh and blood, but against [2] principalities, [3] against powers, [4] against the rulers of the darkness of this age, [5] against spiritual hosts of wickedness in the heavenly places" (Ephesians 6:11–12). We see this five-fold pattern historically in the warfare of ancient Israel and her enemies. Moses, for instance, warred with the five kings of Midian (see Numbers 31:8). Joshua killed the five kings of the Amorites (see Joshua 10:16–26). Israel was harassed by the five capital cities of Philistia (see 1 Samuel 6:17–18). The five-fold ministry gifts are a vital part of the Church's stand against her enemy.

Please see the following entries for descriptions of the individual five-fold ministry gifts. Other gifts to the Church are discussed in Part 8: "What Gifts Does the Holy Spirit Impart to Believers?"

86. What Is an Apostle (Part 1)?

Apostles are first mentioned in Scripture when Jesus "went out to the mountain to pray, and continued all night in prayer to God. And when it was day, He called His disciples to Himself; and from them He chose twelve whom He also named apostles" (Luke 6:12–13). His purpose in appointing these twelve was "that they might be with Him and that He might send them out to preach, and to have power to heal sicknesses and to cast out demons" (Mark 3:14–15). These twelve were: Peter,

Andrew, James, John, Philip, Bartholomew, Thomas, Matthew, James, Thaddaeus, Simon and Judas Iscariot.

Later, Peter asked Jesus about the ultimate outcome for those who "have left all and followed You. Therefore what shall we have?" Jesus replied, "You who have followed Me will also sit on twelve thrones, judging the twelve tribes of Israel" (Matthew 19:27–28). This indicates for us that apostleship falls into two categories: First are the "twelve apostles of the Lamb" whose names are written on the twelve foundations of the wall of the Holy City (Revelation 21:14). This number is fixed, unalterable and will never be exceeded. The second category of apostles is discussed in the entry that follows.

This indicates that the Twelve whom Jesus chose from among His disciples and named as apostles are also the Twelve whose names are written in the foundation of the Holy City. What about Judas? In Acts, chapter one, we read that Matthias was chosen to replace Judas Iscariot as one of the Twelve (see Acts 1:26). Later, when King Herod killed the apostle James (see Acts 12:1–2), another James, "the Lord's brother," was added to complete the Twelve (see Galatians 1:19). It was this second James who presided over the Council of Jerusalem (see Acts 15:13) and wrote the book bearing his name. It also seems prudent to include Paul in this discussion, since he stands unchallenged as the greatest writing apostle. He met the resurrected Christ and talked with Him (see 1 Corinthians 9:1). Is he God's choice for taking the place of Judas Iscariot on the twelfth throne?

Ultimately there is mystery regarding the "twelve apostles of the Lamb."

87. What Is an Apostle (Part 2)?

The second category of *apostle* is defined in Scripture by the Greek word *apostolos*, which appears more frequently than English translations generally indicate. It means "sent ones," "delegates," "ambassadors" or "messengers." For example: "If anyone inquires about Titus, . . . or if our brethren are inquired about, they are messengers [apostolos] of the churches" (2 Corinthians 8:23). Approximately 25 apostles are identified in the Greek New Testament. Barnabas is one example: "When the apostles Barnabas and Paul heard this, they tore their clothes" (Acts 14:14). No other apostles have ever been or will ever be equal with the "twelve apostles of the Lamb." In a lesser way, however, those who hold the office are legitimate bearers of this title.

Did apostleship continue past the early Church? Yes. In the book of Revelation, Jesus commends the church at Ephesus because it "tested those who say they are apostles and are not, and have found them liars" (Revelation 2:2). These believers examined those claiming apostleship. There would be no need for this testing if no one could hold the office legitimately.

But what about today? Is apostleship, as one of the five-fold ministry gifts, still operational for the Kingdom? Yes, again. This gift given by Jesus at the time of His Ascension is an important function to help equip His Church (see Ephesians 4:8, 11). While every believer can consider him or herself as one being "sent out" by virtue of the Great Commission, the men and women who serve as apostles are called to the "office" of apostle to oversee, advise, counsel, when such is needed and where it is accepted.

Apostles are often involved in the pioneering and strengthening of new churches. They are engaged in evangelism—pioneering the preaching of the Gospel—with the accompanying of signs and wonders— more so than any other office gift. Evangelists are also noted for the accompanying signs and wonders. Prophets, pastors and teachers also see signs and wonders, just not as many.

We are warned about false apostles who function in their own presumptive power and not God's assignment (Revelation 2:2). Authentic apostles do not volunteer for ministry but are called, some globally. Like Paul, many struggle with that divine summons. Some resist it. But "[God's] hand is stretched out, and who will turn it back?" (Isaiah 14:27). Are these people without imperfections? Not at all! But they are aflame with holy love for Christ and His Bride. Do they promote or advertise themselves as apostles? No. They are concerned with truth—not titles. They seek God—not gold. Purity not praise.

There is a tendency regarding the five-fold ministry gifts, particularly with apostleship, to think that Jesus selected them because they had special qualifications that we do not have. That is not true. The qualification for their work with Jesus was the presence of the Holy Spirit that rested upon them. Without His anointing they were just as human as we. The apostles and prophets were people "with a nature like ours" (James 5:17). Not only were they subject to fail but frequently did so. Paul rebuked Peter to his face because of his inconsistencies regarding the Jews (see Galatians 2:11). Trophimus was left at Miletus sick (see 2 Timothy 4:20). Paul and Barnabas' quarrel ended their joint ministry when Mark abandoned them (see Acts 15:36–41). To Timothy, Paul wrote "Demas has forsaken me, having loved this present world" (2 Timothy 4:10).

Rather than compare ourselves unfavorably to the early apostles, let us rejoice that God uses us all in various ways in spite of our weakness. The Holy Spirit works His perfect will through imperfect people. God does not want ability; He wants only our availability.

As we consider our humanity, it becomes important for the Church in our day to follow the example for which Jesus commended the Ephesian church—examining those who move in the office of apostle. In fact, everyone moving in the five-fold ministry gifts in the Body of Christ, whether apostle or pastor or teacher, must be put to the test of Scripture. Beware those who are prideful, arrogant, self-serving, controlling. "Always pursue what is good" (1 Thessalonians 5:15) and remember: "Many false prophets have gone out into the world" (1 John 4:1), some who claim to be apostles.

What proof do we seek in those recognized as apostles? Paul answers that question. Of himself, he said to the Corinthians, "The signs of an apostle were accomplished among you with all perseverance, in signs and wonders and mighty deeds. . . . I myself was not burdensome to you" (2 Corinthians 12:12–13). Observe that Paul identifies three character traits: Perseverance (patience), not being burdensome to the saints, and working in "signs and wonders and mighty deeds."

In varying degrees, these qualities must be present in those claiming apostleship today.

88. What Is a Prophet?

There is a distinct difference between someone speaking a prophetic word and someone who functions in the five-fold ministry gift of prophet. We have examples of both in the book of Acts and Paul's letter to the Corinthians. Agabus, a brother in the church at Antioch was called a "prophet." He forewarned the Church of an approaching great famine, which proved true (see Acts 2:27–28). In the same passage we read of Philip the deacon who had four daughters who prophesied (Acts 21:9). Philip's daughters experienced the charismatic gift of prophecy but did not hold the office.

The spiritual gift of prophecy can function in any Spirit-filled believer (see 1 Corinthians 12:10). As Paul explained to the Corinthian church, "You can all prophesy one by one, that all may learn and all may be encouraged" (1 Corinthians 14:31). Observe that prophecy in this regard is not foretelling the future but for the purpose of "learning" and "encouragement." The ministry of prophecy was a vital function in the early Church and should be flourishing today. Much crisis could be avoided through its proper use.

The ease with which the prophetic gift can be abused, however, poses a serious problem for the Church. This is probably the reason Paul forewarned: "Do not despise prophecies. Test all things; hold fast what is good" (1 Thessalonians 5:20). Paul seemed more concerned about wrong use of this gift than any other. We benefit from his warning. The men and women who speak prophetically in the assembly are to be judged openly, immediately and publicly: "Let two or three prophets speak, and let the others judge. But if anything is revealed to another who sits by, let the first keep silent. . . . For God is not the author of confusion but of peace, as in all the churches of the saints" (1 Corinthians 14:29–30, 33).

This passage is interesting because it begins by addressing those recognized as prophets. But Paul does not relegate the right to prophesy only to them. He makes room for people like the daughters of the evangelist Philip, who likely had the gift of prophecy, as well as others who are not known for their prophesying, but who might receive a revelation. Though they are not called "prophets," they, too, are allowed to speak. Paul says, "You can all prophesy in turn."

The late John Wimber noted an interesting progression regarding prophecy. First, from this Scripture we understand that anyone can prophesy simply by virtue of being a Christian and having the activity of the Holy Spirit in his or her life. Second, some have this gift—*gracelet*—of prophecy occurring frequently and generally become known in the local church as being prophetic. Third, if the occurrence of this gift occurs regularly, those individuals will be seen as having a prophetic ministry. Fourth, if the gifting is stronger still, the individuals will be recognized beyond the local church; they will be able to minister to other churches and communities. This last level generally involves the maturing of a prophetic person to the point of being recognized as a prophet or prophetess. This illustration holds true for the next office, that of the evangelist, as well. It is important for the Church to develop language that recognizes these different levels.

89. What Is an Evangelist?

As the early believers fled persecution, they became overnight evangelists: "Those who were scattered went everywhere preaching the word" (Acts 8:4). Persecution helped spread the Gospel across the Roman Empire. There is a distinction between someone operating in the five-fold ministry gift of evangelist and another believer's evangelizing in the ordinary routine of life. Anciently, for instance, two women might meet at the community spring, with the Christian eager to share her testimony about Jesus' work in her life. It might be about the healing of her daughter or her own personal baptism with the Spirit. Her evangelizing might then draw the other woman to Christ. This ministry of evangelism is one in which every believer should be engaged.

While the Greek translation does not necessarily imply one's traveling, it does emphasize one's witnessing so enthusiastically that travel may become a necessary part. In this way, Philip, one of the original deacons, later became an evangelist in the five-fold pattern (see Acts 21:8). Anyone called to the five-fold ministry gift of evangelist gives his or her life exclusively to that work by traveling, preaching, establishing churches, assisting in organizing congregations, as well as helping to oversee the work until the congregation is self-sustaining. In this capacity the evangelist's work is very similar to the apostles'.

Another similarity is the fact that the New Testament evangelists also moved in great power enabling them to experience healings and miracles. Does this mean that great men and women of God who evangelized heroically but who did not move in signs and wonders were not true evangelists? Absolutely not. They were people of their times, constrained by their understanding of the Gospel and the continuation of the gifts. They were truly called of God and used by God. We should always honor the great work done through them.

At the same time we must recognize that the New Testament evangelist is portrayed as one moving in signs and wonders. Even the scattered disciples of Jerusalem who had to leave due to the persecution were seen as having the power of God upon them. Acts 11:1, 19–21 is a significant passage in this regard, because the apostles—if we apply the term both to the Twelve and to those so named who were not of the Twelve—were not scattered; they did not leave Jerusalem. Thus, we see that it was not the apostles alone whom God used for signs and miracles.

Two other passages of Scriptures seem to support this understanding of believers who, regardless of their office or lack of office, could experience supernatural healings and even miracles. In Mark 16:15–18 Jesus gives a directive to "those who believe." It is not limited to apostles and evangelists and includes several signs, such as laying hands on sick people with the result that they are healed. The other is from Jesus in His Upper Room discourse. John 14:12 states, "Most assuredly, I say to you, he who believes in Me, the works that I do he will do also; and greater works than these he will do, because I go to My Father." This passage does not say that this type of ministry would be limited to the apostles and evangelists, but "whoever believes in Me."

90. What Is a Pastor/Shepherd?

The concept of pastor is the same as that of shepherd—one who not only cares for the flock but loves it devotedly (see John 10:11). A pastor without loving dedication for the congregation is not qualified to serve. Jesus called such people "hirelings"; their motivation is not love for the sheep but for the cash they gain (John 10:12). Speaking through the prophet Jeremiah, God said, "'Woe to the shepherds who destroy and scatter the sheep of My pasture!' says the LORD. . . . 'You have scattered My flock, driven them away, and not attended to them. Behold, I will attend to you for the evil of your doings,' says the LORD" (Jeremiah 23:1–2).

Jesus, the Good Shepherd who gave His life for the sheep, is our example (see John 10:11). Paul instructed the elders of the Ephesian church to "take heed to yourselves and to all the flock, among which the Holy Spirit has made you overseers, to shepherd the church of God which He purchased with His own blood" (Acts 20:28). Note that overseers are "among" the flock. The "Chief Executive Officer" concept has no place in the Church and no support from the Kingdom. Other names used to identify the pastoral post are *presbyters* and *elders*—from the Greek *presbuteros* and *episcopos*, which is also translated "bishop." Both words describe the same New Testament ministry, each showing a different aspect of the work.

The New Testament describes two ways that elders are selected, especially if one sees the titles of *presbuteros* and *episcopos* as the same. Not only do we see the Church selecting its elders and deacons, also we see that the apostles set the *presbuteros* in their churches (see Acts

14:23; Titus 1:5). Titus is left in Crete by Paul to appoint elders in every town as Paul had instructed him. The New Testament has room for both congregational and apostolic appointments of *presbuteros,* though not of deacons who appear to always be appointed by the local church. Even so, God accepts the choice of the Church, anoints and empowers it, when the choice has been made after diligent prayer.

Peter exhorted the pastors to "shepherd the flock of God which is among you, serving as overseers, not by compulsion . . . but being examples to the flock; and when the Chief Shepherd appears, you will receive the crown of glory that does not fade away" (1 Peter 5:2–4). Like the Good Shepherd, the pastor leads the flock into "green pastures" and "beside the still waters" (Psalm 23:2).

91. What Is a Teacher?

In instructing Timothy about the qualifications for the five-fold-ministry gift of teacher, Paul emphasizes that this gift is not inferior to the others. Teachers are to be instructed in the same truths and possess the same qualifications as he has required in relation to all other ministries (see 2 Timothy 2:2). As instructor, he or she lays the foundation upon which other ministries will build. Paul even gives the same personality requirements, specifically commanding that a servant-teacher must not be quarrelsome but be gentle to everyone, qualified, patient and humble. Such a person must be innocent of thievery, adultery, blasphemy and other violations (see Romans 2:21–24). At the same time Paul compares the teacher's role to that of a solider (see 2 Timothy 2:3–3). He even assumes that there will be opposition, which the teacher can best overcome through a gracious and nonthreatening demeanor (see 2 Timothy 2:24–25).

Paul puts great emphasis on a teacher being a living example before the students and not one who merely tells students how to live (see 1 Corinthians 4:14–17). Also, teachers should speak from the direct inspiration and anointing of the Holy Spirit. It is important that the students hear what the Spirit is saying to the Church (see Revelation 2:7).

The teacher must not be a mere lecturer but also one who interacts with the students. In recalling the period in his own life in which he was a student, Paul explains that he was taught "at the feet of Gamaliel" (Acts 22:3). The practice in that day was for students to sit on the floor, near the feet of the instructor, where there would be eye contact and interaction between students and teacher. While the teacher can impart much through intellectual and scriptural knowledge, the best communication of the truths of God comes in a heart-to-heart presentation.

PART 8

What Gifts Does the Holy Spirit Impart to Believers?

92. What Did Early Christians Believe about Spiritual Gifts?

Ignatius (c. 35–c. 108), student of the apostle John, third pastor at Antioch whose ministry paralleled the apostles' and extended into the second century, exercised the gift of prophecy and relied upon its operation in the Church.

Justin Martyr (100–165) wrote that Christians in his day operated in miraculous "gifts of the Spirit of God."

Irenaeus (122–c. 202) recorded that "we have heard of many of the brethren who have foreknowledge of the future, visions and prophetic utterances; others, by laying on of hands, heal the sick and restore them to health. . . . We hear of many members of the church who have prophetic gifts, and, by the Spirit speak with all kinds of tongues."

Tertullian (c. 160–c. 220), the greatest theologian of his day, wrote that new Christians should rise from the waters of baptism expecting the gifts of the Spirit to come upon them. Obviously, the gifts had not vanished in his time. Quite the contrary.

Eusebius (263–339), early historian and Christian polemicist, wrote of believers in his day exercising all the spiritual gifts. Words of wisdom, knowledge, faith, healings, tongues and numerous miracles were commonplace among them.

Augustine (354–430), the great pastor-bishop and writer, in his early ministry happily acknowledged the reality of spiritual gifts when some seventy miraculous healings occurred in his congregations. In his day, Christians cast out demons and experienced "falling under the power of the Spirit."

93. What Two Distinct Works Does the Holy Spirit Provide for Believers?

The book of Acts identifies five groups of believers who experienced salvation and spiritual baptism in separate phases. You will observe that salvation always comes first. In that first event the believer's spirit is quickened, made alive in Christ and born again. The individual is saved for heaven. In the second, the saved believer is equipped for authentic, empowered life and New Testament ministry on earth. Miraculous gifts of the Spirit are infused into the believer's temple-body and, subsequently, released in visible operation.

Note that these two experiences can occur closely together; there need not be an expanse of time between them. The Apostolic Constitutions, an early Church document related to moral conduct, indicates that hands were laid upon the newly baptized within seconds to be delivered and filled with the Holy Spirit.

Paul explained these two events when he wrote, "I long to see you, that I may impart to you some spiritual gift, so that you may be established" (Romans 1:11). Paul had already addressed them as "beloved of God, called to be saints." Even so, he wanted to minister to them personally for them to receive spiritual gifts—apparently through the "laying on of hands"—that they might be established.

Observe these five examples of believers being saved and later filled with the Holy Spirit. These were distinctly separate experiences:

The Original Disciples

Salvation: The day of the resurrection, Jesus "breathed on them, and said to them, 'Receive the Holy Spirit'" (John 20:22). The new birth was a provision of the New Covenant and could not be experienced until the resurrection had taken place. The disciples were apparently the first to experience the New Covenant provision.

Baptism with the Spirit: On the day of Pentecost, 120 believers were together in the Upper Room. The sound of a rushing mighty wind filled

137

the room, and they were filled with the Holy Spirit and began to speak in tongues (see Acts 2:1–4).

The Samaritans

Salvation: Philip went to the city of Samaria and preached Christ. The Samaritans believed and were baptized (Acts 8:5, 12).

Baptism with the Spirit: When the apostles at Jerusalem heard about this, they sent Peter and John to Samaria, who prayed for them to receive the Holy Spirit: "Then they laid hands on them, and they received the Holy Spirit" (Acts 8:17).

Saul of Tarsus

Salvation: Saul was traveling to Damascus to search for believers and bring them "bound" back to Jerusalem. Suddenly a light from heaven blazed around him. He fell to the ground and "heard a voice saying to him, 'Saul, Saul, why are you persecuting Me?' And he said, 'Who are You, Lord?' Then the Lord said, 'I am Jesus'" (Acts 9:2–5).

Baptism with the Spirit: Three days later, Ananias went to Saul, laid his hands on him and said that Jesus had sent him in order "that you may receive your sight and be filled with the Holy Spirit" (Acts 9:17). The scales fell from his eyes, and he got up and was baptized.

Cornelius

Salvation: Cornelius, a Gentile, was "a devout man and one who feared God with all his household, who gave alms generously to the people, and prayed to God always" (Acts 10:2). In a vision he saw an angel of God, who told him that his prayers and gifts had "come up for a memorial before God" (verse 4). Cornelius was told in the vision to send to Joppa for Peter, who came and spoke about Jesus to the household, the friends and relatives gathered there. It was a message through which they were "saved" (Acts 11:14, see verse 17).

Baptism with the Spirit: As Peter was speaking, the Holy Spirit fell on them, and they began to speak in tongues and magnify God. Then

Peter said, "Can anyone forbid water, that these should not be baptized who have received the Holy Spirit just as we have?" (Acts 10:47).

Ephesian Believers

Salvation: Paul went to Ephesus and, finding some disciples, said to them, "'Did you receive the Holy Spirit when you believed?' So they said to him, 'We have not so much as heard whether there is a Holy Spirit'" (Acts 19:1–2). They had been baptized in John's baptism. Because they were lacking in their understanding and experience of the Gospel, Paul instructed them more fully and then baptized them in the name of Jesus.

Baptism with the Spirit: Then, "when Paul had laid hands on them, the Holy Spirit came upon them, and they spoke with tongues and prophesied" (Acts 19:6). Paul did not doubt the salvation of the Ephesian believers, but he was concerned over their lack of power. Like many believers today, the Ephesians had received the new birth but not the filling of the Spirit, i.e., the "Promise of the Father" (see Acts 1:4). After the Holy Spirit came upon them, the power of God slammed immediately upon the city in a way that demolished demonic strongholds, broke curses and eventually emptied the world-famous Temple of Diana. Ephesus became one of the greatest Christian citadels in history. The anointing made the difference. Regeneration did not equip the Ephesian believers for their explosive success. Baptism with the Spirit did.

94. What Is the Holy Spirit's "Second Blessing"?

Just before Jesus' ascension from the earth into heaven, He exhorted the disciples to wait in Jerusalem for the gift His Father had promised. He went on to explain that John had baptized with water but they would be baptized with the Holy Spirit (see Acts 1:4–5). Then He said, "You shall receive power when the Holy Spirit has come upon you; and you shall be witnesses to Me in Jerusalem, and in all Judea and Samaria, and to the end of the earth" (Acts 1:8). In a single statement, Jesus connected baptism with the Spirit to the imparting of His power. Though the disciples had worked with Jesus for three years and were born again, they had not yet received their personal anointing for ministry. This spiritual baptism is sometimes called the "second blessing." The first is the new birth and the second is baptism with the Spirit.

It should be pointed out that one can have more than a second blessing. There could be a third, fourth, etc. Each of these experiences of power would also be a significant encounter with the Prince of Peace, power and purity. These are not common, but precious experiences in the life of a believer.

Blessing Number One

The night of Jesus' resurrection, the disciples were huddled together for fear of the Jews when Jesus suddenly appeared in their closed room. They were astonished but He calmed their fear and showed them His hands and side. Scripture says, "He breathed on them, and said to them, 'Receive the Holy Spirit'" (John 20:22). It is probable that in this historic moment He held them face to face and blew His breath into them (see Genesis 2:7; 1 Kings 17:21–22). This "receiving of the Holy Spirit" was forty days before Pentecost. Was it a blessing? Absolutely! What was its purpose? Theologians disagree on this point but it is important to remember that the new birth came with the New Covenant. *Until the day of the resurrection,* these men had been Old Testament Jews. That is now past. As Jesus breathed into them they were regenerated—saved, born again and snatched from the Old dispensation into the New. As of that moment they were New Testament Christians. Are they anointed for worldwide evangelism? No. That will not take place for another forty days.

Blessing Number Two

Forty days later, 120 disciples were gathered in the Upper Room when a loud noise from heaven, sounding like a great wind, filled the house (see Acts 2:1–2). Astonished and overwhelmed, they began rejoicing wildly and "divided tongues, as of fire" came upon each of the 120 (Acts 2:3). To their utter shock, they "were all filled with the Holy Spirit and began to speak with other tongues" (Acts 2:4).

Scripture is careful to explain that others who were not present at Pentecost experienced the same empowering later. Identically, today, multiplied millions around the world have stepped into the Spirit's wondrous baptism. Being born again prepares us for heaven; being baptized with the Spirit prepares us for a powerful life and ministry on earth. This baptism endows us with spiritual gifts and power (see 1 Corinthians 12). Every Christian should be baptized—"filled"—with the Holy Spirit.

Anyone can receive the Holy Spirit's imparting simply by asking. Jesus said: "Everyone who asks receives" (Matthew 7:8). Deep worship is the best preparation to receive. If possible, have another believer lay his or her hands on you in Jesus' name. Remember, Jesus said, "'If anyone thirsts, let him come to Me and drink. He who believes in Me, as the Scripture has said, out of his heart will flow rivers of living water.' But this He spoke concerning the Spirit, whom those believing in Him would receive" (John 7:37–40). The key is "drinking." Present yourself to the Lord. Ask to be filled. Pause in your worship and prayer. Spiritually, drink! drink! drink! You will be filled! The power you receive may manifest alongside the appearance of other "signs and wonders." The Holy Spirit distributes "to each one individually as He will" (1 Corinthians 12:11).

95. What Do the Terms *Pentecostal* and *Charismatic* Mean?

The distinction between *Pentecostal* and *charismatic* is primarily historical. Pentecostal churches began with the Azusa Street revival in Los Angeles, California, in 1906 and spread immediately around the world. Charismatic churches grew out of mainline denominations after

1960 and the sudden reappearance of the gift of tongues at St. Mark's Episcopal Church, Van Nuys, California. This latter radical change in mainline churches was prophesied to David du Plessis by Smith Wigglesworth in South Africa in 1936. Most Pentecostal churches—which see the gift of tongues as the "initial evidence" of the infilling of the Holy Spirit—are now denominational; most charismatic churches—which hold that tongues might or might not occur at the infilling—are usually independent of each other.

Many churches throughout the world are seeking association with other Spirit-empowered churches in what are called Apostolic Networks. In some countries Spirit-filled churches are called *charismatic* instead of the more familiar North American term *Pentecostal*. The current worldwide Spirit-empowered movement comprises Pentecostal, charismatic (Catholic and Protestant) and Third Wave believers.

96. What Is the Importance of the Gifts to the Church?

There is probably no greater theological ignorance in the Church today than of spiritual gifts. To the Romans Paul said, "I long to see you, that I may impart to you some spiritual gift, so that you may be established" (Romans 1:11). Without the presence and power of spiritual gifts the Church cannot be properly established. In the Greek language the word for saving "grace" is *charisma* and the word for "grace gift" is *charismata*. Observe: The structure of the grace-system connects the two words in an inseparable way. To deny the miraculous gifts of the Holy Spirit is to contradict the biblical structure of grace. Grace as a spiritual gift is translated seventeen times in the New Testament from the word *charismata*. Apart from grace, spiritual gifts cannot exist. Apart from spiritual gifts, grace cannot be fully revealed. Paul encouraged the Church to exercise these gifts.

The modern Church has in large part forbidden them, but there are signs that this is changing. It is difficult, for example, to find an Anglican vicar who does not believe the spiritual gifts are still for today. Most of the churches in Latin America believe the gifts are still for today, and the number of churches in the West is increasing that acknowledge that the gifts did not end with the death of the apostles or the canonization of the Bible.

In rejecting spiritual gifts, part of the modern Church rejects God's provision for her own success. Scripture tells us: "Earnestly desire the best gifts" (1 Corinthians 12:31); "Pursue love, and desire spiritual gifts, but especially that you may prophesy" (14:1); "Since you are zealous for spiritual gifts, let it be for the edification of the church that you seek to excel" (14:12).

97. What Are the Individual Spiritual Gifts?

The New Testament contains six passages in which gifts of the Spirit are identified. All are still active; none has been withdrawn. These gifts are miraculous provisions for the Church's ministry.

> Having then gifts differing according to the grace that is given to us, let us use them: if prophecy, let us prophesy in proportion to our faith; or ministry, let us use it in our ministering; he who teaches, in teaching; he who exhorts, in exhortation; he who gives, with liberality; he who leads, with diligence; he who shows mercy, with cheerfulness.
>
> Romans 12:6–8

> I wish that all men were even as I myself [unmarried]. But each one has his own gift from God [chárisma ek Theoú], one in this manner and another in that.
>
> 1 Corinthians 7:7

For to one is given the word of wisdom through the Spirit, to another the word of knowledge through the same Spirit, to another faith by the same Spirit, to another gifts of healings by the same Spirit, to another the working of miracles, to another prophecy, to another discerning of spirits, to another different kinds of tongues, to another the interpretation of tongues. But one and the same Spirit works all these things, distributing to each one individually as He wills.

1 Corinthians 12:8–12

God has appointed these in the church: first apostles, second prophets, third teachers, after that miracles, then gifts of healings, helps, administrations, varieties of tongues.

1 Corinthians 12:28

And He Himself gave some to be apostles, some prophets, some evangelists, and some pastors and teachers.

Ephesians 4:11–12

Be hospitable to one another without grumbling. As each one has received a gift, minister it to one another, as good stewards of the manifold grace of God. If anyone speaks, let him speak as the oracles of God. If anyone ministers, let him do it as with the ability which God supplies, that in all things God may be glorified through Jesus Christ, to whom belong the glory and the dominion forever and ever. Amen.

1 Peter 4:9–11

Though these may be categorized in various ways, they can be divided loosely into two groupings:

Manifestation Gifts

Word of wisdom: Specific God-revelation of unknown information
Word of knowledge: Miraculous knowledge of a previously unknown fact
Faith: An absolute assurance/expectation of good

Gifts of healings: The miraculous normalizing of disease or injury

Miracles: A sudden, material change, as water into wine

Prophecy: Foretelling and forth-telling

Discerning of spirits: Detecting the presence of spirits—clean and unclean; this gift was also used as a corrective to the gift of prophecy to help determine if the message was from the Holy Spirit, the human spirit or a deceiving demonic spirit

Varieties of tongues: Heavenly praise, prayer or prophetic utterance

Interpretation of tongues: Understanding the message of an unknown tongue

These gifts may be placed into three categories of three each:

Power Gifts: Faith, Miracles, Healings

Vocal Gifts: Prophecy, Tongues, Interpretation of tongues

Cognitive Gifts: Knowledge, Wisdom, Discerning of spirits

Ministerial Gifts

Apostle: One "sent forth" who ministers in scriptural authority and power

Prophet: An exhorter who speaks with revelatory knowledge

Teacher: One who teaches from Scripture

Evangelist: One who travels, sharing the Good News

Pastor: A preaching-shepherd who oversees a flock

Helps: An assistant to others

Administrations: An organizational aide or minister/elder, though not a teaching elder

Ministry: One spiritually motivated for Kingdom service

Exhortation: One who encourages verbally or by example

Speaking: Probably speaking and exhortation are the same

Giving: A supporter in money, time or talent

Leading: An example-giver who leads by illustration

Mercy: A grace-giver and helper

Hospitality: A donor-helper

Chastity: One who maintains sexual purity regarding abstinence

The Trinity is also recognized in the arrangement of spiritual gifts in 1 Corinthians 12:4–6. Observe: "There are diversities of gifts, but the same [Holy] Spirit. There are differences of ministries, but the same Lord [Jesus]. And there are diversities of activities, but it is the same God [Father] who works all in all."

98. What Is Cessationism?

Cessationism is a religious idea with widespread acceptance in many Christian bodies. It claims that God has withdrawn all miraculous gifts, signs, wonders and demonstrations of the Holy Spirit that occurred in early Christian history. All such miracles have "ceased," hence the name. Any such "sign and wonder" today is fraudulent, possibly demonic. According to this concept, God withdrew the Holy Spirit's power from the Church but let the devil keep his. The fact is: The absence of signs and wonders is due to the Church's unbelief and rejection of the Word.

Two theoretical claims are made by cessationists: (1) All miraculous works ended in the AD 90s with the death of the final apostle, John, and (2) miraculous signs were withdrawn in AD 367 when the New Testament was canonized. Let's take the latter as an example.

In an attempt to disqualify the gift of tongues as being valid today, 1 Corinthians 13:8–10 is misapplied. The Scripture is this: "But whether there are prophecies, they will fail; whether there are tongues, they will cease; whether there is knowledge, it will vanish away. For we know in part and we prophesy in part. But when that which is perfect has come, then that which is in part will be done away."

Cessationists consider the wording *when that which is perfect has come* to refer to the New Testament when it was "perfected" or canonized. The fact is this: Those who believe in the inspiration of Scripture agree that Paul's first Corinthian letter was perfect when he wrote it. The New Testament when finally completed was still perfect. Opponents to tongues claim that the moment it was canonized, gifts of knowledge, tongues and prophecy failed (ended). Though left in the New Testament, they were obsolete. The long-awaited "perfect" book was not perfect at all. Instead, parts that had been perfect instantly became imperfect "when that which is perfect had come."

This is religious absurdity.

Ignore it.

99. Why Do Some Reject the Idea of Spiritual Gifts?

The phenomenon of Pentecost startled the devout Jews anciently and has the same effect on devout Christians today. Scripture says: "There were dwelling in Jerusalem Jews, devout men, from every nation under heaven. And when this sound occurred, the multitude came together" (Acts 2:5–6). And:

They "were confused" (verse 6).

"They were all amazed" (verse 7).

"They were all amazed and perplexed" (verse 12).

"Others mocking said, 'They are full of new wine'" (verse 13).

Paul explained it this way: "The natural man does not receive the things of the Spirit of God, for they are foolishness to him; nor can he know them, because they are spiritually discerned" (1 Corinthians 2:14). To the rational mind, speaking in tongues, noise, commotion, falling to the floor—all is disorderly conduct and cannot be godly. Whether anciently or today, the opinion is often the same. Such people are mocked. Their activity is often not recognized as caused by the Holy Spirit.

100. Why Is There Particular Objection to the Gift of Tongues?

The gift of tongues is a "sign" gift (1 Corinthians 14:22). That means it serves a secondary purpose beyond its work of spiritual communication. In this additional function, tongues attacks a person's ego, exposes religious pride and self-centeredness, and reveals attitudes the person might be unwilling to admit are there. Some people get not only uncomfortable but angry when the subject of tongues is mentioned. That happens because the "sign" is working. Tongues, then, helps people discover unpleasant facts about themselves.

101. When Will the Spiritual Gifts Actually Cease?

Not a single New Testament verse indicates that spiritual gifts ended when the last apostle died or would end after its canonization. Still, the day will come when the gifts cease, as the apostle Paul wrote the Corinthians: "Prophecies . . . will fail; . . . tongues . . . will cease; . . . knowledge . . . will vanish away" (1 Corinthians 13:8). But until that day comes, he encouraged them to continue in the gifts: "The testimony of Christ was confirmed in you, so that you come short in no gift [*charismati*], eagerly waiting for the revelation of our Lord Jesus Christ" (1 Corinthians 1:6–7). In that brief statement Paul confirmed that spiritual gifts will endure as long as the Church waits for Christ's return. Gifts bring power to the Church and her ministry. Miraculous gifts provide power for the preached Word.

102. What Does It Mean to Be Slain in the Spirit?

George Whitfield rebuked John Wesley because of people falling while he ministered. Later, it happened in Whitfield's own open-air preaching in the mid-1700s. By the time Whitfield came to Boston, he was wise enough to command people watching in the trees to come down. He knew that when the power of the Holy Spirit fell upon the congregation, many would drop to the ground like stones. Once when a man was knocked from his horse by the power of God, Wesley wrote of him: "Between the saddle and the ground, He mercy sought—and mercy found."

In 1742, in answering accusations made against his "signs and wonders" ministry, Jonathan Edwards explained, "If there be a very powerful influence of the Spirit of God in a mixed multitude, it will cause in some way or other a great visible commotion." His wife, Sarah, lay immobile under the Spirit's power for seventeen days—"swooning," as it was then called. It may have been during that time of immobility that Sarah was in intercession for her husband's ministry and helped sustain the Great Awakening in its move across America.

Pastor James Glindening, a British Puritan of the sixteenth century, asked deacons to lay the fallen under the trees in the churchyard until they recovered. Peter Cartwright, Charles Finney and hosts of other historic preachers witnessed this in their meetings. It even happened in Baptist meetings in early America. At the Cane Ridge, Kentucky, revival in 1801, where as many as five hundred were felled simultaneously, it was called being "slain in the spirit." There is no scriptural name. It may have typified the "drunken" appearance in the Upper Room.

Many feel a sudden weight come upon them, forcing them down. Others sense a strong pull—like gravity—drawing them to the floor. Some go blank; in most cases the person only knows he dropped. In this arrested state people have dramatic encounters with the Lord. It may have been this sensation that occurred in 1 Kings 8:11, at the dedication of Solomon's Temple, when "the priests could not stand to minister because of the cloud: for the glory of the LORD had filled the house of the LORD" (KJV). We read also that the Roman soldiers who came to arrest Jesus "drew back and fell to the ground" (John 18:6). Jerking, shaking and falling are not what the Spirit is trying to accomplish. These are merely side effects of His presence and occur because the human body cannot cope with the sudden invasion of power. The test of successful ministry is a changed life, purer habits, stronger discipleship, healed body. Unfortunately, this holy experience can be falsified either by the one ministering or the one receiving. Even prayer, baptism, worship can be faked. Even so, we continue with what is genuine and godly. Those who falsify such moves of the Spirit are answerable to God.

The following Scriptures provide important insight between falling in the natural and spiritual aspects. Observe this:

> "Peter went up on the housetop to pray, about the sixth hour. Then he became very hungry and wanted to eat; but while they made ready, he fell into a trance" (Acts 10:9–10). Peter's fall was spiritual and the Greek word used is *epipito*.
>
> "As Peter was coming in, Cornelius met him and fell down at his feet and worshiped him" (verse 25). Here the fall was natural and comes from the word *pipto*.
>
> "While Peter was still speaking these words, the Holy Spirit fell upon all those who heard the word" (verse 44). Here Scripture returns to *epipito*.

When Cornelius fell before the apostle Peter, the word is used in the ordinary sense; it has no other implication than an action on Cornelius's part. That is not true in the instance of Peter "falling into a trance" or the Holy Spirit "falling upon all those who heard the word." In this case, it means to be "embraced with affection." Spiritual passion is involved in both of these instances. The same word is used of the Prodigal Son being hugged by his compassionate father (see Luke 15:20). That was a holy embrace of pure fatherly love. This is also the use in the story of the young man killed in a fall (*pipto*) whom the apostle Paul embraced (*epipito*) and restored to life (see Acts 20:10). In every instance in the New Testament *epipito* carries an emotional or spiritual implication. When the angel appeared to Zacharias in the Temple, the fear that fell upon him was holy and heavenly—and was *epipito* (see Luke 1:12). The distinction is not from translation but implication.

103. What Is the Laying On of Hands?

Jesus said, "These signs will follow those who believe: In My Name . . . they will lay hands on the sick, and they will recover" (Mark 16:17–18). Reference to "hands on" ministry appears some 28 times in the New Testament. Only four or five times does it refer to the ordination of ministers and deacons. Other instances regard healing, ministering the baptism with the Spirit, imparting of spiritual gifts and more.

The power in this ministry is more easily understood when we realize that our bodies are the temples of God and that the Spirit of God dwells in us (see 1 Corinthians 3:16). It is the temple of the Holy Spirit inside the human body from which the power is released. There is no "power" in the human hand apart from the Holy Spirit. Religious formalities are unfortunate imitations of the authentic and cannot impart the power Jesus intended.

Power comes from the Holy Spirit who dwells inside the temple of God, which is the human body. The hand has value only because it is an extension of the temple. When a "ministering temple" rightly contacts a "receiving temple," there is frequently a visible movement of the Holy Spirit from the first to the second. The result may be healing, deliverance, baptism or some unidentified purpose. The concept of electric current arching from one terminal to another illustrates this transfer of power. The effect is sometimes dramatic and may be life-changing for the one receiving.

We have such an example when Ananias laid his hands on Saul of Tarsus and said that Jesus had sent him that Saul might "'receive [his] sight and be filled with the Holy Spirit.' Immediately there fell from his eyes something like scales, and he received his sight at once; and he arose and was baptized" (Acts 9:17–18).

Paul wrote Timothy, "Do not lay hands on anyone hastily, nor share in other people's sins; keep yourself pure" (1 Timothy 5:22). In Samaria, Peter laid hands on the people; in Caesarea, he did not (see Acts 8:17; 10:44). In both cases, results were the same. Peter's temple was present and, in the latter case, the power fell without physical contact. The same principle was true when Peter walked the streets of Jerusalem and invalids were healed by the touch of his shadow (see Acts 5:15). There is no healing power in a shadow. Rather, it was the nearness of Peter's temple-body and the anointing radiating from him that brought miraculous results.

104. What Does Scripture Say about Women Preaching?

Jesus gave His first post-resurrection preaching-command to two women at the tomb: "Go and tell" (Matthew 28:10). That command has never been withdrawn from any disciple, male or female. All believers are to "Go and tell." Philip the evangelist had four daughters who prophesied. They obviously spoke in public gatherings. Aquila and Priscilla, Paul's assistants, are mentioned five times in the book of Acts as the apostle's ministry team. Jesus said, "These signs will follow those who believe. . . ." (Mark 16:17). There was no exclusion of women; His offer was for all.

Much violence has been forced upon the Church by demanding women to be voiceless. This position cannot be upheld in the presence of New Testament examples of women in public ministry. It has its basis in misrepresentations regarding a particular instruction Paul gave to the church in Corinth. First Corinthians 14:34 says this: "Let your women keep silent in the churches, for they are not permitted to speak."

This is very direct—and perplexing considering that Paul commended women in public ministry, including Phoebe, who was a deacon (see Romans 16:1). What was Paul saying?

The key is this: The Greek language, in which the New Testament was written, has no word for *wife*. Instead, the text uses the word *woman* [*gune*]. Translators are left to determine whether *gune* means "woman" in the general sense or "wife" in the family sense. The conflict in Corinth that Paul was addressing was actually a domestic problem in which wives in the congregation were usurping certain areas of authority that their husbands held. Paul stopped the conflict by saying, "Let these wives keep silent in the church." Disorderliness in the Corinthians' church was not unusual. Paul rebuked its members—men and women, husbands and wives—for heresy, drunkenness and gluttony (see 1 Corinthians 11:17–21). Their meetings did more harm than good (see verse 17).

Family peace and orderliness should be the rule in every home and carry its harmony into the churches. When the New Testament pattern is followed, everyone in the Church is free to function in the gifts God has given.

105. What Is a Deacon?

From the time of Pentecost onward, the early Church experienced such explosive growth that its own members were sometimes neglected and their needs left unmet. This included widows. The apostles directed the congregation to find "seven men of good reputation, full of the Holy Spirit and wisdom, whom we may appoint over this business." They wanted to give themselves "continually to prayer and to the ministry of the word" (Acts 6:3–4). The church prayed, the individuals—in this case, men—were found, ordained by the laying on of hands, and the apostles were freed for ministry. As a result, "The word of God spread, and the number of the disciples multiplied greatly in Jerusalem."

The presence of "Spirit-filled" deacons provided help within the congregation while the apostles and other preachers did their work without. The deaconship helped fuel the Church for greater growth. Paul, for instance, commended "Phoebe our sister, who is a servant [*diákonos*] of the church in Cenchrea" (Romans 16:1).

The term *deacon* is translated from the Greek word *diákonos* and means "servant" or "minister." It occurs 29 times in the Greek New Testament. While deacons work in close contact with elders, their function is not the same. In caring for widows and orphans, and meeting other needs, the deacon remains servant to the church body. He or she serves the church table. The true meaning of *deaconship* has been lost in many congregations where the deacon is regarded as an executive with power to hire or fire the pastor. This is a dangerous usurpation of the role.

The functions of bishops and deacons are mentioned together in Philippians 1:1 and 1 Timothy 3:1, 8. The qualifications are much the same, but not identical. The bishop is required to be "able to teach" but the deacon does not share that responsibility. Both must be persons of prayer, lovers of truth and godly examples to unbelievers.

106. What Is an Elder?

An elder is a leader in the Church who has been recognized as fulfilling the Scripture's mandates for that office and set apart by the laying on of hands (see 2 Timothy 1:6). The term for *elder* in New Testament Greek is *presbuteros*, meaning a mature leader in the congregation. Eldership may be based on seniority of age or seniority of wisdom and devotion to Christ. Paul stressed this when he said a bishop should not be a novice (see 1 Timothy 3:6). In Titus 1:5–9, Paul used the words *bishop* (*episcopos*) and *elder* (*presbuteros*) interchangeably. While there are other distinctions between the two, there is a camaraderie that unites them. The elder's function is not political but spiritually administrative. Scripture always identifies elders in the Church as plural, not singular. The pastor is also an elder.

Paul is very exact in identifying the role of elder. Among other duties, an elder must be able to teach sound doctrine, expose heresy, be of an honorable reputation, and if the elder has children, they must be of godly and honorable conduct. Elders work concurrently with the pastor, being aware of any needs and prompt in caring for them. An elder must be an example to the flock (see 1 Peter 5:3), shepherd the flock (see 1 Peter 5:2), be a capable teacher (see 1 Timothy 5:17; Titus 1:5, 9), anoint and pray for the sick (see James 5:14), and provide oversight for the flock (see 1 Peter 5:2). In cases of controversy, the elder must be a loving and unbiased judge (see Acts 15:2, 6, 22–29; 16:4). Numerous other Scriptures detail the work of the elder.

Much depends on the godliness of the elder, but this must be the prevailing attitude in all who minister in the church. Where there is conflict in Church leadership, the Holy Spirit will be grieved and the congregation will be deprived of His anointing.

PART 9

What about Satan and His Demons?

107. Who Is Satan?

The name *Satan* is derived from the Hebrew word meaning "adversary." He is a fallen angel, a created being, who possesses no creative power of his own, and whose chief weapon is deception. Scripture identifies him as Lucifer, the "light bearer" or "son of the morning," and provides ample details about his rebellion and exile from heaven (see Isaiah 14:12–15). John identifies him as the "great, fiery red dragon" that was cast to the earth and swept a third of the stars with him. This apparently refers to the angels who were under his archangel authority and who rebelled with him (see Revelation 12:3–4).

While we have no scriptural guide, it seems that three archangels served the Trinitarian nature of the Godhead. The other two were Gabriel and Michael. On another significant point the Bible is silent: What was the origin of Lucifer's sin? Prior to the rebellion, what enabled him to become evil? How was sin possible in heaven? The Bible's first reference to the devil is his appearance in the Garden of Eden. He is mentioned many times in Scripture and finally in the Bible's conclusion when he is cast into the lake of fire. Other references are these: 1 Chronicles 21:1; Job 1:6–12; Zechariah 3:1–2; Matthew 4:1; Mark 3:23–24; John 13:2.

108. What Is the Origin of Evil?

Theologians and philosophers have struggled for millennia for answers about the origin of evil. We know only of the first appearance of sin in Lucifer, "son of the morning," and his capacity for contaminating others with evil (see Isaiah 14:12). Scripture is silent as to how sin originated in him. It appears that Lucifer was one of three archangels who ministered to the Trinity. They were: Lucifer, the worshiper; Michael, the messenger; and Gabriel, the warrior. It is possible that the book of Revelation alludes to each as possessing authority over one-third of lesser angels. Lucifer, in a fallen state, is described as a "great, fiery red dragon . . . [who] drew a third of the stars of heaven and threw them to the earth." This same beast "stood before the woman who was ready to give birth, to devour her Child as soon as it was born" (Revelation 12:3–4).

While we do not know sin's origin, we do know Satan's final state: "The devil, who deceived them, was cast into the lake of fire and brimstone where the beast and the false prophet are. And they will be tormented day and night forever and ever" (Revelation 20:10).

109. What Is Satanism?

Most world cultures recognize Satan—the devil—as an authentic reality. It is obvious that evil is a powerful, active force in the world. Atheistic Communism, which denies the existence of any spiritual reality, has, in its blindness, produced some of the worst human brutality records. Joseph Stalin deliberately starved millions of people to death. Adolf Hitler, in murdering millions of Jews and destroying huge parts of an otherwise happy society, was a satanic practitioner and occultist. This is Satanism in its public, political form. The devil delights in human brutality and has demonstrated that fact in every generation.

The spectrum of Satanism is wide, moving from its international display into the secrecy of an organized coven of witches and warlocks, or the subtlety of a person's vicious lies, hatefulness and spiteful deeds. People can become a ploy of Satanism and be unaware they are being used. The devil's chief tool is deception, and his works can dominate families, organizations and religious groups for generations. Churches can become infected with it. Cults employ it to control their subjects. In some instances Satanism takes the form of worship with participants performing ritualistic sacrifices—human and animal—dancing before Satan and adoring him as god.

Young people are frequently brought under the grip of Satanism through psychic palm reading, Ouija boards or Tarot card games. These are enticing tools that pull the unwary into the dark world of evil. God's message toward all of it is an absolute no. There is no middle ground allowed in serving both God and Satan (see 2 Corinthians 4:4).

110. What Is the Spirit of Jezebel?

It is significant that Jezebel, wife of King Ahab, who lived more than eight hundred years before Christ, should still be of concern when the final book of the Bible was written. In it, Jesus rebuked the church at Thyatira for allowing Jezebel, who called herself a prophetess, to seduce the members into sin (see Revelation 2:18–22). Jezebel's father was Ethbaal, king of the Sidonians and a worshiper of Baal; though queen of Israel, Jezebel was a devoted follower of this demonized cult. She demolished the kingdom of Israel, killed God's prophets, stole from its citizens, and promoted idolatry and witchcraft.

Today, we recognize Jezebel as a spirit, a living active force of conquest, moving worldwide, century to century, deceiving her way into good families, churches, ministries, even governments. There is probably no unclean spirit more dangerous to the Church than that of Jezebel. Failed lives, broken homes, distraught and wounded people lie in her wake. Jezebel often works through a demonized person—man or woman—to do her work of controlling others, particularly leaders. Jezebel can appear charming, loving and eager to help. In the end it is a destroyer of the people of God. She achieves this through lying, seduction, intimidation, manipulation or outright force, often deceiving by her pretension to be helpful. She is a queen; dethroning her is one of the most fearsome tasks a church faces.

The woman Jezebel was killed when two eunuchs threw her from the balcony. The good news for us today is that ardent prayer, fasting, words of knowledge, wisdom and other spiritual gifts can break her hold.

111. What Are Demons?

Demons are spiritual parasites who need a physical host in which to live. Having no bodies of their own, they can only fulfill their lust by expressing it through the body of another. They dread the "dry places," which is their only other option (see Matthew 12:43). Like leeches, they can even anesthetize the place of their wound so that their invasion goes undetected. In many cases, a demon will mentally mesmerize his prey to the degree that the victim believes the spirit's will is his own.

Once established, the demon considers the person's body as "my house" (Luke 11:24). Worse still, if not addressed, such dominating control can be passed from one generation to the next. These are called family "strongholds" (2 Corinthians 10:4). This includes undesirable physical, mental, moral, emotional, religious traits. These, in turn, can open their victims to addiction, explosive anger, self-abuse, depression, repeated failure, jealousy, adultery and a wide variety of perversities. Demons hate God and find pleasure in defacing those who are created in His image and likeness.

The Bible gives us much detailed information about demons but does not tell us how or when they originated. We know only that Satan, their ruler, appeared early in the Genesis account as a serpent (see Genesis 3:1), and that demons existed at the same time. The prophet Isaiah described Satan's fall, and the book of Revelation indicates that he took one-third of the angels with him (see Isaiah 14:12; Revelation 12:4). At this point we cannot form doctrinal opinions; we know only that demons are real, they are dangerous, and their greatest power is deception. With it, they are very successful. When confronted, they defend themselves desperately. Apparently, demons are indestructible and will remain alive with Satan and his fallen angels in the lake of fire (see Revelation 20:1).

The good news is they can be bound and banished from believers by the authority of Jesus. Jesus never sent His disciples to preach without equipping them with His same authority and power (see Matthew 10:8). On one occasion the disciples returned to Jesus with great joy, shouting, laughing and saying, "Lord, even the demons are subject to us in Your name" (Luke 10:17). Of future believers, Jesus said: "In my name they will cast out demons" (Mark 16:17). Thirty percent of Jesus' recorded ministry was spent in direct conflict with unclean spirits. Casting them out of their victims was a cardinal part of His ministry (see Mark 1:25–26).

112. Can Christians Be Possessed by Demons?

No, Christians cannot be possessed by demons. *Possession* implies ownership. Saved people are "owned" by Jesus Christ and cannot be co-owned by the devil. The spirits of born-again people are secure in Christ.

Christians can be attacked, vexed and oppressed by demons. Demons can severely infest the bodies and minds of Christians. The New Testament Greek word *diamonizomai*, or its English equivalent, "demonized," has no connotation of the devil's ownership; it speaks only of humanity's susceptibility to demonic attack.

The rule is this: A demon can go anywhere sin and disease can go. For a Christian to be immune to demons in his body or brain, he would also have to be free from sin and disease. Such a person does not yet exist. Paul explained that our "mortal" has not yet put on "immortality." Nor has our "corruptible put on incorruption" (1 Corinthians 15:51–57). As long as we are on the earth, in our present corruptible state, we will be vulnerable to demons. Jesus healed a woman with a severely twisted back by casting out a "spirit of infirmity" (Luke 13:11). He also called her a "daughter of Abraham," meaning she was a woman of faith. The demon was in her physical body; not her redeemed spirit. It oppressed her but did not possess her. So it can be with us. Unclean spirits can invade the body and mind of a saved believer; they cannot enter his or her spirit.

113. How Do Demons Enter a Person?

Sometimes the abuse done to us, such as trauma or ancestral curses flowing down the family line, gives legal entry. Forgiveness of the per- petrators and breaking of strongholds can remove the demonic grip on a person or family.

Sin is a conscious choice that opens the door to demons in our lives. Sinful acts such as participation in occult organizations, occult rites, superstition, hate-groups, uncontrolled anger, unforgiveness and mysti- cism are some of the ways demons gain access. God has given humans a mental "will" by which we make moral choices to protect ourselves. The will is like a protective wall surrounding the mind that enables us to choose between right and wrong, good and evil.

Many people do not realize that their actions can predispose them to demonic control; the illicit use of drugs and alcohol is particularly dam- aging in this regard. Certain plants such as peyote cactus, mushrooms and marijuana have a psychiatric effect on the brain. Other plants such as corn and grapes produce alcohol that may be equally destructive. Why is this? Of themselves, the plants are innocent. But drugs attack that protective wall, weakening or momentarily destroying it. With the mental protection down, the person is unguarded and demons rush in. While the effects of the alcohol or drugs eventually disappear, the person may remain spiritually infected and in need of deliverance ministry.

114. How Does One Know if Deliverance Is Needed?

Christians need to be aware that compulsive behaviors, ongoing sinful behaviors, and ancestral and family patterns that do not respond to repentance, prayer and ordinary Christian means are suspect. Health problems, emotional instability, depression, uncontrollable temper, persistent failure, superstition, addiction, undesirable conduct, violence, disease, alcoholism, compulsive behavior and manipulation are just a few indicators of the possible presence of unclean spirits. Not everyone realizes that these are not simply family "traits" or that they can be stopped. Granted, not all human problems are demonic in their origin. If, however, such a problem remains unresolved, demons will take advantage of it.

Since demons and curses are spiritual in nature they can be corrected only by spiritual means. Medical, psychiatric or other forms of therapy, excellent as they are, may relieve symptoms but cannot sever problems that are spiritually based. Such areas can be penetrated solely by the ministry of the Holy Spirit. This is done only in the authority of Jesus' name. If unclean spirits are present they are compelled to leave.

Even if no symptoms present themselves, it is beneficial for every Christian, especially pastors and those in church leadership, to routinely receive "discerning of spirits" ministry and deliverance for themselves. No one is immune to demonic attack. We live in a dirty world. Unclean spirits invade the body and mind; they cannot enter the spirit of a saved believer. A demon has no physical body of its own; to fulfill its lustful desires it must use the body of someone else. For that reason, they are desperate for a body—even choosing the body of a pig rather than be left without one at all (see Matthew 8:28–32).

Christians who fail in their commitment to Christ are frequently accused of "backsliding" when that is not the problem. The real failure is that most of the time the Church never helped them understand the full benefits of the cross—specifically, deliverance from demons. Jesus never said there would be an "Apostolic Church" and a "Post-Apostolic

Church" with different practices, teachings, expectations and achievement. He established one Church, not two, which was to continue unchanged to the "end of the age." Whether ancient or modern, Christianity must retain the same love, truth and power. Many Spirit-empowered believers today are returning to historic Christianity—including casting out demons and rescuing victims from lives of repeated failure and defeat.

115. How Is One Delivered?

The steps to deliverance are not complicated. Scripture says, "Submit to God. Resist the devil and he will flee from you" (James 4:7). How is this done? The victim should:

Repent of all sin.
Forgive everyone who has caused him or her harm.
Renounce every occult influence.
Surrender to Jesus Christ.
Then rebuke the unclean spirit and command it to go.

Any believer or ministry team assisting in the deliverance can "lay hands" on the victim in the name of Jesus, anoint him or her with oil and, speaking with confidence and quiet assurance, command the demon to leave. Fasting is often beneficial (see Matthew 17:21). Demons respond to authority (see Mark 1:25). They do not obey emotion and noise, only authority.

Demons, on the other hand, can be noisy (see Mark 1:26; Acts 8:7). In the ministry of Jesus, those who were demonized sometimes fell to the ground and "wallowed, foaming at the mouth" (see Mark 9:20). Ugly? Yes, but the people were set free. Jesus did not allow demons to speak. They can be commanded to be silent during the deliverance process.

The word for "spirit," *ruwach* in Hebrew and *pneuma* in Greek, is also used for "wind" or "breath." Demons frequently resist by shutting off the victim's breath and gagging him or her. The victim can offset this and assist in the expulsion by coughing. If symptoms of the demon's exit occur, such as heavy breathing, hiccups or coughing, do not suppress them. Demons may well attempt to intimidate their victims and those involved in deliverance ministry. If the amount of time required becomes too lengthy, bind the spirits in the name of Jesus Christ and resume later.

Jesus intended the contemporary Church to do the same works as the ancient Church. This includes exercising authority over demons and driving them out. We can move into deliverance ministry confidently, trusting Christ and the power of His name.

116. Can Demons Reenter a Person after Being Cast Out?

Jesus taught that a demon who is expelled goes "through dry places, seeking rest, and finds none." The demon then reasons that he will "return to my house from which I came" and attempt to reenter. If he finds that house now empty and unoccupied, he will round up other spirits—ones that are even more wicked than himself—and go back inside to live. "The last state of that man," said Jesus, "is worse than the first" (Matthew 12:43–45).

Demons can return only to an empty, unprotected "house" (person). A willful act of sin on the part of the individual is what allows their reentry; they cannot enter by mere choice. If the person allows fear to replace faith, for instance, the heart attitude becomes sinful and provides the demon that needed opportunity. Following deliverance, the victim must be filled with the Holy Spirit (and remain so), develop a godly lifestyle, become a student of Scripture and maintain in active, worshipful relationship with the Body of Christ.

117. Who Can Provide Deliverance Ministry?

Deliverance ministry is the term currently applied to exorcism or the casting out of demons. Jesus gave this authority to the early disciples and never revoked it (see Luke 10:19). He gave it to all true believers in every generation. Jesus said, "These signs will follow those who believe: In My name they will cast out demons" (Mark 16:17). The responsibility for deliverance still applies to the Church today and the power to do it is available. While every believer is potentially capable of ministering in this authority, not every one is scripturally informed and prepared. Quite simply, disciples today who stand in the authority of His name may exorcize demons from themselves or others.

While Jesus was teaching in one of the synagogues, He saw a woman who had been bent double by "a spirit of infirmity [for] eighteen years" (Luke 13:11). He called her to Himself, laid His hands on her and declared her "loosed" from her infirmity. Observe that Jesus did not heal her; instead He cast out a spirit of infirmity and immediately she was well again. Many Christians in our day suffer from prolonged illness because of spirits of infirmity that cannot be diagnosed medically. In many cases deliverance ministry would set them free.

According to Jesus every true believer can cast out demons. Jesus intended that the modern Church would do the same works as the ancient Church. This includes exercising authority over demons and driving them out. In Philippi, the apostle Paul encountered a young woman possessed by a fortune-telling spirit. Speaking directly to the demon, he said, "I command you in the name of Jesus Christ to come out of her" (Acts 16:18). The spirit obeyed immediately and the woman was set free. Why did it happen? Paul was a believer moving in authority.

It is important for those ministering in deliverance to ask the Holy Spirit's protection and the covering of Jesus' blood. Also remember Jesus' words: "Nothing shall by any means hurt you" (Luke 10:19).

118. Is Every Bad Circumstance Demonic in Origin?

We can all make foolish decisions and bring problems on ourselves without the devil being to blame. Not every bad circumstance is demonic. It is also true that the devil will take advantage of every opportunity we provide. Study this example. A woman falls and breaks her leg. It was her own carelessness that caused the injury. While in recovery she becomes self-pitying, angry, jealous, abuses her medication and does other things that provide Satan with an open door. What began as mere human error has become a workplace for powers of darkness. Her broken leg may heal perfectly, while a new problem moves into the woman's life. In such cases, yes, deliverance is needed. It may be self-administered if she is truly honest about herself.

Granted, the answer to the question "Can the devil make a person fall?" is yes. If he can make someone fall morally, he can make someone fall physically. Our spiritual warfare with powers of darkness is a never-ending battle. But the One who is in the believer is greater than the one who is in the world (see 1 John 4:4; Revelation 12:11). Can we tell the difference in what is God-caused or Satan-caused? Part of the time. God has expressed His will for us and His works in His covenant. Jesus proclaimed this in His first sermon in Nazareth when He declared that the Spirit of the Lord was upon Him and had anointed Him to preach, to heal, to liberate and to proclaim the acceptable year of the Lord (see Luke 4:18). This was the expression of God's covenant and purpose for mankind. Nowhere did Jesus say He had come to blind, destroy and kill. God does not blind, deafen or destroy His people; He would not undo what Jesus suffered on the cross to achieve for us.

But Paul blinded a man! True. And Paul said of the deceitful and fraudulent man, "You son of the devil, you enemy of all righteousness, will you not cease perverting the straight ways of the Lord? And now, indeed, the hand of the Lord is upon you, and you shall be blind, not seeing the sun for a time. And immediately a dark mist fell on him" (Acts 13:10–11).

Insurance companies refer to earthquakes, hurricanes, floods and the like as "acts of God." Is this true? No. Most disasters are caused by the prince of the power of the air, his demons and human greed (see Ephesians 2:2; James 4:1). Believers who are embraced in God's covenant, who are born again and who have received the blessing of Abraham still live in territory dominated by powers of darkness. We are exposed to them on a daily basis and frequently fall victim to their attacks. Even so, we are warned about the "wiles of the devil" and taught how to flee them (see Ephesians 6:11).

119. After Deliverance, What Does a Person Need for Healthy Development?

Deliverance from an unclean spirit is frequently an immediate, instantaneous experience. When this is not the case, the person must have follow-up sessions until free. Following deliverance, it is absolutely essential that the person be filled with the Holy Spirit. That individual's mental attitude must be made healthy, godly and normal. Patterns of jealousy, resentment, pessimism and skepticism must be broken; negativity must be replaced by positive, constructive affirmations of faith. It matters not if the deliverance came from self-effort or team-ministry; the person's tongue must be brought under control of the Holy Spirit (see James 4:1). Spiritual disciplines such as prayer, fasting, Scripture study and worship with other believers need to become part of the person's life. Unlike deliverance, renewal of the mind usually requires time, discipline and determination. Both require protective effort on the part of the believer. If the mind is not renewed, the person is left unprotected and becomes an easy target for the devil's future infestation.

120. Who Discipled the New Age Movement?

In 1949, the unchallenged world high priestess of the occult, Alice A. Bailey, died. Her career as a medium and psychic reader began thirty years before, when she accurately predicted the year of her death. Bailey's parents were Anglican missionaries to India. She married an Anglican priest, divorced him and moved to America. It seems that while in India, Bailey had become involved with Hindu spirits. Sorcerers around the world eagerly acknowledged her as Satan's appointed messenger of the New Age and successor to Helena Petrovna Blavatsky, the earlier champion of the Theosophical Society. Bailey wrote some 24 books of instructions for disciples of the New Age that were published by the Lucifer Trust.

By the time of Bailey's death, a network of more than five thousand organizations was listed in worldwide New Age directories. These included industrial organizations, international music groups, highly organized and well-financed clubs, witchcraft covens, political bodies, religious societies and others. Bailey's voluminous writing spanned three decades of intense activity in which she instructed her followers to wait 25 years from the time of her death before "going public." That year, 1974, they were to "come out of the closet" and make their influence fully known. Millions of Americans who never heard of Alice Bailey are unaware of the driving force of her influence.

121. What Is the Christian's Response to the Pull of the Occult?

The Bible warns repeatedly against every form of Satanist power and sorcery. Make no mistake about it: Satan is real and extends his power eagerly by planting demons inside naive and unsuspecting people. In the Old Testament those practicing witchcraft were treated as criminals and put to death. That included palmistry, astrology, tarot cards, channeling and all other forms of black-art known today. Ouija Boards—which are extremely dangerous—are sold in children's toy stores.

As Christians, we must separate ourselves from every form of satanic power. In the Old Testament many forms of sorcery were practiced by pagan nations and God forbade Israel to touch "what is unclean" (2 Corinthians 6:17). Anyone who has participated in sorcery in any degree needs to repent, seek God's forgiveness and receive deliverance ministry. If there are books, amulets or other items connected to witchcraft in the house, they must be destroyed, their power broken and all traces put beyond the reach of recovery.

PART 10

What Are Foundations of the Faith?

122. Why Are Bible Doctrines Important?

No Bible doctrine is complete within itself or stands apart from any other scriptural truth: "The Scripture cannot be broken" (John 10:35). "All scripture is given by inspiration of God" (2 Timothy 3:16). In the fulfillment of its particular role, each doctrine returns to the perfect oneness of Christ. It is part of the "restoration of all things" (Acts 3:21). In studying doctrine it is important to know that God wills for us to be "filled with the knowledge of His will in all wisdom and spiritual understanding" (Colossians 1:9). In writing to the Ephesians, Paul explained that he—though he was "less than the least of all the saints"—was given grace to preach about "the fellowship of the mystery, which from the beginning of the ages has been hidden in God" but now "might be made known by the church" (Ephesians 3:8–10).

123. What Is Systematic Theology?

The word *theology* is a combination of two Greek words—*theos,* meaning "God," and *logos,* meaning "word"—and, in this instance, refers to the written Word of God. Systematic theology is an organized study of Bible truths that is designed to produce a clearer understanding of Scripture. The logos introduces us to the rhema word, which is the revelation of the logos: The first reveals what God has said; the second reveals what God is saying. Theology should not be the study of different Bible topics but a study of one systematic flow of divine truth containing many parts.

124. What Is Original Sin?

Original sin refers to Adam's transgression and the polluting of all his posterity with his same fallen nature. As his decedents, we sin because the sin nature is in us before birth. No one is exempt from this tragic reality. Scripture says, "All have sinned and fall short of the glory of God" (Romans 3:23). We do not become sinners after we are born; we are born with the sin nature already in us. Paul explained this: "Through one man [Adam] sin entered the world, and death through sin, and thus death spread to all men, because all sinned. . . . Death reigned from Adam to Moses, even over those who had not sinned according to the likeness of the transgression of Adam" (Romans 5:12, 14).

Sin is the violation of God's law. But sin is more than an act: It is a controlling nature. We sin because we are sinners; not to become sinners. David wrote: "Behold, I was brought forth in iniquity, and in sin my mother conceived me" (Psalm 51:5). David not only acknowledged his sin nature, but rejoiced that God had already supplied the remedy: "Wash me, and I shall be whiter than snow" (verse 7).

Since sin is an inherent nature in us, we are powerless to free ourselves from it. For this reason, God, in His love and grace, imputed our sin to the account of Jesus Christ. The Father "made Him who knew no sin to be sin for us, that we might become the righteousness of God in Him" (2 Corinthians 5:21). When Jesus cried out on the cross, "It is finished!," He meant the transaction was complete. Our debt of sin was fully paid. How do we claim that freedom? The apostle John explained: "He came to His own, and His own did not receive Him. But as many as received Him, to them He gave the right to become children of God, to those who believe in His name" (John 1:11–12).

It is this sin nature in our spirits that is destroyed by regeneration. The physical body remains temporarily sinful until the final trumpet sounds and the dead are raised, now "incorruptible." When that occurs, the words first spoken through the prophets Isaiah and Hosea will have come to pass: "'Death is swallowed up in victory.' 'O Death, where is your sting? O Hades, where is your victory?' The sting of death is sin, and the strength of sin is the law. But thanks be to God, who gives us the victory through our Lord Jesus Christ" (1 Corinthians 15:54–55).

125. What Is the Incarnation?

When the angel Gabriel said to Mary "You will conceive in your womb and bring forth a Son, and shall call His name Jesus" (Luke 1:31), she did not realize that the greatest event of all creation was soon to be performed in her own body. Heaven and earth would lock together in her womb.

Previous to His transference into the womb of Mary, Jesus preexisted eternally with the Father and Spirit as fully God. The Spirit's work of the incarnation refers to Jesus' embodiment into a human body; part of that word, *carne*, means flesh. In this event, employing the "body You have prepared for Me" (Hebrews 10:5), God would remain fully God and also become fully human, and then submit Himself to sin's painful consequence. Through this act of Jesus' incarnation, God's plan to rescue humanity would be finalized. The defeat of sin and the restoration of mankind to God's original plan would become reality.

God is love; love cannot exist without an object. Through the Fall the objective of God's love was taken from Him. The perfect solution for restoration was the incarnation of Jesus Christ. Through Him, the atoning sacrifice would be made to God for mankind. This would be the greatest display of love ever demonstrated.

Scripture explains that the Father "made Him who knew no sin to be sin for us, that we might become the righteousness of God in Him" (2 Corinthians 5:21). The blood Jesus gave at the cross for the redemption of mankind was both human and divine; it alone had the power to wash away sin (see Romans 5:9). This blood was far greater than that which Moses sprinkled on Jewish houses in Egypt (see Exodus 12:21–22). Jesus' blood had power to wash away sin permanently.

126. How Is Jesus Fully God and Fully Man?

Was Jesus truly human? Though possessing Godhood, Jesus, "being found in appearance as a man . . . humbled Himself and became obedient to the point of death, even the death of the cross" (Philippians 2:8). Speaking of His own life ending in crucifixion, He said, "No one takes it from Me, but I lay it down of Myself. I have power to lay it down, and I have power to take it again" (John 10:18). As man, He had power to lay down His life but could not raise it again. As God, He had power to take it up again, but could not lay it down. As the God-Man, He had power to do both. In His manhood Jesus was hungry (see Matthew 4:2; 21:18), ate food (see Luke 24:42–43), experienced joy (see John 15:11) and sorrow (see Matthew 26:37), fell asleep (see Luke 8:23), sweated (see Luke 22:43–44), could be angered (see Mark 3:5) and bled (see John 19:34). He "was in all points tempted as we are, yet without sin" (Hebrews 4:15).

"The Word became flesh and dwelt among us, and we beheld His glory, the glory as of the only begotten of the Father, full of grace and truth" (John 1:14). Why did the Father deem this necessary? That through the blood atonement "we might become the righteousness of God in Him" (2 Corinthians 5:21).

127. What Is Meant by the Bodily Resurrection of Jesus?

There is no more basic belief in Christianity than that of the actual, physical resurrection of Jesus Christ from the dead. Two thousand years after that historic event in Jerusalem, His resurrection message is still vibrating mankind with its truth. A careful study of Scripture shows that Jesus did not exit the tomb when the angels appeared "like lightning" and the stone was rolled away. When that happened, He was already gone. His body had risen through the rock that encased Him; that very stone had been made by Him when Creation first began (see Colossians 1:17). Roman soldiers sent to guard the place were knocked unconscious to the ground, paralyzed with fear at the angels' appearance, and the Roman seal Pilate had ordered for the cave was smashed. Jesus was already resurrected—gone—free from all human control (see Matthew 28:1). The two Marys were staring into an empty tomb.

It was He, the eternal Word by whom "the worlds were framed," who had finished the act of redemption and restoration for mankind (see Hebrews 11:3). God's ultimate display of passion had been made (see John 3:16). With it came grace, love, eternal life for everyone who believes.

The resurrection was the first explosive wind—soon to be followed by Pentecost—that would send the message of resurrection life around the world. Death, hell and the grave were all defeated by the final blow of Jesus' resurrection. Evangelization of that love could no more be stopped than could the Roman seal confine Jesus to the tomb. How does the resurrection affect the Gospel message? The Church, which Paul explained was another revelation of "His Body" (1 Corinthians 12:27), would also experience resurrection power and carry the message of His love to the end of the earth (see Mark 16:15).

128. What Is Meant by God's Foreknowledge?

God not only knows everything that will ever be but knew it before time began. That is one of the qualities of sovereignty that makes Him God. While the truth of His foreknowledge permeates Scripture, the first appearance of that word regards the sacrifice of Jesus and is found in Peter's rebuke to the people of Israel: "Jesus of Nazareth, . . . being delivered by the determined purpose and foreknowledge of God, you have taken by lawless hands, have crucified, and put to death; whom God raised up, having loosed the pains of death, because it was not possible that He should be held by it" (Acts 2:22–24). This reference to God's foreknowledge relates specifically to Jesus.

Another reference to God's foreknowledge is this: "For whom He foreknew, He also predestined to be conformed to the image of His Son, that He might be the firstborn among many brethren. Moreover whom He predestined, these He also called" (Romans 8:29–30). And, "God has not cast away His people whom He foreknew" (Romans 11:2). The last New Testament reference to God's foreknowledge regards those "elect according to the foreknowledge of God the Father" (1 Peter 1:2). This reference is to the "pilgrims of the Dispersion" (verse 1), that is, believers within the Jewish diaspora.

129. What Is the Atonement?

The word *atonement* occurs many times in the Old Testament regarding the death of sacrificial animals being substituted in the place of a guilty person. The blood of the blameless becomes a replacement for the blood of the guilty. The word's etymology can be demonstrated by dividing it as "at-one-ment," i.e., estranged people become reconciled, restored, reunited, made "one" again—in this case brought back into relationship with God. Paul explained that God demonstrated His great love for us "in that while we were still sinners, Christ died for us." Because we are now "justified by His blood, we shall be saved from wrath through Him. . . . And not only that, but we also rejoice in God through our Lord Jesus Christ, through whom we have now received the reconciliation [the at-one-ment]" (Romans 5:8–9, 11). Atonement took place at the cross. Regeneration takes place in our hearts because of the atonement achieved by Christ at the crucifixion.

130. What Are the Five "Sola" Principles?

In the Protestant Reformation, five cardinal principles quickly emerged that identified theological distinctions between the Reformers and the sixteenth-century Catholic Church. These have continued as a safe guide for believers into modern times. The Reformers' Latin is retained below. Simply identified, they are these:

1. *Sola Scriptura* or "Scripture Alone": The Bible is the inspired Word of God, the only guide for matters of personal faith and Church practice. Creeds, confessions of faith, religious ordinances and traditions must be supported specifically by Scripture as the inspired Word of God and its final authority.

2. *Sola Christus* or "Christ Alone": Jesus is the only Mediator between God and man, the only price of mankind's redemption, and the final Judge and authority in the resurrection. His is the only name necessary by which humanity can be saved, and the only One to be worshiped as Savior.

3. *Sola Gratia* or "Grace Alone": The divine love, mercy and grace of God Almighty alone are to be acknowledged in mankind's redemption. The grace-reality specifically excludes works on the part of an individual in achieving salvation: Salvation comes by divine grace or "unmerited favor" only, not as something merited by the sinner. Salvation is an unearned gift from God, which was achieved by Jesus Christ.

4. *Sola Fide* or "Faith Alone": Divine faith, which has been miraculously breathed into us by the Holy Spirit, enabling us to receive grace, excludes all self-righteousness and personal achievement. This doctrine confirms that we are saved by grace through faith. And that faith is not of ourselves, but has been imputed to us by God alone. Personal good works are the result of a new nature imparted to us through salvation and the indwelling of the Holy Spirit. Being justified by faith alone, we are vindicated, absolved of all sin and declared "righteous" by the blood of Jesus Christ.

5. *Sola Deo Gloria* or "Glory to God Alone": Since salvation is accomplished solely through the grace, will and action of the Almighty, and not by the self-righteousness of any individual, all glory and praise goes to Him alone. The gift of the all-sufficient atonement of Jesus on the cross, with the Holy Spirit's provision of faith in that atonement, brings justification to the believer. It was He, God Almighty, who imparted His own Spirit into us that we might be rescued from sin and equipped for eternal life.

131. What Is the Grace of God?

There is no language on earth with a word that can do proper justice to the word *grace*. Behind the word stand the nature, love, power, wisdom and authority of God. It is an all-inclusive concept—trying and failing—to reveal His fullness. In speaking of the wisdom of God as it relates to our salvation, one historic hymn writer said, "Grace all the work shall crown, / Through everlasting days; / It lays in heaven the topmost stone, / And well deserves the praise." The display of grace reached its climax at the whipping post and the cross. The shout of Christ for the Father to "Forgive them!" was followed by "Why have You forsaken Me?" Emphasis is on two words: *them* and *Me*. "Why have You forsaken Me?" is the only prayer of Jesus recorded in the New Testament to which the Father did not respond. Heaven remained silent as the scapegoat died alone. There was mercy for rebels but none for Christ. The price of our redemption was paid by grace.

132. What Is Faith?

Faith is a spiritual force that reveals itself in a variety of ways. First, it is a tangible, spiritual energy imparted to us by the Holy Spirit. It comes into our dimension from the heavenly realm, passes through receptive believers here, then penetrates and effects change in the circumstance it touches. Jesus was the easy receptacle to receive and send out this power. He explained, "The words that I speak to you I do not speak on My own authority; but the Father who dwells in Me does the works" (John 14:10). Jesus was acknowledging that the words and power did not originate with Him but merely passed through.

Second, the New Testament offers some eighteen detailed accounts of Jesus healing someone. In twelve of those instances, He pointed to the person's faith as being a factor. Faith reveals itself both in the one ministering and the one receiving ministry. God acknowledges our faith but is not dependent on it. Emotion may accompany faith, but faith is not an emotion. We know this: "Without faith it is impossible to please Him" (Hebrews 11:6). Recognizing their lack, the disciples came to Jesus saying, "Increase our faith" (Luke 17:5). So should we also routinely seek His empowering. Jesus also said, "Everyone who asks receives" (Matthew 7:8). Hope is oftentimes mistaken as faith but it is not the same. Hope is an "anchor of the soul" (Hebrews 6:19), which holds us steadfast, secure, awaiting the arrival of faith.

Third, faith may come in the form of a gift that appears suddenly—but powerfully—in a believer to meet a particular need (see 1 Corinthians 12:9). This charismatic gift of faith is a precise empowering of the Holy Spirit that appears, accomplishes a specific purpose and disappears. It is temporary.

Fourth, saving faith is a specific gift of the Holy Spirit that enables us to respond to the Gospel's offer of salvation. It is through saving faith that we can believe in our hearts that Jesus is the Son of God—our only means of redemption—and be born again.

Fifth, faith is the soul's expression of quiet trust, assurance, confidence in God. Faith enables us to rest in Him.

Finally, we sometimes speak of "our faith" as a doctrinal identification with a certain Christian group.

133. What Is Saving Faith?

The unregenerate human does not possess faith, yet Paul makes it very clear that the experience of being saved is dependent on faith. How is this possible?

Scripture tells us that initial faith—saving faith—is God's gift to us: "For by grace you have been saved through faith, and that not of yourselves; it is the gift of God, not of works, lest anyone should boast" (Ephesians 2:8–9). This faith, which enables us to "believe to the saving of the soul," is called *prevenient grace* (see Hebrews 10:39). Such faith usually appears as an inner witness when we hear the Gospel, assuring us it is true. At this crucial point we have the choice of responding to the gift of faith and being saved, or quenching it and remaining in our lost condition.

If we choose to respond in faith, Paul tells us the results: "If you confess with your mouth the Lord Jesus and believe in your heart that God has raised Him from the dead, you will be saved. For with the heart one believes unto righteousness, and with the mouth confession is made unto salvation" (Romans 10:9–11).

134. What Is Justification by Faith?

Justification is God's act of removing the eternal guilt and penalty of our fallen nature and simultaneously declaring us righteous in Christ. This "divine exchange" took place initially at the whipping post when Jesus "who knew no sin" became "sin for us, that we might become the righteousness of God in Him" (2 Corinthians 5:21). Being unregenerate, we are "dead in trespasses and sin" and cannot rescue ourselves. God, therefore, calls us by the Gospel—the Good News—and through grace provides the faith whereby we are able to believe "to the saving of the soul" (Hebrews 11:39).

Jesus said, "If you do not believe that I am He, you will die in your sins" (John 8:24; see Hebrews 10:39). Our personal belief is mandatory. Through it, the Gospel offers us the full benefits of Christ's righteousness, atonement, redemption and resurrection. On the cross Christ assumed our sin and imparts to us His righteousness. Our state of grace is "not according to our works, but according to His own purpose and grace which was given us in Christ Jesus before time began" (2 Timothy 1:9).

Paul further explains, "Having been justified by faith, we have peace with God through our Lord Jesus Christ, through whom also we have access by faith into this grace in which we stand" (Romans 5:1–2).

God's provision of faith is a grace-gift. You were awakened by the Holy Spirit and enabled to believe the Gospel. In that awesome moment you were made just as innocent as if you had never sinned. You were "justified by faith"!

135. What Is Salvation by Grace?

Salvation is God's free gift; it is not earned by our good deeds: "For by grace you have been saved through faith, and that not of yourselves; it is the gift of God, not of works, lest anyone should boast" (Ephesians 2:9; see Romans 1:16–17). The Gospel "is the power of God to salvation for everyone who believes, for the Jew first and also for the Greek. For in it the righteousness of God is revealed from faith to faith; as it is written, 'The just shall live by faith.'"

When the Philippian jailor asked Paul and Silas, "What must I do to be saved?," the immediate reply was, "Believe on the Lord Jesus Christ, and you will be saved, you and your household" (Acts 16:31). Believing was the release of faith that God provided: "The grace of God that brings salvation has appeared to all men" (Titus 2:11). Salvation comes in our believing that Jesus Christ is the sufficient "propitiation for our sins, and not for ours only but also for the whole world" (1 John 2:2).

Note: We have access by faith into this grace. Then, once we are saved, faith continues to expand exponentially in us. As a result of the baptism with the Holy Spirit, faith may also assume the nature of a spiritual gift, which can impact others powerfully (see 1 Corinthians 12:9).

136. What Is the Difference between Faith and Hope?

Faith is holy expectation. Where there is no expectation there is no faith. When we face moments in which faith has seemingly fled, we must remember that even the apostles said to Jesus, "Lord, increase our faith."

Hope, on the other hand, is an "anchor of the soul, both sure and steadfast," which keeps us secure, awaiting the arrival of faith (Hebrews 6:19). At whatever point hope begins to expect, it has ceased being hope and has become faith.

137. What Does It Mean to Be Born Again?

Our first birth in flesh prepares us for life on the earth; the second birth equips us to live with God in glory. We are saved from sin, rescued from hell, made ready for heaven. This is achieved by our believing in our hearts that Jesus is the Christ and Son of God (see John 3:16; Romans 10:8–10).

We have a perfect example of this in Acts 16:22–34. Paul and Silas had been jailed and, chained in the blackness of the inner cell, were praying and singing hymns through the long dark hours. Suddenly at about midnight, an earthquake shook the very foundations of the prison—"and immediately all the doors were opened and everyone's chains were loosed." The jailer, who had been awakened by the com-motion, saw the open prison doors and assumed that his prisoners had fled. Knowing that he would be executed for allowing these high-profile prisoners to escape, he drew his sword and was about to kill himself when Paul called out to him not to harm himself, for they had not left.

The jailer was overcome at this point, recognizing that something amazing had happened. "He called for a light, ran in, and fell down trembling before Paul and Silas. And he brought them out and said, 'Sirs, what must I do to be saved?' So they said 'Believe on the Lord Jesus Christ, and you will be saved, you and your household.'" Im-mediately after washing their wounds, still in the early morning hours, the jailer and his family were baptized. The Bible says that "he was filled with joy because he had come to believe in God—he and his whole family."

Jesus talked about this experience of being born again with Nicode-mus, a prominent Pharisee. "Most assuredly," Jesus said, "I say to you, unless one is born again, he cannot see the kingdom of God."

Nicodemus took Jesus' words in the earthly sense and responded with a logical question: "How can a man be born when he is old? Can he enter a second time into his mother's womb and be born?" (John 3:3–4).

Jesus went on to talk about the new birth—a miraculous work of the Holy Spirit. When this occurs, our lifestyle, habits, desires, personal choices and inner nature change. We become "new creatures." Anyone who is born again "is a new creation; old things have passed away; be-hold, all things have become new" (2 Corinthians 5:17; see Galatians 3:27). In fact, if there is no change it is questionable that the new birth has genuinely taken place. When we are born again, God reconciles us "to Himself through Jesus Christ" (2 Corinthians 5:18) and makes us overcomers: "For whatever is born of God overcomes the world. And this is the victory that has overcome the world—our faith. Who is he who overcomes the world, but he who believes that Jesus is the Son of God?" (1 John 5:4–5). This salvation experience is achieved through the specific work of the Holy Spirit.

138. What Is the Purpose of Water Baptism?

Scripture tells us, "In those days John the Baptist came preaching in the wilderness of Judea, and saying, 'Repent, for the kingdom of heaven is at hand!' . . . Then Jerusalem, all Judea, and all the region around the Jordan went out to him and were baptized by him in the Jordan, confessing their sins" (Matthew 3:1–2, 5–6).

Peter explained the purpose of water baptism: "There is also an antitype [example] which now saves us—baptism (not the removal of the filth of the flesh, but the answer of a good conscience toward God), through the resurrection of Jesus Christ" (1 Peter 3:21–22). By submitting to baptism we are saying to God, "Wash me. Cleanse my conscious. I commit myself in sincere discipleship to You." Baptism does not regenerate us or remove our original Adamic sin. According to Peter, it cleanses our consciences from the effects of sin.

Paul had numerous, willful sins committed against Christians from which he needed cleansing. Baptism provided that answer of a "good conscience." In recounting his conversion and baptism, he wrote how Ananias, whom Paul called "a devout man according to the law," came to him after the Damascus Road experience. Ananias spoke to him (known as Saul at this time), saying, "Brother Saul, receive your sight." Ananias then told Paul that God had chosen him not only to see and hear the risen Christ, but to be His witness. Ananias then said, "And now why are you waiting? Arise and be baptized, and wash away your sins, calling on the name of the Lord" (Acts 22:12–16).

In baptism we are "buried with Christ," though it is water—not soil—through which we portray ourselves as dead, entombed and awaiting resurrection. Though there are various forms of baptism practiced today, it is baptism by immersion through which we are given a striking picture of the "earth" closing over the candidate. No one goes into the grave alone; we are buried with Christ. Paul explained it this way: "We were buried with Him through baptism into death. . . . If we have been united together in the likeness of His death, certainly we also shall be in the likeness of His resurrection" (Romans 6:4–5). All of this is portrayed in the rite of baptism. Everyone who is baptized "in the name of the Father and of the Son and of the Holy Spirit" (Matthew 28:19) is now able to "walk in newness of life."

139. What Is Regeneration?

Several words are used interchangeably to identify the spiritual experience of being born again. *Regeneration* is one of these. *Regeneration* is the term used more frequently in theological discussions than in public preaching. To be regenerated is the same as being born again, reborn, saved, born from above, etc. It means to bring back to spiritual life what was dead. In this sense, regeneration is the end result of the Gospel's call to the lost "to open their eyes, in order to turn them from darkness to light, and from the power of Satan to God, that they may receive forgiveness of sins and an inheritance among those who are sanctified by faith in [Jesus]" (Acts 26:18).

140. What Is Hardness of Heart?

One of the great dangers Christians face is allowing their hearts to become hardened. Heart-hardness can arise from a variety of sources with severe and long-lasting effects. This happened to the first disciples and kept them at one point from recognizing that Jesus was with them in the midst of a crisis. Jesus had just fed the five thousand and sent the disciples ahead of Him by boat across the Sea of Galilee. The night became stormy and their boat was caught in it. They were in a panic when Jesus appeared to them walking on the water. Thinking He was a ghost they screamed in terror. He calmed their fears, climbed into the boat, and the winds ceased. Scripture says that they had "not understood about the loaves, because their heart was hardened" (Mark 6:52). A short time later, as the disciples once again pondered their food supply, Jesus asked them if their hearts were still hardened (Mark 8:17).

Many today do not realize that hardness of heart is blinding them to truth, to the joys of life and to God's intended purpose for them. Why do people harden their hearts?

1. They feel disappointment in themselves.
2. They endure abuse from others.
3. They have unresolved conflicts, present and past.
4. They misunderstand circumstances.
5. They seek a form of "protection" from being touched by hurts.
6. They desire power to control situations and other people—a form of witchcraft.

What does hardness of heart do to a person?

1. One's conscience becomes dull or even closed off to the voice of the Holy Spirit, as if "seared with a hot iron" (1 Timothy 4:2).
2. It produces mental stress, anxiety, emotional breakdown.
3. It obscures clear thinking and encourages wrong decisions.
4. It causes physical illness.
5. It distorts and obscures reality.
6. It attacks and seeks to destroy all relationships.
7. It destroys humility, sensitivity and creativity.
8. It promotes ego and pride.
9. It blinds a person to truth and opens the way to greater error.
10. It cultivates harshness and religious legalism.

141. What Is Apostasy?

The Bible uses some of its most noxious language and illustrations to describe the believer who renounces Christ and returns to his former unsaved lifestyle. Peter compared him to a dog devouring its own vomit and the sow that was washed returning to wallowing in the mire.

Our English word *apostasy* comes from the Greek *apostasia*, which means "to defect, rebel against, deny, fall away." We use it regarding a believer who abandons Christ. People who have apostatized have knowingly forsaken their love for God and rejected Him from their lives. In effect, apostasy is the reversal of conversion. The person having been a believer renounces his faith in Christ and joins the ranks of the unsaved. Is he still born again? Calvinists say yes—if he were ever truly saved. Arminians say no.

In instances other than apostasy, people become discouraged, feel they cannot achieve the Christian lifestyle and "backslide." This is not apostasy. The apostate has gone beyond the point of return; not so with the backslider who can repent and turn back to God. We have a beautiful example of this in Jesus' story of the Prodigal Son who repented and came back to his father's house (see Luke 15:18). Tragically, Judas Iscariot was an apostate. Finding no relief in returning the betrayal money to the priests, he hanged himself (see Matthew 27:5). Esau, brother of Jacob, is another such failure. Though seeking restoration with tears he was rejected (see Hebrews 12:17).

The same Hebrew writer warned that if anyone sins willfully after he has received the knowledge of the truth, he no longer can claim Jesus' sacrifice for his redemption. Instead he faces God's judgment and fiery wrath. As if that were not frightening enough, the writer reminds us that everyone who rejected Moses' Law died without mercy. Of how much worse punishment will he be thought worthy, he asks, who has trampled the Son of God underfoot, counted the blood of the covenant by which he was sanctified a common thing, and insulted the Spirit of grace? To such a one God says, "'Vengeance is Mine, I will repay. . . .

The LORD will judge His people.' It is a fearful thing to fall into the hands of the living God" (Hebrews 10:30–31). An old hymn-writer described it this way: "The weary soul who tries and faints / And walks the ways of God no more / Is but esteemed almost a saint / And makes his own destruction sure!"

To the backslider, Jesus still stands with open arms saying, "Come to Me . . . and I will give you rest" (Matthew 11:28).

142. What Is Adoption into God's Family?

This beautiful doctrine explains that the unrighteous person, who is unrelated to God and has no claim to sharing in His family, is "adopted" and made a legal heir as if he or she had been family-born (see Galatians 4:4–7). Adoption is a legal transaction. An adopted child is afforded the same rights and privileges as children born into the family. The apostle John explained that Jesus "came to His own, and His own did not receive Him. But as many as received Him, to them He gave the right to become the children of God, to those who believe in His name" (John 1:11–12). He has "made us accepted in the Beloved" (Ephesians 1:6).

143. What Is Sanctification?

The biblical concept of sanctification contains numerous benefits that are frequently unrecognized by the believer. The word means not only to be "set apart" but also to be "set into a state of proper functioning."

The condition of "proper functioning" can benefit every area of the Christian's life.

Paul illustrated this principle when he wrote Timothy that he would "set in order" things that were lacking (1 Corinthians 11:34). While he did not use the Greek word *hagiasmos*, which is translated "holiness" or "sanctification," he illustrated its principle by "setting in order" the ministries and people who were not functioning in the fullness of God's purpose. Sanctification cleanses the mind, impacting the total person spiritually, physically and emotionally. Sanctification unifies one's mental capacity, organizing it for greater productivity and maximum achievement. This is accomplished by separating the person from negative influences that distract and handicap. Mismanagement is minimized and the person is moved into a state of proper functioning.

Sanctification and renewing of the mind are companion forces and create a state of productivity and achievement that can be gained no other way. In that condition the former carnal attractions lose their grip. In this sense, sanctification is a condition of such fruitfulness and fulfillment that "old things pass away."

As humans, we cannot make ourselves holy. We can yield to God who can sanctify and in the process enable us to consecrate ourselves to Him. Sanctification does not make us sinless. Our corruptible has not yet "put on incorruption" nor has our mortal "put on immortality" (1 Corinthians 15:53–54). Perfection will not be achieved until the resurrection. The demonstration of sanctification in us is past, present and future.

According to Reformed theology, we were sanctified or set apart when we were chosen in Christ before the foundation of the world (see Ephesians 1:4–5). Arminian theology places more emphasis on the believer's current state (see Ephesians 4:22–26). Both are essential Bible truths. Calvin and Wesley each had a concept of sanctification that complimented the other. In every aspect, sanctification is of great benefit to the believer and we should pursue it.

144. What Is the Apostles' Creed?

The Apostles' Creed is an ancient statement of Christian faith that was finalized in its present form by the year AD 700. It is a summary of basic New Testament doctrine. Church scholars believe it was written to counteract the advance of Gnosticism and other heresies that were invading the early Church. It is not the work of the original Apostles as early Christians supposed, though its truths were first preached by the Apostles. Like the Nicene Creed, the Apostles' Creed, with slight wording changes, still serves as a statement of faith and is recited in every Sunday service in many churches. Note: The words *holy catholic Church* refer not to the Roman Catholic Church but to the Church universal.

> I believe in God, the Father almighty, creator of heaven and earth. I believe in Jesus Christ, his only Son, our Lord, who was conceived by the Holy Spirit, born of the Virgin Mary, suffered under Pontius Pilate, was crucified, died, and was buried; on the third day he rose again; he ascended into heaven, he is seated at the right hand of the Father, and he will come to judge the living and the dead. I believe in the Holy Spirit, the holy catholic Church, the communion of saints, the forgiveness of sins, the resurrection of the body, and the life everlasting. Amen.

145. What Is the Nicene Creed?

In AD 325, the First Council of Nicaea (present-day Iznik, Turkey) issued a statement of doctrinal belief that became the test of orthodoxy for Christians into modern times. Roman emperor Constantine convened the Council to distinguish orthodox positions for the Church on beliefs such as the Trinity and the full humanity and deity of Jesus Christ, largely to counter Arianism. The Nicene Creed has experienced several word changes. This version below is the wording offered in the

1979 *Book of Common Prayer*. Note: The words *holy catholic and apostolic Church* are not a reference to Roman Catholicism, which at that time had not been so identified. The word *catholic* in its original sense means "universal"—i.e., the "Body of Christ."

> We believe in one God, the Father, the Almighty, maker of heaven and earth, of all that is, seen and unseen. We believe in one Lord, Jesus Christ, the only Son of God, eternally begotten of the Father, God from God, Light from Light, true God from true God, begotten, not made, of one Being with the Father. Through him all things were made. For us and for our salvation he came down from heaven: by the power of the Holy Spirit he became incarnate from the Virgin Mary, and was made man. For our sake he was crucified under Pontius Pilate; he suffered death and was buried. On the third day he rose again in accordance with the Scriptures; he ascended into heaven and is seated at the right hand of the Father. He will come again in glory to judge the living and the dead, and his kingdom will have no end. We believe in the Holy Spirit, the Lord, the giver of life, who proceeds from the Father and the Son. With the Father and the Son he is worshiped and glorified. He has spoken through the Prophets. We believe in one holy catholic and apostolic Church. We acknowledge one baptism for the forgiveness of sins. We look for the resurrection of the dead, and the life of the world to come. Amen.

146. What Is the Westminster Confession of Faith?

In 1643, the English Parliament authorized the drafting of the Westminster Confession of Faith as a theological guide for the Church of England. Parliament then called upon "learned, godly, and judicious Divines" to meet at Westminster Abbey and provide a guide "for worship, doctrine, government, and discipline, for the Church of England." Their meetings, over a period of five years, produced the Confession of Faith as well as a Larger and Shorter Catechism. The Confession, which was strongly Reformed/Calvinistic theologically, was accepted by the Anglican Church and adopted by the Church of Scotland. It has remained the standard in most Presbyterian churches worldwide. In minor ways it was revised and adopted by Congregationalists in 1658 as the Savoy Confession and in 1689 by English Baptists who renamed their version the London Confession of Faith.

For more than three centuries, churches around the world have adopted the Westminster Confession and the Catechisms as their standards of doctrine. Of all modern Confessions, it has been the most influential worldwide. As is true in other Calvinistic documents, it is relatively silent on the subjects of the Kingdom of God and the Holy Spirit's baptism, gifting and power. In 1742, Baptists in America republished the London Confession of Faith, naming it the Philadelphia Confession, and added two new topics: the "laying on of hands" on every newly baptized believer and the singing of psalms in worship. In a short time, unfortunately, both practices were abandoned.

147. What Is the Judgment Seat of Christ?

Paul wrote that "we must all appear before the judgment seat of Christ, that each one may receive the things done in the body, according to what he has done, whether good or bad" (2 Corinthians 5:10). It is important to remember that our salvation in heaven is a gift from God, an inheritance purchased by Christ on the cross, and is not a reward for our good works (see Titus 3:5).

Scripture is emphatic about this point: Heaven is not a reward but an inheritance (see Matthew 5:12; 16:27; Luke 6:23). That being so, the Judgment Seat of Christ, which dispenses rewards, will not determine hell or heaven but the extent of gifts each believer receives in heaven. Jesus said that He would come in the glory of His Father and reward everyone according to his works" (Matthew 16:27). What those rewards will be, we do not know. But we do know that whatever good anyone does, he or she will receive the same from the Lord (see Ephesians 6:8). Jesus promised that if we give, it will be given to us in return, a full measure, pressed down, shaken together and running over (see Luke 6:38). Heaven is ours only because of the loving favor and grace of the Almighty Father. It is not by our works. Heaven comes wholly from His loving favor that was bequeathed to us before time began (see Ephesians 1:4). With that also come wonderful rewards.

148. What Is the Great White Throne Judgment?

Paul wrote about the Judgment Seat of Christ (see Romans 14:10; 2 Corinthians 5:10), and John wrote about the Great White Throne Judgment (see Revelation 20:11–15). Peter referred to the Great White Throne Judgment as the "Day of the Lord" and described it in fearsome terms (see 2 Peter 3:10). Please read these portions of Scripture carefully; the events are not the same, and great care must be given not to confuse the two.

Basically, the distinction between them is this: The Judgment Seat of Christ is when the redeemed will be judged according to their works and rewarded proportionately in heaven. Jesus referred to this when He said He would come in the glory of His Father with His angels and reward all redeemed individuals according to their works (see Matthew 16:27). The names of these saved ones are all found written in the Lamb's Book of Life (see Revelation 20:12).

The Great White Throne Judgment is the event when the unsaved are judged and consigned to hell. The Bible does not tell us when these two judgments will take place; it is possible that they will be simultaneous or one instantly following the other. On that point Scripture is silent. What is important is the fact that both the saved and unsaved will be told why they are in their specific places. The writer to the Hebrews speaks of those who do not "draw back to perdition, but . . . believe to the saving of the soul" (Hebrews 10:39). The saved are not redeemed because of their good works but because they believed in Jesus and trusted Him as Savior. The word *perdition* refers to hell. Mankind has the choice of drawing back or believing in Christ and becoming born again.

Is it necessary for one to believe in Jesus to be saved? Yes. Jesus said, "If you do not believe that I am He [the Messiah], you will die in your sins" (John 8:24; see Romans 1:16). Scripture also acknowledges that there are disciples in secret who nonetheless are genuine believers (see John 19:38). There will be no self-defense at the Great White Throne Judgment. The argument that "I was not told" will be unspoken. Paul explained that the knowledge of God has been manifested to humanity even since the beginning of time. That includes His invisible attributes, His eternal power and Godhead (see Romans 1:19–21). With the unavoidable testimony of creation before them, they could have called on the Lord and His grace would have responded.

149. What Is the Second Death?

Sin, death, disease for mankind and a polluted universe were not the original plan of God. Observing His own creation, He pronounced everything He had made "very good." The Hebrew word for good (*towb*) appears fourteen times in the first three chapters of Genesis. In showing Adam the Tree of Knowledge of Good and Evil (the tree also was "good"), God warned him not to touch or eat from it. The result would be death. Adam had the ability to choose between right and wrong. He disobeyed God's warning, and brought the consequence upon himself and his posterity.

With his wife, Adam disobeyed, and death came with two effects: *Spiritually*, he died on the spot and lost all his rights for relationship with God. Restoring himself to God was totally impossible. *Physically*, he was banished from Eden and the process of death began its long-term effect in his body. From that moment on, Adam began aging. His death, however, was not final. The body perishes but the inner person of the spirit lives on eternally.

The crisis had not originated with Adam nor with his wife, but with Satan, the prince of darkness. As for Satan, God already had a plan that would not be fully disclosed until John wrote "the book of the Revelation." John described the end time when "Death and Hades" will open and surrender the ones buried in them. Then Satan, demons, fallen angels and all the unsaved of mankind will be brought forth, all to be judged according to their works, and all to be cast into the lake of fire (see Revelation 20:13–15). This is the Great White Throne Judgment and the "second death" that follows it. Other references are Hebrews 9:27–28; Revelation 2:11; 20:6, 14.

150. What Is Hell?

The New Testament uses four different words from which *hell* is translated. The first three are: *sheol* (Hebrew), *hades* and *tartarus* (Greek)— all three of which mean "the unseen world" or simply "the grave." The fourth word from which *hell* is translated is the Hebrew word *gehenna*, which is the only one associated with burning. Jesus used this word ten times in the New Testament. Originally, Gehenna referred to a narrow valley on the south side of Jerusalem that, in early years, was used for the worship of Molech. This was a monstrous demon that demanded the burning sacrifice of children and infants. It was a horrific site of torment and suffering. Parents who participated were required to stand emotionless and unmoving as the screaming babies were burned alive in the arms of the idol. In an act of repentance, later Jews converted the site into a trash dump where the carcasses of dead animals, garbage and city waste were burned. Of this place, Jesus said, "Their worm does not die and the fire is not quenched" (Mark 9:44).

The book of Acts, speaking of the descent of Christ after death, says, "His soul was not left in hades, nor did His flesh see corruption" (Acts

2:31). The story of the rich man and Lazarus describes hades as a place of torment (see Luke 16:19–31). Here Jesus tells of a wicked person suffering fiery torment in hades; all the while, Lazarus is comforted in the bosom of Abraham (Paradise). The book of Revelation (20:14) reveals that in the end, hades itself is cast into the "lake of fire." This is probably a reference to hades as the "grave." Instead of using the word *hell*, Paul writes of God's "wrath" and "everlasting destruction" (Romans 2:7–9; 2 Thessalonians 1:9). He describes "fiery indignation" (Hebrews 10:27) and "perdition" (2 Peter 3:7). Jude writes of "blackness of darkness" (Jude 13). The book of Revelation contains the image of a "lake of fire and brimstone" where the devil, the beast and false prophet will be "tormented day and night forever and ever" (Revelation 20:10) along with those who worship the beast or receive "the mark of his name" (Revelation 14:11).

There can be no doubt for Christians that hell is real and a place to be avoided. A theological counter-revolt exists among many Christians today regarding the reality of hell; human sympathy rejects the idea of eternal suffering for anyone. We are not at liberty on this point—as on any other—to make doctrinal changes in Scripture. Jesus believed in the pains of hell; so do we.

151. What Is Heaven?

To the believer, heaven is not only the abiding place of God but the ultimate destination of all saved people. It is the site of eternal rest where love, joy, peace and happiness reign supreme. Heaven offers reunion with departed loved ones, total freedom from pain, and liberty such as was never known on earth. The devil, demons, darkness will be banished, never to be a concern again. In heaven all crises, trials, adversities are banished and reconciled. God will "wipe away all tears from our eyes" (see Revelation 7:17; 21:4). There, the saved not only "rule and reign" with Him but share in the never-ending joy of ultimate freedom. The saved are carried beyond the earthly state lost by Adam in Eden and given the freedom of the universe. Scripture uses the word *heaven* in three different dimensions:

The first heaven: earth's atmosphere. "The LORD will open to you His good treasure, the heavens, to give the rain to your land in its season, and to bless all the work of your hand" (Deuteronomy 28:12). "Nevertheless He did not leave Himself without witness, in that He did good, gave us rain from heaven and fruitful seasons, filling our hearts with food and gladness" (Acts 14:17).

The second heaven: outer space. "The stars of heaven and their constellations will not show their light" (Isaiah 13:10).

The third heaven: God's dwelling place. "Indeed heaven and the highest heavens belong to the LORD your God, also the earth with all that is in it" (Deuteronomy 10:14). "Will God indeed dwell on the earth? Behold, heaven and the heaven of heavens cannot contain You" (1 Kings 8:27). "Let your light so shine before men, that they may see your good works and glorify your Father in heaven" (Matthew 5:16). "May You hear the supplication of Your servant and of Your people Israel, when they pray. . . . Hear in heaven Your dwelling place" (1 Kings 8:30).

PART 11

What Are Some Doctrinal Variations?

152. What Is Pentecostal Theology?

Pentecostals stand on Scripture as the inspired Word of God and the Christian rule of faith and practice. Pentecostal churches are not cessationist. In a protective way they defend the validity of 1 Corinthians 12–14 and other passages that endorse miraculous works of the Holy Spirit. That being so, they place great value upon Christian evangelism and are leaders in the numbers of personal conversions and churches growing worldwide.

An abbreviated statement of Pentecostal belief is this: The Scriptures are inspired. They believe in the one true God: Father, Son, Holy Spirit. They believe in the deity of the Lord Jesus Christ; the fall of mankind; salvation through the Lord Jesus Christ; the ordinances of the Church (including baptism in water and Holy Communion); baptism with the Holy Spirit with the gift of tongues being the initial evidence; the believer's pursuit of a sanctified life; divine healing; the Millennial reign of Christ; the final Judgment; the new heavens and the new earth; heaven for the saved and hell for the lost.

The Assemblies of God, which is the largest of all Pentecostal bodies, was founded in 1914 in Hot Springs, Arkansas, with three hundred people in attendance. One century later, there are 12,849 Assemblies of God churches in the U.S. with more than three million members and supporters. Worldwide, more than 67 million believers crowd into Assemblies of God congregations, making it the world's largest Pentecostal denomination. This growth is typical of first-century Christianity. The major danger Pentecostal churches face is their own success. Some of their larger churches are avoiding historic Pentecostal style in preference for more acceptable mainline appearance.

153. What Is Charismatic Theology?

The charismatic renewal made its initial appearance in an Episcopal Church on April 3, 1960, but was quickly joined by Spirit-filled believers from a wide spectrum of other mainline denominations. Though not Pentecostal in background, they quickly found cohesiveness with Pentecostals in Scripture's truth—particularly, the Holy Spirit's work in the modern Church. In itself, the unity of charismatics is remarkable. Today the great bulk of charismatic congregations hold, unyielding, to the historic message of the Bible—i.e., Scripture is inspired; God is One but Trinitarian in revelation of Himself as Father, Son and Holy Spirit; the New Testament is a covenant, confirmed with the sprinkling of blood, of which no part can be deleted and all is to be believed (see Hebrews 12:24).

Probably, the greatest point of divergence between Pentecostal and charismatic churches regards demons. The issue exists because of a difference in terminology. Charismatics believe Christians can be oppressed by demons and need deliverance. For that reason, an important part of charismatic ministry is casting demons out of anyone who is oppressed—including Christians. Pentecostals say no, demons cannot "cross the bloodline" into born-again people. Charismatics explain that our bodies have not yet been through the resurrection—our "corruptible" has not yet "put on incorruption," nor has our "mortal . . . put on immortality" (1 Corinthians 15:53). The body is still defiled and a demon can go anywhere sin and disease can go. The question is not one of "possession" but "oppression." Even so, the difference continues. This, however, has not become a divisive issue between the two groups and in most cases a strong bond of fellowship exists between them.

154. What Is Spirit-Empowered Theology?

It is possible to learn facts about God, Jesus' resurrection, the Holy Spirit's fiery anointing at Pentecost and other Bible accounts—and none of it qualify as authentic theology. In reality, genuine *theos*—"God"— and *logos*—"Word"—only becomes *theology* when the Holy Spirit opens our spiritual eyes and allows us to see beyond the page. It is in this other spiritual dimension where the Word actually resides (see 2 Corinthians 3:6). We may hold a Bible in our lap with its wonderful stories spread on every page, delight in its wisdom, rejoice in its message, but never actually see into the true Bible itself. The study of Scripture cannot be compared to the study of math, science or medicine, wonderful as they are. In authentic theology we expose ourselves to the light of God and in return He reveals Himself to us.

We might liken the distinction to admiring a painting of a seascape as opposed to visiting the ocean where the painting was made. In the first, beautiful as it is, we are looking at a flat surface—the Bible page; in the other, we can see to the distant horizon and miles into space. The wind of the Spirit whips us; the fragrance of empowered air energizes us.

For that reason, spiritually empowered theology is not something we can learn in seminary. The primary work of Spirit-empowered theology is that it releases us from the grip of religious gravity and carries us into the vastness of truths we never knew existed. Are such Spirit encounters possible? Yes. Pity the congregation whose pastor never experiences them; instead, that pastor comes to the pulpit from an office lined with books and not from a God-encounter in that place of study. The ministry of the Gospel can be presented only by those who have visited the mountaintops of divine revelation and descend glowing in heaven's glory.

155. What Is the Word of Faith Doctrine?

The Word of Faith doctrine emphasizes the power of faith and positive confession to rid the Christian of undesirable circumstances, such as sickness, poverty or failure. In addition, it warns that the potential for good in one's life can be destroyed by negative thinking and speaking. By claiming the promises of Scripture, a believer can "speak to the mountain" and that mountain must bow to the authority of Jesus (Mark 11:22–23). This concept is often derided as the "name it and claim it" principle. Basic concepts promoted by the Word of Faith movement are these: (1) God speaks His biblical Word to us; (2) We receive and believe His Word; (3) In response, we speak and act on His Word; (4) God confirms His Word with signs following; (5) The promise of Scripture becomes reality to us.

A chief criticism rose when some Word of Faith teachers began emphasizing success as a sign of spiritual achievement and used wealthy displays as proof of their right interpretation of Scripture. In addition, their assurances that God wants every believer to experience perfect health and financial prosperity led to destructive charges of sin or lack of faith in believers who could not attain this perfection. The origin of the movement is debated. Some claim it began with E. W. Kenyon (1867–1948), a Methodist pastor who embraced the Pentecostal Movement; others point to Kenneth Hagin (1917–2003), a disciple of Kenyon. Both men greatly emphasized the role of faith.

156. What Is the Prosperity Gospel?

God's provision for our prosperity and abundant living is taught throughout Scripture. The Old Testament prophet Malachi exhorted the people to bring all their tithes to God's storehouse that they might experience

205

the abundance of His blessing (see Malachi 3:10). According to Scripture, it is God's will that we "prosper in all things and be in health" in the same measure that our souls prosper (3 John 1:2). To achieve this, He has entrusted us with the capacity and responsibility to care for our own physical health and well-being in the same manner that we care for our souls. The two are deeply related.

It is in awareness of this principle that Paul taught the believers at Philippi that God would supply all their needs "according to His riches in glory by Christ Jesus" (Philippians 4:19). The apostle could be assured of this, because he had earlier acknowledged that they were "partakers" of grace (Philippians 1:7). It is grace that conforms us to Christ in every way possible—spirit, soul, body. While Jesus promised a "good measure" to those who give generously, He expected their motives to be true charity and not self-aggrandizement. Though we are told to expect a generous return on our giving, we are also cautioned not to flatter ourselves or be vain before others (see Romans 12:3).

It was during the healing revivals of the 1950s that a different view of prosperity theology appeared in the United States. The basic concept is that sickness, poverty, failure, etc. are curses that can be broken only by faith.

Today, two prosperity gospels are being preached: One is authentic, based on the Bible, blessing believers and honoring God. The other emphasizes the importance of classic dress, impressive automobiles and external appearances—and is quick to denounce someone who is not equally "prosperous" as having inadequate faith. This position ignores the wisdom of Solomon who said, "The race is not to the swift, nor the battle to the strong, nor bread to the wise, nor riches to men of understanding, nor favor to men of skill; but time and chance happen to them all" (Ecclesiastes 9:11).

Are we faith-believers? Absolutely! "Without faith it is impossible to please Him" (Hebrews 11:6). At the same time we observe Scripture's teaching to care for the health of our souls, even as we partake of God's grace, knowing that this is also a fair determiner of our needs being met.

157. What Is Calvinism or Reformed Theology?

The doctrinal system known as Reformed theology or Calvinism emphasizes God's absolute sovereignty regarding salvation. Five points are primary: (1) humankind's total depravity in sin; (2) God's unconditional election, or personal choice, of all who will be saved; (3) God's limiting redemption to the chosen (elect) only; (4) the elect's inability to resist God's call to salvation; and (5) the perfect keeping of all the elect without the loss of any. An acrostic, using the word *TULIP*, was developed to illustrate these five doctrines. Simply stated, they are identified as: *T*otal depravity, *U*nconditional election, *L*imited atonement, *I*rresistible call and *P*erseverance.

While the system is the result of other minds, John Calvin (1509–1564) was its primary contributor and the one whose name it bears. Legitimate criticism has come against the system because of what appears as harsh legalism: If one is elect, he will be forcibly regenerated and saved; if one is not elect, he cannot be saved—regardless. Calvin was contemporary with Martin Luther, a strong voice in the Reformation, and later established his headquarters at Geneva, Switzerland, where he became a prodigious writer. Calvinism produced many great minds over the centuries, but has shown less motivation for missions and evangelism.

158. What Is Arminian Theology?

Jacobus Arminius (1560–1609) was a minister in the Dutch Reformed Church in Amsterdam, an acclaimed theologian and professor of theology at Leiden University. Though he accepted certain biblical tenets of Calvinism, he focused more on God's love than on His power. Arminius maintained that all could be saved and embraced in Christ's redemption. He taught that human free will exists without violating the sovereignty or power of God. His opinion was widely received and soon became a serious competitor to the Calvinistic system that was the official doctrinal position of Holland. Today his modification is endorsed by an overwhelming majority of churches worldwide. That is, they embrace the concepts that Jesus offers Himself freely to all, and that all are able to accept Him and be saved.

Arminian theology basically holds to the following tenets. Regarding election: God elected those who He knew would of their own free will believe in Christ and accept Him. Regarding atonement: In His atonement, Christ provided redemption for all mankind, making everyone savable. Regarding depravity: No one can save himself; the Holy Spirit must effect the new birth. Regarding prevenient grace: The Holy Spirit's preparatory work enables the believer to savingly respond to the Gospel. Regarding perseverance: Believers are enabled to live a victorious life, but are capable of falling from grace and being lost again.

159. What Is Free Will?

The doctrine of free will and the apostle Paul's writings on the sovereignty of God, election and predestination are usually seen as opponents to each other. This is not so. A divine harmony exists in all Scripture. Our challenge is to find it.

God has endowed us with a free will so that we can honor Him with our choices. Free will is the freedom of self-determination and action independent of external causes. A robot cannot honor its creator by its predetermined behavior. It is on this point that Calvinism and Arminianism come to an immediate disagreement.

Calvinism says, "A person who is spiritually dead in sin cannot make the choice to accept Jesus Christ and be born again. That person does not have a free will, so must be effectively 'called' and regenerated from above."

To this Arminianism replies, "But you also believe that Christ died for the elect only, and the non-elect are doomed to hell before they are born."

To that, the Calvinist falls silent. The accusation is valid.

Paul, who was the greatest New Testament writer on theology, said, "God our Savior . . . desires all men to be saved and to come to the knowledge of the truth. For there is one God and one Mediator between God and men, the Man Christ Jesus, who gave Himself a ransom for all" (1 Timothy 2:3–6). Scores of New Testament passages emphasize the necessity in personal belief in Jesus to be saved. Jesus Himself made this point very clear when He said to the Jews, "If you do not believe that I am He, you will die in your sins" (John 8:24). Everyone can make the personal choice to believe in Jesus—and making that choice is necessary to be saved.

160. What Is Election?

Early in His ministry Jesus told the disciples, "You did not choose Me, but I chose you" (John 15:16). The Lord spoke to Ananias, saying, "Go [pray for Saul], for he is a chosen vessel of Mine" (Acts 9:15). By divine prerogative, God has the right and the power to choose anyone for any purpose He wants. Beginning with Abraham, then Isaac, finally Jacob, whose name He changed to Israel, God elected the entire nation of Jacob's descendants. From them, He chose individuals—Moses, Joshua, numerous others and finally a maiden named Mary—through whom the Messiah/Christ was born.

Does divine prerogative—His choice, His election—conflict with our free will or our necessity to believe personally in Jesus Christ in order to be saved? Not at all.

Scripture is perfect in balance regarding this. While "God from the beginning chose you [elected you] for salvation through sanctification by the Spirit and belief in the truth, to which He called you" (2 Thessalonians 2:13–14), equally "Christ also suffered once for sins, the just for the unjust" (1 Peter 3:18), "He died for all" (2 Corinthians 5:15), and God desires that everyone be saved (see 1 Timothy 2:4). Jesus conquered sin and death. Every person on earth can make the choice by free will to accept His free gift or not. And at the same time, everyone who will ever make that choice is already known—chosen, elected—by the Lord.

Correctly said, the doctrine of God's election has a companion doctrine of our believing. We do not find one taught in the Scripture without the other. Personal election on the part of God and personal believing on the part of the sinner are inseparable truths. If we teach a form of election that does not insist upon individual response on the sinner's part to God's prevenient grace, we are not teaching the full truth of God. In the marriage of Christ and His Bride, as in weddings today, husband and wife each say yes to the other. Similarly, Jesus warned the Jews, "If you believe not that I am He, you shall die in your sins." That is, "You cannot be My Bride if you do not believe in Me."

Again, personal believing is the key: God's choice is administered through His foreknowledge of those who "believe the truth."

161. What Is Predestination?

When rightly understood, the doctrine of predestination is one of the most beautiful concepts in Scripture. Paul was its greatest New Testament proponent, though its truth runs as a fiber through the whole of the Old Testament as well. It has been vilified, damaged by misunderstanding and preached out of harmony with or to the neglect of other

Bible truths. The word itself identifies its role: Predestination has to do with destiny. The Greek word *proorizo* is the source from which our word *predestinate* is translated. Part of that word, *rizo*, is the foundation for our English word *horizon*, referring to the limit of our human vision. Predestination predetermines a "limit" for us. Our English word relates it exclusively to destiny.

In our fallen, unregenerate state, we could not rescue ourselves. God, foreseeing that, pre-fixed human destiny—changing it from disaster to glory by predestinating believers to heaven and immortality. This is grace in its highest revelation and was based on God's perfect foreknowledge of our need (see 2 Thessalonians 2:13). Violence is done to this truth when it is presented apart from our responsibility to believe the Gospel. Jesus said, "I said to you that you will die in your sins; for if you do not believe that I am He [the Messiah], you will die in your sins" (John 8:24).

According to Ephesians 1:3–6, 11–12 and Romans 8:29, predestination does three things for us: (1) It allows us to be adopted as God's children, (2) it conforms us to the image of Christ, and (3) it gives us a heavenly inheritance. Do not be afraid of predestination. It is your friend.

Predestination is frequently confused with foreordination, which may or may not concern events in time. It is a serious mistake to apply predestination to the concept of time. Predestination has to do with our destiny; it has nothing whatever to do with things such as disasters, tragedies or catastrophes that befall the planet or people on it. The end result of predestination is to bring us into God's presence and glory—not to kill us in disaster. God has expressed His will, His word and His intended actions for us in His covenant of grace.

Please hear this: "Christ has redeemed us from the curse of the law . . . that the blessing of Abraham might come upon the Gentiles in Christ Jesus, that we might receive the promise of the Spirit through faith" (Galatians 3:13–14). God's provision for the believer in this life is to receive the "blessing of Abraham."

162. What Is the Doctrine of Transubstantiation?

Regarding the sacrament of Holy Communion, the Catholic Church, which affirms that Jesus died "once for all," holds that the material substance of the sacrament transubstantiates into the actual flesh and blood of Jesus. He does not die again; rather, the mass serves as a "perpetuation" of His death and an acknowledgment that He continues to offer Himself to His Father as a living sacrifice. The word comes from the Latin *trans*, meaning "across," and *substantia* meaning "substance." The first known use of the term *transubstantiation* appears in the eleventh century when it was suggested by Hildebert de Lavardin, Archbishop of Tours. The doctrine was adopted by the Fourth Lateran Council (1215), later formalized at the Council of Trent (1545–1563), and finally reaffirmed at the Second Vatican Council (1962–1965). To non-Catholics the idea is too modern to be scriptural.

163. What Is the Doctrine of Consubstantiation?

Consubstantiation is the explanation commonly associated with Martin Luther that in the sacrament of Holy Communion the body and blood of Christ coexist in union with the bread and wine, without the elements undergoing actual change. The bread and wine remain bread and wine, while the substance of the body and blood of Christ are spiritually present. Luther illustrated the principle by the example of iron put into the fire, whereby both fire and iron are united in the heat and yet each continues its original state unaltered.

164. What Is the Doctrine of Memorial Only?

This position of memorial only, held by most evangelicals, denies the presence of anything miraculous in Holy Communion. The bread and wine are simply parabolic reminders of the body of Jesus and His death on the cross. By prayer, the elements are consecrated and received with thanksgiving, but have no other significance than being a solemn commemoration.

PART 12

What Are Some Doctrinal Heresies?

165. What Is Preterism?

The basic claim of preterism is that the prophecies of the Bible have all come to pass. Events that are described in the books of Daniel and Revelation were fulfilled in the first and second centuries, respectively. In addition, all prophecies concerning Israel have been fulfilled. God's plans for Israel as a nation are complete. Individual Jews may be saved, but as a historic people they have disappeared into the commonality of all other nations. Preterism basically teaches that the Kingdom of Christ was not established at Pentecost, but at the destruction of Jerusalem in AD 70 when Rome conquered Israel, and that the Second Coming of Christ occurred at that time. It promotes the idea that all New Testament passages relating to the Second Coming of Jesus for the saved have nothing to do with the actual return of Christ; these promises are not to be understood literally but metaphorically. Nor was the resurrection a physical event. Jesus returned mystically, this claim goes, when the Jewish Temple was destroyed.

166. What Is Oneness or Jesus Only?

The Pentecostal revival that began in Los Angeles in 1906 soon came under attack by splinter groups that weakened its unity and integrity. One of those was the appearance of the "Jesus only" doctrine, otherwise known as "oneness" theology. The controversy began in 1914 in a debate that quickly erupted into angered division. Basically, the argument attempts to reconcile Jesus' teaching on baptism with Peter's teaching on baptism—Matthew 28:19 and Acts 2:38, respectively.

Those insisting on baptism in the name of "Jesus only" soon assumed other ideas foreign to the initial movement. Not only must baptism be administered in the name of Jesus only, but it must be done by a minister ordained and endorsed by churches upholding that view. Religious legalism appeared. Another doctrinal change insisted that without speaking in tongues it was impossible to be saved. These concepts were far removed from those who were honored by the Holy Spirit's initial falling at the Azusa Street event. Of the several Pentecostal bodies identified with the "Jesus only" concept today, the United Pentecostal is the largest and most influential. The Hebrew name for God, *Elohim*, which appears in Genesis 1:1, and some 2,700 other places in the Old Testament, is a plural name but is ignored.

167. What Is Ultimate Reconciliation?

Ultimate reconciliation is not a theological system; its varied adherents agree on the claim that hell is not eternal. All hell's occupants, including Satan, demons, fallen angels and lost souls will ultimately be "reconciled" to God and transported to heaven. Jesus did not support this claim. Speaking of hell, He said, "If your hand causes you to sin, cut it off. It is better for you to enter into life maimed, rather than having two hands, to go to hell, into the fire that shall never be quenched—where 'Their worm does not die and the fire is not quenched'" (Mark 9:43–44).

Ultimate reconciliation is not new. Origen Adamantius, a second-century Christian theologian from Alexandria, Egypt, endorsed the idea. He was an excellent writer in many branches of theology but embraced concepts unacceptable to his peers and us today. Among them was his endorsement of ultimate reconciliation. This idea might appeal to our sympathies but cannot be supported scripturally.

168. What Is Neo-Platonism?

Without question, Plato was one of the most influential people in the history of mankind. He is thought to have lived from 428 to 348 BC. Plato, with his teacher, Socrates, and his student, Aristotle, molded the style in which modern society still thinks. It is believed that Plato's entire works have been preserved intact for more than 2,400 years. His academy in Athens, where his teaching became famous, was the world's first institution of higher learning. Though his emphasis was not religious, his philosophical approach to the nature of the human soul and body had great impact on Christian and secular minds alike. This is especially true in the fields of science, philosophy and mathematics. Saint Augustine drew heavily upon Plato and became one of the leading theological voices in the Church. Christian leaders from the Middle Ages to modern times have drawn heavily upon his concepts.

About six and a half centuries after Plato's death, a new philosophical system known as Neo-Platonism was introduced at Alexandria, Egypt, by Plotinus (AD 205–270) and a band of his followers. This new religious cult contained elements from Plato, Judaism, Christianity and mystical sources, and claimed that through philosophical contemplation, the human soul could be united with the universe. While on earth, disciples could experience a spiritual mesmerizing that joined them to material things about them. In this way human perfection and happiness could be achieved without waiting for an afterlife. To Neo-Platonists, there was no such thing as evil; it was only the absence of good. They also denied darkness; it was only the absence of light. At death everyone returned to the same eternal "source." Reincarnation was also an important part of the Neo-Platonist belief. It is easy to recognize these same pagan teachings in the world today. Yoga, for instance, offers a path to "enlightened consciousness."

As Christians we are happy in Christ, knowing that we are "complete in Him" (Colossians 2:10). It is in Him that "we live and move and have our being" (Acts 17:28)!

169. What Is Arianism?

Arius, Bishop of Alexandria, Egypt (AD 250–336) deviated from basic Christian belief regarding the Holy Trinity, and taught that Jesus was created by the Father before time and prior to His birth by the virgin Mary. Since Jesus was a created being, made by the Father, He could not be equal to the Father. Instead, Jesus was a creature—divinely made—but still a created being. Arius based most of his theory on Jesus' statement that the Father was greater than He (see John 14:28). First Corinthians 8:5–6 was also cited as proof text that only the Father was the true God. Arius failed to recognize that Jesus' greatest display of humility was His voluntary submission to the Father. This did not strip Him of His equality with the Father.

The teachings of Arius spread widely, including to high-ranking members of the clergy. In AD 325, a council of bishops and churches was convened in the city of Nicaea primarily to deal with Arius' growing influence. Emperor Constantine, whose personal Christianity was questionable but who wanted Church uniformity in the Empire, presided over the council. Arianism was declared heretical, and Arius, then 85 years old, was stripped of his ministry and banished to Illyricum on the east coast of the Adriatic Sea. Two of his outspoken supporters were banished with him.

170. What Is Gnosticism?

The word *gnosis* means "knowledge," and the cult that claimed its special revelation became the most difficult heresy the early Church had to confront. Gnostic concepts came from a combination of Zoroastrianism, Platonism and Christianity, and heralded a plurality of heavens and gods. In some of his writing, the apostle John appears to have targeted Gnosticism as the enemy of his day. Gnostics believed that salvation was not necessarily found in Jesus Christ but that a secret knowledge—which they had—led to redemption. While they held conflicting views on a number of issues among themselves, they did agree on several basic ideas.

First, there were two major gods—one righteous, the other evil. The evil god, named Demiurge, made the world. The righteous "god" did not. This concept in part is neo-platonic, originating in Greece, and probably was introduced into the Holy Land during Alexander the Great's occupation of the area several centuries before Christ.

Second, all physical things were fundamentally evil.

Third, Demiurge was god of the Old Testament, and the Jews followed this evil god. The higher "god" sent Jesus to bring salvation. Since Jesus was perfect, He could not have been physical; He only appeared physical. His resurrection was not actual; it only appeared to be so.

Buried in the heresy was enough truth as to confuse the unlearned. On this point Irenaeus wrote of them: "Error, indeed, is never set forth in its naked deformity, lest being thus exposed, it should at once be detected. But it is craftily decked out in an attractive dress, so as, by its outward form to make it appear to the inexperienced . . . more true than the truth itself." Much of today's Church battles with concepts of Gnosticism without recognizing it. We call it modernism or free thought.

171. What Is Antinomianism?

The expression *Antinomianism*—meaning "anti-law"—appeared soon after the Protestant Reformation (c. 1517) and is still used today to identify those who justify sinful behavior by claiming to have been set free from the Law. The theological argument, a misinterpretation of Galatians 3:13, might be expressed thus: "I am saved by grace, not by good works; therefore my own works, good or bad, can have no effect on me. I am free from the curse of the Law."

The rebuttal to such reasoning is that the person who has been renewed in grace is repulsed by sinfulness. That one no longer needs the restraint of the Law because grace has changed him or her from within. If "old things have passed away" and "all things have become new," it will show in the person's desire to please God (2 Corinthians 5:17). Where there is no apparent change externally, there is also no reason to believe that change has taken place internally. We have the example of Zacchaeus the publican who, after his saving encounter with Jesus, restored everything he had stolen fourfold (see Luke 19:8).

Grace saves us from sin; it does not save us *to* sin. Peter gave the very stern illustration of the washed sow returning "to her wallowing in the mire" (2 Peter 2:22). By that he meant that genuine regeneration will unavoidably demonstrate itself in an externally changed life. The clean sow returns to the mire because internally she experienced no change. Jesus compared a renewed life to a tree that brings forth good fruit. And a tree with no fruit? His attitude was, "Cut it down" (Luke 13:7). Jesus' most severe warning was to those who claimed to have cast out demons in His name, but to whom He said, "I never knew you: depart from Me, you who practice lawlessness!" (Matthew 7:23).

The position of Antinomianism is a dangerous one. Don't go there!

172. What Is Annihilationism?

Annihilationism, also known as extinctionism, is the concept that hell is not eternal, and that Satan, fallen angels, demons and the unsaved do not abide there perpetually. Instead, they are destroyed and exist no more. This is contrary to Scripture. Even Martin Luther hypothesized about "soul death," that is, annihilation. To deny the eternal nature of spirit-life, however, allows us to reject other Bible truths simply because we do not agree with them. When the apostle John wrote about Satan being tormented "forever and ever" he used the same Greek words regarding God who lives "forever and ever" (Revelation 15:7; 20:10).

Thus, to deny the eternal nature of hell allows us to deny the eternal nature of the Creator. This we cannot do. Hell and its punishment are as eternal as heaven and its glories. When Jesus gave the account of the rich man and Lazarus who died, He explained that the beggar was transported to the bosom of Abraham, but the rich man was cast into hell (Luke 16:23). According to Jesus, the torment of the rich man did not end abruptly; it was as ongoing as Lazarus' bliss. Other Scriptures relative to death and hell are these: Genesis 3:19; Psalm 146:4; Ecclesiastes 9:5; Ezekiel 18:20; Malachi 4:1–3; Matthew 10:28: Hebrews 10:26–27; 2 Peter 3:7.

173. What Is Dualism?

Universally, people in every age, environment and religious conviction have dealt with dualism—at its heart the belief that two equal and independent powers are at war in the universe: God, who is good, and Satan, who is evil. It is heretical to consider God and the devil as equal and opposite powers. Satan, a created being, appeared immediately in the Garden of Eden to seduce the first humans and gain control over them and all mankind (see Genesis 3:1). His success was achieved through subtlety and deceit. For Christians, the challenge is to reject the devil's lies of supremacy and believe Scripture's declarations that Satan was defeated at the cross, that "he who is in you is greater than he who is in the world" (1 John 4:4).

When Jesus appeared, He offered life "more abundantly" (see John 10:10). His invitation to all mankind was for all who "labor and are heavy laden" to come to Him for rest (Matthew 11:28). The failure of much of modern Christianity comes from avoiding the very obvious truth of Scripture for relief through self-made doctrines (see Jeremiah 2:13). Jesus said it this way: "You must be born again" (see John 3:7; see 1 Peter 1:23). Paul explained that when we are born again we become new creations, old things pass away and all things become new (see

2 Corinthians 5:17–18). This prepares us for the resurrection when our misconceptions about dualism end forever.

174. What Is Universalism?

The idea of ultimate reconciliation claims there will be no distinction between the saved and unsaved soul after death; all will be redeemed and taken to heaven. God's mercy is too great to allow any one to perish and be deprived of His love. Scripture denies this (see Revelation 19:20; 20:10, 14–15).

The word *universal* in that context is not to be confused with Unitarian-Universalist doctrines. A body of churches by that name, and headquartered in Boston, Massachusetts, rejects the idea of punishment after death—or the existence of hell. This denomination does not have a creed and includes many atheists, agnostics and other non-Christians in its fellowship. In this regard, it is interesting to know that following America's "Great Awakening," in the early 1700s, Dr. Charles Chauncy, pastor of First Church, Boston, denounced the Awakening as being purely emotional. At the time, New England was filled with strong, Bible-believing churches from the Pilgrim era. Many, however, embraced Chauncy's claim, rejected the move of the Spirit, and later became part of a liberalist, Scripture-rejecting movement. In disdaining their opportunity for authentic awakening, these churches followed Chauncy into total denial of Scripture.

PART 13

What Are God's Plans for Israel?

175. What Was God's Covenant with Abraham?

When Abram was 99 years old and still holding to God's promise that he and Sarai would have a son, God appeared to him and confirmed the covenant He had made. It involved primarily the number and stature of Abram's descendants and the land God was giving them. Abram fell on His face as God spoke.

> "As for Me, behold, My covenant is with you, and you shall be a father of many nations. No longer shall your name be called Abram, but your name shall be Abraham; for I have made you a father of many nations. I will make you exceedingly fruitful; and I will make nations of you, and kings shall come from you. And I will establish My covenant between Me and you and your descendants after you in their generations, for an everlasting covenant, to be God to you and your descendants after you. Also I give to you and your descendants after you the land in which you are a stranger, all the land of Canaan, as an everlasting possession; and I will be their God."
>
> Genesis 17:4–8

Observe: God's covenant is "everlasting." It is still in full power today. God has not changed His mind and the land of Israel is still a lawful possession of the Jews. Also, be aware: His promise to bless those who bless Israel still applies. The enlarging of the name Abram to Abraham was apparently a parabolic sign that God was similarly enlarging his posterity.

176. What Is the Blessing of Abraham? Can Gentiles Receive It?

Abraham was chosen by God to be the one through whom He would reveal His covenant (Scripture), the Messiah-Redeemer and blessings to mankind. Specifically, God told Abraham, "I will bless you and multiply your descendants" (Genesis 26:24). There are several aspects to this blessing. First and most important, was the privilege to know God. Second, Abraham became a very intellectual, wealthy man. His descendants today through his sons Isaac and Ishmael are some of the wealthiest people on earth—the Jews through their intellect; the Ishmaelites through the oil beneath their land.

My research has shown that there is no other ethnic group more productive, creative, originative than the Jews. They excel intellectually and, when given liberty, flourish financially. This, in part, is the "blessing of Abraham" that has never been lifted from them. For example, the world's total population is about seven billion people; Jews, with about fourteen million citizens compose only two-tenths of one percent of that number. In spite of their minute minority, they lead the world in the number of Nobel Peace Prize winners—129. One-fifth of all winners are Jewish. Jews are also regarded as the most philanthropic people on the planet.

This intellectual and financial aspect of the "blessing of Abraham" has continued working through them in spite of humanity's abuse of them and their worldwide dispersion. The Jewish practice of charity giving—*tzedakah*—has grown into a worldwide complex of philanthropic and nonprofit organizations. Jewish benevolence annually distributes more than $3 billion in public welfare. Much of that benefit goes to non-Jews through public benevolence, scholarships and other endowments. Even those who have persecuted them are welcome to participate in Jewish charity.

Jews are natural heirs. Gentiles who receive Abraham's blessing by faith in Jesus Christ become heirs: "Christ has redeemed us from the curse of the law . . . that the blessing of Abraham might come upon the

Gentiles in Christ Jesus, that we might receive the promise of the Spirit through faith" (Galatians 3:13–15). And: "The children of the flesh, these are not the children of God; but the children of the promise are counted as the seed" (Romans 9:8). As spiritual children of Abraham, by faith, we receive the covenant's provision of acceptance with God through the promised Messiah.

177. What Is the Significance of the Jewish Feasts?

Historically, Israel observed seven feasts annually, which were called "holy convocations" or "appointed times" (see Leviticus 23). Most continue today. These special occasions were reminders of God's care and provision for His people nationally and individually. The seven feasts were celebrated as part of three main festivals. Beginning in the spring, the first festival included the feasts of (1) Passover, (2) Unleavened Bread and (3) Firstfruits. The next festival was (4) Feast of Weeks. The autumn festival included feasts of (5) Trumpets, (6) the Day of Atonement and (7) Tabernacles.

To the Jews, these celebrations memorialized two realities: God's protection and provision for their nation. As a tribe, they were His elect; chosen and precious. To Christians, each feast communicates a vital truth about events surrounding the sacrificial death and glorious return of Jesus Christ when He "tabernacles" with His people forever (see Revelation 1:7). Understanding the significance of these God-appointed Jewish festivals helps us see more clearly the complete plan of redemption.

1. *Passover* begins on the fifteenth day of the Hebrew month Nisan and lasts for seven days in Israel and eight days in the Diaspora. (The Diaspora refers to dispersed Jews who are not living in their homeland.) The Passover celebrations begin with the Seder

supper. Passover speaks of redemption from sin; the time when Jesus Christ, the Lamb of God, was offered as an atonement for our transgressions. As the blood of a lamb, which was sprinkled on the doorposts of Jewish homes in Egypt, forced the Angel of Death to pass over them (see Exodus 12), so those covered by the blood of Jesus, the Lamb of God, will escape the spiritual death that comes upon those who reject Jesus Christ. Of all the Jewish festivals, Passover is of the greatest importance to Christians, as the Lord's Supper was instituted at Jesus' final Passover meal with the disciples (see Matthew 26:17–27). In passing the elements and telling the disciples to eat of His body, Jesus was presenting Himself as the ultimate Passover Lamb.

2. *The Feast of Unleavened Bread* warns us about the yeast-like contaminating effects of sin.

3. *The Feast of Firstfruits*, which came three days later on the first day of the week, speaks of Christ as the "first fruit" from the dead. Because of Jesus' resurrection, we can trust the Father for our own resurrection and His continuous provision for our future.

4. *The Feast of Weeks*—Pentecost, to the Church—occurs fifty days after the Firstfruits festival, and celebrates the successful end of the grain harvest. It portrays the outpouring of the Father's bounty. The word *Pentecost*, meaning "fiftieth," is a Greek term, not Hebrew, and foretold Jesus' promise to send "another Helper" who would indwell believers and empower them for ministry (John 14:16). The outpouring of the Holy Spirit fifty days after Jesus' resurrection was accompanied by astonishing "signs and wonders" and left many inhabitants of Jerusalem in a state of utter confusion. To believers it was the guarantee that their future resurrection would also come to pass (see Ephesians 1:13–14). While Pentecost was the ultimate blessing to those receiving it, to others it was only wild emotionalism and alcoholic drunkenness.

The remaining three have their spiritual fulfillment at the time of the Lord's return.

229

5. *The Feast of Trumpets* begins the Jewish civil New Year and is the celebration known as Rosh Hashanah. Beginning at sunset, families and friends gather to pray and celebrate, eating honey and apples to symbolize the hope for a sweet and blessed new year. It is a beautiful occasion. To the Church it signifies Christ's triumphant return to earth in His Second Coming. "For the Lord Himself will descend from heaven with a shout, with the voice of an archangel, and with the trumpet of God. And the dead in Christ will rise first" (1 Thessalonians 4:16). Additionally, the sounding of the trumpet also forewarns the pouring out of God's wrath on the earth as told in the book of Revelation.

6. *The Feast of the Day of Atonement* was the greatest day in Israel's history, and occurred ten days after the Feast of Trumpets. On this day the High Priest, trembling with fear, entered the Holy of Holies and sprinkled sacrificial-animal blood on the Mercy Seat atop the Ark of the Covenant. If accepted by God, atonement was made and Israel's sins were forgiven. If not accepted, the priest fell dead. No other moment in Israel's year surpassed the importance of this one. This feast is prophetic of the time when the final number of Gentiles is saved, when God has called the last Israelite to Himself, and when the gates of heaven are opened before the redeemed (see Romans 11:25–26).

7. *The Feast of Tabernacles* (or *Booths*) was the seventh and final feast of the Lord, and took place five days after the Day of Atonement. For seven days, the Israelites presented offerings to the Lord, during which time they lived in huts made from tree limbs and palm branches. Sleeping at night in booths recalled the Israelites' wilderness sojourn prior to their possessing the land of Canaan (see Leviticus 23:43). It also portrayed their utter safety in being able to sleep outdoors without the protection of a walled city. This feast signifies the future time when Christ brings ultimate peace to the earth. "For He must reign till He has put all enemies under His feet. The last enemy that will be destroyed is death" (1 Corinthians 15:25–26). For eternity, people from every tribe, tongue

and nation will "tabernacle" with Christ in the New Jerusalem (see Revelation 21:9–27).

While the four spring feasts look back at what Christ accomplished at His first coming, the three autumn feasts point us toward the glory of His Second Coming. The early feasts show the source of our hope in Christ—His finished work of atonement for sins—and the later feasts give the promise of what is to come—eternity with Him.

178. What Was Jesus' Conflict with the Jews Concerning the Sabbath?

From the time of Moses, Israel attempted to obey the Law in all things. Unknown to them, that period was now closing and, without explanation, Jesus began demonstrating how life would be after the Law's conclusion. His challenge was fiercely resisted, but He maintained that He had not come to destroy "the Law or the Prophets" but to fulfill them. Reminding the Jews of the Law's authority, He said, "Till heaven and earth pass away, one jot or one tittle will by no means pass from the law till all is fulfilled" (Matthew 5:17–18).

Even so, as told in Matthew 12:1–8, one Sabbath day He took His disciples through the grainfields, broke off the heads of wheat, rubbed the kernels in His hands to break away the husks, and began eating. The Jews were horrified at His actions. He then reminded them that David once took his soldiers into the Tabernacle and ate the showbread, which was not lawful for them. Challenging the Pharisees on another example, He reminded them that the priests were allowed to work in the Temple on the Sabbath and were blameless. More alarmingly, He referred to Himself and said, "I say to you that in this place there is One greater than the temple." The people who heard this were startled, but He continued, "For the Son of Man is Lord even of the Sabbath." With that, Jesus did many of His greatest miracles on the Sabbath Day.

When was the Law fulfilled? The shout from the cross, "It is finished!" (John 19:30), forever ended righteousness being achieved by the Law. From that point on, it would be the imputed righteousness of Christ that would bring mankind into right standing with God.

179. What Are the Times and Fullness of the Gentiles?

When Jesus prophesied about the destruction of Jerusalem and His Second Coming, He said that not one stone of the great buildings of the Temple would be left upon another, but would all be thrown down (see Matthew 24:1–2). One of the stones to which Jesus referred was 45 feet long, 15 feet wide and 12 feet high, and weighed 570 tons. Other stones were equally huge. Jesus' statement sounded absurd. In the year AD 70, however, Roman General Titus destroyed the city, leaving the massive stones pushed aside—and helping us realize the awesome strength of the Roman army. Jesus also explained that "Jerusalem will be trampled by Gentiles until the times of the Gentiles are fulfilled" (Luke 21:24). The deliverance of Jerusalem from Gentile rule in 1948 could easily be understood as the fulfillment of this Scripture—except for the fact that we have not seen "the Son of Man coming in a cloud with power and great glory" (verse 27).

Romans 11:25 states: "I do not desire, brethren, that you should be ignorant of this mystery, lest you should be wise in your own opinion, that blindness in part has happened to Israel until the fullness of the Gentiles has come in. And so all Israel will be saved." Paul spoke of this as a "mystery"—and it has so remained. We should not be surprised that competent Bible scholars disagree about its meaning. "The secret things belong to God"—and some shall so remain.

180. What Is the Diaspora?

Jews who remain scattered worldwide today are known as the Diaspora—i.e., the "dispersed." This distinguishes them from Jews who have returned to the homeland of Israel. While adjusting to local Gentile circumstances worldwide, Jews have maintained their own distinct identity. In that separation minor differences have developed. Two of the most prominent groups are the Ashkenazi, with long ancestral residence in Germany, France and Eastern Europe, and the Sephardic, who are identified more with the Middle East, Spain, Portugal and North Africa. A smaller group is the Mizrahi, whose ancestors came from North Africa and the Middle East. It is believed that Ashkenazi Jews composed only three percent of the world's Jewish population in the eleventh century. In 1931 they accounted for 92 percent. Other Jewish sects are Yemenite, Ethiopian and Oriental. Today, some six million Jews live in the U.S.

Traditionally, one is not a Jew who is not born of a Jewish mother. In our day, medical evidence has confirmed that mitochondrial DNA is passed exclusively from mother to child. The Jews were right long before modern science confirmed their practice.

181. What Is at the Root of Muslim Anger?

Many Muslims who are descended from Ishmael—Abraham's son by Hagar—still carry the bitterness of his being ejected from his father's tent and deprived of his love. Not only so, but Scripture tells how Hagar left him under a desert bush and walked away, certain they were both about to die. Abandonment and loss of family love was, is, will always be the greatest rejection a child can know. The double crisis of the loss of Abraham as father and abandonment to the desert by their mother still burns in Muslim hearts. Later, Abraham's grandson Esau, who was cheated out of his birthright blessing, married an Edomite woman and destined his posterity to Islam. He, too, suffered from rejection and loss of family favor.

182. How Have Christian Nations Abused the Jewish People?

Over the centuries Jews have suffered incredible violence at the hands of Christians. These were not a few isolated incidences, but century after century of deliberate, wicked behavior against them. Jews were banished from nearly every country in Europe, burned alive at the stake, murdered by whole villages, suffered their children being forcibly taken from them and their property confiscated. Others were forced into Catholic conversions. Instead of being shown the love of Christ, they were treated with repulsion and contempt. As early as the Council of Nicea (AD 325), Christian documents spoke of the Jews in evil and degrading ways. In 337, the first Christian emperor of Rome, Constantine, who had ended persecution against Christians, made the marriage of a Jew to a Christian punishable by death. Two years after that, converting to Judaism became a criminal offense. Emperor Theodosius, in 379, encouraged the destruction of synagogues. One bishop directed the burning of a synagogue and called it "pleasing to God."

In AD 380, Christianity became the state religion of the Roman Empire and a greater threat to the Jews. Cyril, Bishop of Alexandria, Egypt, expelled all Jews from that city in 415. By that time, the "mystery of lawlessness" (iniquity), which Paul warned was coming, had gained full dominance over most of the churches (2 Thessalonians 2:7). The spread of Catholicism and its claim of imperial power meant, for Jews, centuries of tragedy. Violence against them became horrific.

In 1099, Christian Crusaders, who were promised absolution for all sin as payment for their being warriors, struck Jews and Muslims alike.

In fact, Jews were safer with Muslims than professing Christians at that time. In one instance the Crusaders forced all of the Jews of Jerusalem into a central synagogue and set it on fire. Those who tried to escape were shoved back into the burning building and perished.

In 1229 the Spanish Inquisition began with Pope Innocent IV authorizing the use of torture before killing victims. Horrible methods were employed against Jews and non-Catholics. Jews were given the choice of leaving the country (with nowhere to go) or converting to Catholicism. Jewish children over six years of age were forcibly taken from their parents and given a Church education. In 1298, Jews suffered a new wave of persecution in Austria, Bavaria, France and Germany, when 140 Jewish communities were destroyed; another hundred thousand Jewish men, women and children, were killed in a six-month period.

Across Europe, Jews were not allowed to own land, be farmers or enter certain other trades. Even so, they became the intellectual backbone of Europe. When they succeeded as bankers and businessmen, they were hated the more. In 1306, one hundred thousand Jews were exiled from France with nothing but the clothes on their backs, food for one day and no place to go. Many starved to death, children dying first. In 1236, Pope Gregory ordered Church leaders in England, France, Portugal and Spain to confiscate all Jewish books. In 1261, Duke Henry III of Brabant, Belgium, ordered that "Jews . . . must be expelled from Brabant and totally annihilated so that not a single one remains, except those who are willing to change." In 1267, the Synod of Vienna ordered Jews to wear horned hats. Jews were exiled from England in 1290, forcing some sixteen thousand to abandon their homes. In 1320, forty thousand French shepherds went to Palestine as the "Shepherd Crusade," and on the way destroyed more than a hundred Jewish communities. Again, no Jew was spared.

Through the centuries the story continued. The United States participated in the anti-Jewish action in 1939 when the MS St. Louis, a German ocean liner, sailed to America with 915 Jewish refugees from Germany; the Jews were denied entry. At the time, Hitler was storming across Europe with his anti-Jewish madness. The ship had already been refused in Cuba and other ports of call. It finally returned to Europe where World War II was raging. Many of the passengers died in Nazi concentration camps.

In 1941, the Jewish Lithuanian population numbered around 220,000. The capital, Vilnius, was the Jewish center of rabbinical learning and influence in Europe. There, as elsewhere, the Jews provided the nation with its intellectual and financial elite. During the German invasion of June 1941, Nazis murdered 206,800 Jews with the aid of "Christian" civilians. Many were clubbed to death.

By the end of the war, some six million Jews had died in Nazi gas chambers and concentration camps. Adolf Hitler quoted Martin Luther's anti-Jewish writings to justify his horrific crimes. Currently in the U.S. and Europe, anti-Semitic attitudes are growing alarmingly—as is the marginalization of the Church. The mass influx of Muslim migrants and refugees into Europe and the West, along with the rise of secular humanism, fuels this distress.

Christianity has an unpayable debt to the Jews, and no amount of apologizing can ever remove our guilt. Our only recourse is to love them as Christ loves them and help defend their future.

183. What Is Replacement Theology?

Replacement theology claims that all the promises, covenants and blessings provided Israel in the Old Testament have been taken from the Jews and given to the Church. Christians have replaced Israel totally in the Old Testament covenant relationship.

If this be so, we have been demoted.

God's historic covenant with Israel promised only earthly land and prosperity; the Church—comprising all who come under the New Covenant, Jew and Gentile alike—has been promised heaven and eternity with God. Additionally, if the Hebrew covenant has been transferred to the Church, what about Hebrew Law? Paul goes to great length to explain how believers have been redeemed from Israel's "curse of the law" (Galatians 3:13). God forbid that we return to the Old Covenant in any capacity!

As to Israel's future as a nation, Paul further explains:

> Blindness in part has happened to Israel until the fullness of the Gentiles has come in. And so all Israel will be saved, as it is written: "The Deliverer will come out of Zion, and He will turn away ungodliness from Jacob; for this is My covenant with them, when I take away their sins." Concerning the gospel they are enemies for your sake, but concerning the election they are beloved for the sake of the fathers. For the gifts and the calling of God are irrevocable.
>
> Romans 11:25–29

The fact is this: The Church will remain the Church; Israel will remain Israel, and God will ultimately complete His plan for the Jewish nation.

184. What Is Meant by Blindness in Part Happening to Israel?

Paul, a Jew, and one who loved the Jewish nation, explained to the church at Rome why so many of his own kinsmen were not receiving the Gospel: "Blindness in part," he said, "has happened to Israel" (Romans 11:25). This partial spiritual darkness has, for a time, prevented the Jews from hearing, believing or wanting the Gospel message. Israel's blindness and rejection of Jesus will end simultaneously when God's time of favor for the Gentiles comes to an end. At that point, God will pour His Spirit on the "family of David" and other inhabitants of Jerusalem. This holy deluge will force the Jews to look on Him whom they pierced (see Zechariah 12:10–11). That scene will bring incredible mourning to the entire Jewish nation. The prophet Zechariah describes it like a family mourning over the tragic death of their firstborn son.

Painful as it will be, it will also be the time when God takes away Israel's sin. The same Deliverer who rose out of Zion two millennia ago will again arise within their midst and "turn away ungodliness from Jacob" (see Romans 11:26). Those who were once avowed enemies of the Gospel will suddenly become its greatest lovers and defenders. This mourning will be national throughout the land of Israel and in every Jewish home around the world. Their grief for rejecting Jesus and their sin of unbelief will be beyond description.

Scholars hold varying opinions, but "the fullness of the Gentiles" may climax with the total collapse of pseudo-Christianity (see 2 Thessalonians 2:3), followed by a massive worldwide revival in which billions are saved and the Holy Spirit is poured out on the Jews (see Isaiah 11:9; Habakkuk 2:14). Perhaps it was this period of which King David prophesied that God would have mercy on Zion for her "set time" had come (Psalm 102:13). Israel's blindness is partial, not total, and temporary, not permanent; her restoration to the Lord will take place.

God forewarned Moses twice that the Jewish nation would forsake Him, break His covenant, worship heathen gods and be devoured by terrible crises. This rebellion is one for which God declared three times that He would hide His face from them (see Deuteronomy 31:16–19; 32:20). This "hiding of His face" was obviously true during the Nazi regime in Europe when some six million Jews perished in horrific ways. Thankfully, God's mercy is unending and through the prophet Ezekiel He said, "'I will not hide My face from them anymore; for I shall have poured out My Spirit on the house of Israel,' says the Lord GOD" (Ezekiel 39:29). Israel, like the church, will yet experience its own Pentecost, be filled with the Holy Spirit, rescued from national sin, and acknowledge Jesus as Lord.

185.

What Is Meant by Christians Being Grafted into Israel?

In Romans 11:11–24, Paul compares Israel to a cultivated olive tree and the Gentiles to a wild olive tree. The purpose of grafting is to provide a good root system for a plant that does not produce one of its own. Israel's root is the one true and only God, the Holy Scriptures, the prophets and, specifically, the "blessing of Abraham" (see Galatians 3:14). The Gentiles' ancestral root is pagan. By being grafted into Israel, we become established "upon the foundation of the apostles and prophets" (Ephesians 2:13–22). Non-fruit-bearing Jewish branches were broken off so that Gentiles could be grafted in (see Romans 11:17).

With that grafting came a warning from Jesus: "Every tree that does not bear good fruit is cut down and thrown into the fire" (Matthew 7:19). Once when Jesus approached a fig tree hoping for fruit but finding none, He cursed it. Later, when He and His disciples passed it again, Peter said, "Rabbi, look! The fig tree You cursed has withered away."

The grafting-in of Gentiles into the Jewish root does not mean that God quit loving the Jews or abandoned His plans for their future. Through this grafting, Gentiles have been made partakers of the covenant benefits and heirs to the blessings of God. The finality of Israel's being "broken off" came in AD 70, when Titus, the Roman general, destroyed Jerusalem, demolished the Temple, shattered the all-important archives and ancestral records and carried the Jewish survivors into slavery. Not one Temple stone was left standing upon another. This was the exact fulfillment of Jesus' prophecy (see Matthew 24:2).

The Arch of Titus, still standing in the Forum area of Rome today, shows Roman soldiers carrying away victoriously the golden Temple menorah in the company of Jewish slaves. There have been numerous tribes of people since ancient times who, even without persecution and rejection, have vanished from the earth. Not so with Israel. God Himself guarantees their survival. Even in their dispersion and incredible abuse, the Almighty keeps His covenant with Abraham.

239

186. Will Israel See a National Conversion to Christ?

Through two millennia of dispersion and worldwide scattering, the Jews have preserved their historical identity. This would have been impossible had it not been for the saving hand of God who said: "Once I have sworn by My holiness; I will not lie to David: His seed shall endure forever, and his throne as the sun before Me; it shall be established forever like the moon, even like the faithful witness in the sky" (Psalm 89:35–37). Jesus mentioned signs in the moon in Luke 21:25. In the 1948 restoration of the Jews to their ancestral land, God kept His promise to David and His covenant with Abraham. Maintaining possession, however, has been a continuous political and military struggle for the Jews.

Today there are still more Jews in the Diaspora (those scattered worldwide) than are living in the State of Israel. Paul asked the question about their spiritual state: "Have they stumbled that they should fall?" He answered quickly, "God forbid!" God is sustaining Israel in her dispersion until the time of her national conversion. Being now in a time of waiting, Israel is like John the Baptist, who was in the desert until the "day of his manifestation to Israel" (Luke 1:80).

The time of Israel's foreordained national conversion is known only to God. Paul explained, "All Israel will be saved, . . . [for] concerning the election they are beloved for the sake of the fathers" (Romans 11:26, 28).

PART 14

What Are Significant Events in Christian History?

187. How Did the Early Church Develop?

In the early days of Christianity, the apostles remained in Jerusalem while many of the disciples were scattered everywhere—"preaching the word" (Acts 8:4). As Christianity spread across the Roman Empire and beyond, most churches went "underground" to survive persecution. There were no printed Bibles, and preachers oftentimes had to rely on the Holy Spirit's illumination and their memory of Scripture. The only communication system was word of mouth and, in their remote stations, minor differences among Christian practices developed. This was especially true where Christianity moved into different cultures and languages. Christians were bonded to each other by their devotion to Christ and the continuing presence of the Holy Spirit. The concepts of Catholic and Protestant were unknown.

Disciples who secretly carried the Word sometimes found themselves as pastors of exploding churches. These in turn gave birth to other congregations in outlying areas, and in this way the system of bishops was born. There was no political church government controlling their affairs. In time, bishoprics developed and church government became more territorial. This occurred even under the threat of persecution.

In AD 311, Galerius, Eastern emperor of the Roman Empire and persecutor of the Church, was on his deathbed and asked Christians urgently to pray for him. That was followed on April 30 of that year by an order for their persecution to cease. With it came a request. He said, "In return for our tolerance, Christians will be required to pray to their god for us." Persecution stopped and within five days Galerius was dead. Two years later (313), Constantine joined with Licinius (Western and Eastern emperors, respectively) to issue the "Edict of Milan," which officially ended all persecution against Christians within the Empire. When the death threat against believers ended, churches became public, and divisions began to occur over doctrine or practice into the many church bodies we know today.

Note: The title *pope*, meaning "papa" or "father," was originally given to all bishops throughout the Church. In the late fourth and early fifth centuries, Popes Siricius and Ennodius narrowed its use to the Bishop of Rome.

188. What Was the Council of Nicaea?

By the year AD 325, Christianity had become such a dominant force in the Roman Empire that any crisis involving the churches also concerned the emperor. A theological dispute, known as the Arian controversy, arose, which challenged the divinity of Christ and the Trinity of God. Specifically, Arius, who was a priest in Alexandria, Egypt, maintained that the Son of God had been created as an act of the Father's will. He had not existed eternally before birth by Mary. Arius also denied the reality of the Holy Trinity.

Roman Emperor Constantine I, having through combat joined the East with the West, summoned eighteen hundred bishops to meet in Nicaea, Bithynia, in order to quell the argument over Arianism and define orthodoxy—this was the First Council of Nicaea and the first ecumenical council of the Church. Only 318 of the bishops attended. Emperor Constantine, who was not a baptized Christian at the time, presided over the council. Long after the meeting in Nicaea adjourned, Constantine continued his worship of the sun god, and made provision for his troops to reverence a variety of other deities. Christianity seemed to be another part of his religious collection.

At the council, Constantine directed the bishops to decide the issues by majority vote—and sound theological decisions were made. The overwhelming majority, 250 of the 318 present, held to biblical positions regarding Jesus and the Trinity. An official statement adopted by the council is known today as the Nicene Creed. In AD 381, at the Council of Constantinople, the wording was expanded regarding the Holy Spirit. This is the form generally in use today.

When the Council of Nicaea ended, Arius and two of his supporters were stripped of their churches and exiled to Illyria. While Arius' doctrine was heretical, his banishment established a model for a dangerous Church practice: physical punishment to discipline uncooperative members.

Five years after the Council of Nicaea, on May 11, 330, Constantine dedicated the new city of Constantinople in his own honor. He invited the goddess Tyche to live in the city. His statue, with a replica of this goddess in his hand, stood atop one of the columns in the Forum area. Constantine was baptized by immersion a few days before his death. In the archeological ruins of Ephesus near Izmir, Turkey, the ruins of an ancient church dating to this era can be found in which the baptismal pool can still be seen.

189. When Was Christianity Made the Official Religion of the Roman Empire?

There have been few eras more crucial in the history of the Church than the reign of Roman Emperor Theodosius (379–395). On February 27, 380, he declared "Catholic Christianity" to be the only legitimate religion in the Empire. As the State Church, it would be composed of churches that endorsed the Nicene Creed of 325 and accepted their identity as the "official" Church of Rome. The following year he convened the Council of Constantinople (considered the second ecumenical council) and conferred with some 150 bishops for three months—May, June and July. The Nicene Creed was reexamined and concepts regarding the work of the Holy Spirit were enlarged.

Numerous churches and bishops, however, did not attend the council. They feared the direction Theodosius was taking the Church. He had already authorized the destruction of all Jewish synagogues across the Empire. In compliance, one bishop had participated in such a burning and called it an act "well pleasing to God." In another instance, following a riot, thousands of Roman citizens were killed, for which Theodosius was blamed. He acknowledged his sin publicly and repented. Many pastors and churches knew the emperor had a violent nature and distanced themselves from him. Even though they embraced the Nicene Creed, they were still regarded as heretics.

Three churches today claim to be the historical continuation of the Council of Constantinople: the Catholic Church, the Eastern Orthodox Church and the Oriental Orthodox Church. We appreciate all of them.

190. Why Did Eastern and Western Christendom Separate?

By the end of the first millennium, most of Christianity had taken three religious forms. Two were Latin-speaking Roman Catholicism in the Western Mediterranean and Greek-speaking Eastern Orthodoxy claiming areas covered today by Iraq, Iran, the old Persian Empire and as far east as India. Scattered among both of these West and East Territories were independent congregations that were opposed to ritual. The third, the Oriental Orthodox Church, had discontinued communion with other church bodies in the fifth century. Its family comprises Ethiopian, Coptic, Armenian, Syrian, Indian and Eritrean churches.

In 1054, Pope Leo IX attempted to make the Greek-speaking Eastern Churches submit to Rome and come under his jurisdiction. His supposed authority was a little-known document from the reign of Emperor Constantine. The paper, dated March 30, 315 or 317, allegedly bestowed on the pope imperial "power, and dignity of glory, and vigor, and honor imperial . . . supremacy." Included were "all the churches of God in the whole earth." The document contained a Christian confession of faith by the emperor and a testimony of how he was healed of leprosy, converted and baptized by Pope Sylvester I. The act of bestowal was done in gratitude. It was not until the mid-fifteenth century, with the improvement of classical scholarship and textual criticism, that the document was proved false. Some of its Latin words were incorrect—not known in the fourth century.

The statement *all the churches of God in the whole earth* challenged the authority of the Eastern churches, which did not acknowledge the preeminence of the pope, but, rather, considered any leader of the Church to be "first among equals." Also divisive was the decision the Western churches had made centuries earlier when translating the Nicene Creed into Latin: A clause had been added stating that the Holy Spirit proceeds not from the Father but from the Father and the Son. The imposition of this change in the creed—the *filioque* clause—was a serious point of contention for the Eastern churches.

The Eastern Orthodox Church reaffirmed Constantinople as its capitol—thus becoming distinct from the Western Catholic Church. In some cases, both churches shared the same geographical areas. Both forms had become highly ritualistic and politically controlling. The city of Rome and the papacy dominated the West. In the East, the Ecumenical Patriarch of Constantinople ruled from the ancient church of Hagia Sophia (Holy Wisdom). This beautiful structure, built by Emperor Justinian I between 532 and 537, is still standing. In 1453, Muslims captured the city of Constantinople and converted the church into a mosque. Today it is a museum.

Eastern and Western Churches, each claiming apostolic succession (as does the Oriental Church), also claimed supremacy over the other, and ultimately each excommunicated its opponent. These excommunications were lifted in 1965 when Pope Paul VI and Ecumenical Patriarch Athenagoras I met in Jerusalem and revoked the excommunication decrees.

191. What Were the Crusades?

The Crusades were seven failing military/religious campaigns begun in 1095 by Pope Urban II for the purpose of freeing the Holy Land from Muslim control. Seljuk Turks were attacking Christian pilgrims on their way to Jerusalem, and the Byzantine (Eastern) emperor called for help. The Pope responded by recruiting several hundred thousand Catholic soldiers for the effort. Each became a "crusader" by taking a public oath. In return for their services, they were promised complete indulgence from all sin. Warriors came from every nation in Western Europe and had varying motivations for taking up "The Cross." Some did not volunteer but were sent by their monarchs as a way for the royalty to be part of the war.

After the first crusade, there followed an ongoing two-hundred-year struggle for control of the Holy Land. Six more major crusades and a number of minor ones took place. One of those, the Shepherds Crusade, killed thousands of Jews and destroyed their villages. In 1291, the final crusade ended in failure with the fall of the last Christian stronghold at Acre. The ruins of numerous crusader castles and fortifications still stand across the Middle East. *Crusade* means "marked by the cross" and is taken from a French word *croisade*.

192. What Was the Inquisition?

The Inquisition, established by the Catholic Church, called Sanctum Officium or Holy Office, was a religious reign of terror begun officially by Pope Innocent III in 1140 for the purpose of annihilating rival Christian groups. He announced: "Anyone who attempts to construe a personal view of God which conflicts with Church dogma must be burned [alive] without pity." He forbade the reading of Scripture and ordered that any house where the Bible was found be demolished.

Under Church sanction, the bishop of Lodève distributed across Europe a special directory of recommended torture methods. Another, *Directorium Inquisitorum* (*Guidelines for Inquisitors*), was composed by Nicolas Eymerich, Inquisitor General of the Inquisition of the Crown of Aragon. These were the authoritative textbooks for the use of Inquisitors. In 1483, an enlarged and revised *Directorium* was put into practice. Several ancient groups—the Christian Cathars and Albigenses as well as Waldenses—were special victims of the Inquisition. Jews were also targeted.

Forms of torture were demonic and inhumane: The "Rack" to which victims were strapped, slowly broke arms, legs, neck, and pulled bones out of their sockets. The "Iron Maiden" slowly penetrated the victim's body with long spikes. Other victims were tied, hands strapped behind their backs, with heavy iron weights attached to their feet. They were hoisted to the ceiling, then dropped repeatedly to the floor. Bones shattered on each fall. Victims who still survived were tied to a cross and their legs broken in additional places. Some had their tongues cut out. All was done with a priest standing by to record the victims' confessions.

It is estimated that over the years of the Inquisition's operation more than five million Europeans suffered. The terror also came to Latin America where it put to death thousands of non-Catholics in equally horrific ways. The original instruments of cruelty may still be seen today in Lima, Peru, and in Spain. As recently as 1947 in Morro Castle, Havana, Cuba, a wax-image of an execution in process was on display. It showed a victim, executioner and priest in lifelike representation. The last official Spanish execution for heresy occurred in 1826 when a schoolmaster was hanged because he substituted the phrase *Praise be to God* in place of *Ave Maria* ("Hail Mary") during school prayers.

193. What Was the AD 1378 Western Schism in the Catholic Church?

In 1378 three papacies arose simultaneously in Europe, each laying claim to being the sole authentic Catholic Church: one, with headquarters in Rome, was endorsed by the Holy Roman Empire; another based in Avignon, France, was supported by the French government; and, for a short time, the third in Pisa, Italy, was endorsed by a small number of cardinals and bishops. Each claimed to be the true Catholic Church stemming from the Council of Constantinople in AD 381. The papacy in Rome gained ascendency over Pisa and Avignon and the "Holy See" was reestablished.

194. What Was the Protestant Reformation?

The Protestant Reformation was a violent struggle within the Roman Catholic Church begun in 1517 by Martin Luther, a German Augustinian priest. Luther challenged abuses by the papacy; specifically, the cash purchase of forgiveness for sin for those already dead and in purgatory. Another priest, Johann Tetzel, came to Wittenberg, Germany, Luther's parish, to raise funds for the building of St. Peter's Basilica in Rome. He declared that every sin of loved ones in purgatory could be forgiven by an offering of sufficient cash. His reputed chant was, "As soon as the coin in the coffer rings, the soul from Purgatory springs."

Luther was enraged and nailed a list of 95 theological protests to Roman Catholicism on the Castle Church door. His "Disputation on the Power and Efficacy of Indulgences" is also known as "the 95 Theses." The summary, which began by criticizing the sale of forgiveness, also claimed that the pope had no authority over purgatory, and that Catholic doctrines of salvation by good works, penances and prayers to the saints had no foundation in Scripture. Salvation, said Luther, was by grace alone, through faith alone, in Christ alone. Luther's protests quickly gained momentum across Germany and northern Europe.

In 1618, open warfare broke out between papal and Protestant forces; history remembers it as the Thirty Years' War. Some of the most clandestine work in battling Protestantism was done by the new Catholic Order of the Jesuits. This group held many sympathies identical to those of the Inquisition. No religious organization requires a more blood-chilling, murderous oath than the Jesuit Extreme Oath of Induction. (It can be found online.) Governments later became so fearful of the Jesuits that they were outlawed in 39 nations. When the War of the Reformation ended in 1648, much of Europe lay in ruins. Disease and starvation radically reduced the surviving population. Vagabond soldiers roamed much of the countryside preying on survivors. Northern Europe had successfully broken ties with Rome and the Lutheran/Reformed churches had become a reality. One priest had successfully challenged the pope and won. Catholicism never regained power over northern Europe.

One of the expectations of the Reformation was that the Christian Church would continue reforming itself in its beliefs, practices and organizations. It is a principle of Protestantism to protest not only external abuses of all kinds but also the errors and imperfections that it progressively discovers within itself. This has not been done. Most denominations have hardened into an unchangeable mold that prevents the Holy Spirit's new revelation.

195. What Was the Moravian Revival?

In the early 1700s, a congregation of some three hundred Anabaptists, Calvinists, disciples of John Huss, Ulric Zwingle, Caspar Schwenckfeld and other non-conformists, sought refuge on the estate of Count Ludwig von Zinzendorf in Saxony, East Germany. Religious persecution was blazing across Europe, driving the populace to flee.

Like the count, who was only 27 years old, most members of the community were young. In the beginning they quarreled over doctrines of baptism, predestination, holiness, etc. until the Count encouraged them to concentrate on their mutual love for Jesus. It was the cross, he reminded them, not doctrines about the cross that purchased their redemption. With that understanding, they united in covenant agreement and began seeking the Lord in travailing prayer. God heard and answered.

A few days later, August 13, 1727, at morning Communion, the power of God fell upon the community in such force that men working in the fields ten miles away felt its impact. Soon afterward, the children were anointed with three hours of anguished intercession. This event exploded into a night-and-day prayer meeting that continued nonstop more than one hundred years. Early in that period, the Holy Spirit instructed the group to send missionaries to the Island of St. Thomas in the Virgin Islands. Their mission was to African slaves who had never heard the Gospel.

No one left immediately—instead, they prayed another ten years. When the day came to make the choice as to who would be first to go, they wrote Scripture quotations on slips of paper and placed them in a box. After agonizing prayer, each person drew out one of the notes. Whether he stayed in Moravia or went to the mission field was determined by the instruction he held. It was either Leonard Dober or David Nitschmann, partners, who opened and read the instruction: "Send the lad with me, and we will arise and go" (Genesis 43:8).

Believing they were God's choice, the two men walked more than a hundred miles to Copenhagen, Denmark, where they volunteered to work as deckhands on a ship to St. Thomas. Without God's protection, they knew that they, too, could be pressganged onto a ship and never seen again. They arrived safely in the Caribbean and were followed by Frederick Martin; he was soon imprisoned in the fortress dungeon at Charlotte Amalie. Tobias Leopold then arrived and went to the island of St. Croix. Other missionaries came to the Virgin Islands and together established slave churches, which survive to this day. Others flooded out of Germany like water over a spillway, and within 25 years more than

251

two hundred missionaries had gone to every continent on earth. Even Greenland heard about the Holy Spirit's awesome power.

In the zeal of first-century believers, these Spirit-baptized youths took the flame of the Spirit to every country in North and South America, much of Asia and Africa. Only a few came to the U.S.; most preferred un-evangelized areas.

Of the eighteen missionaries who went to the Virgin Islands, more than half perished the first year. Tobias Leopold died on St. Croix, shouting the message of the Gospel. At the same time in England, a young Anglican priest named John Wesley sat listening to the Moravian bishop, Peter Boehler, when he felt his heart "strangely warmed." Through him and his brother Charles, the Methodist Church was born.

Few other eras in world history have impacted mankind evangelically as did that blazing period of the Moravian revival. When the hundred-year-long prayer meeting ended, every denomination had been touched by the call to missions and was vigorously engaged in taking the Gospel to the ends of the earth.

196. What Was America's Great Awakening?

In the 1730–1740s, colonial America was shaken by a visitation from the Holy Spirit that awakened churches and changed the religious face of the nation. Jonathan Edwards (1703–1758), a principal voice in the movement, was a New England pastor whose historic sermon, "Sinners in the Hands of an Angry God," swept through Northampton, Massachusetts, with "signs and wonders." The Holy Spirit fell in such power that numerous people swooned—were "slain in the spirit"—and collapsed to church floors. Repentance in the form of agonized shouting filled the buildings and churchyards. Some of the slain remained motionless for many hours while others clung to trees groaning and weeping noisily.

In addition to being a theologian, Edwards was an acknowledged scientist, psychologist and philosopher. Theologically, he was a cessationist and did not believe the charismatic gifts of the Spirit were still active—even so, he experienced the power. Charles Chauncy, pastor of First Church, Boston, as well as Lutheran, Anglican, Reformed congregations and others, opposed the revival, claiming it was mere human emotion. Edwards was joined by Englishman George Whitefield whose ministry brought additional signs and wonders to the revival.

In 1741, Yale University dean, the Rev. Samuel Johnson, became alarmed at the effect George Whitefield's preaching was having on the students. Whitefield, who was contemporary with John and Charles Wesley and a personal friend of Benjamin Franklin, experienced "miraculous signs" attending his ministry. The dean wrote a friend in England about these strange physical manifestations affecting those who heard Whitefield preach. Not only the students, he lamented, but whole congregations were being seized with some kind of bizarre power. Johnson, in criticizing Whitefield and other revivalists, described their preaching as "hideous outcries," but failed to mention that a wave of God-fearing morality, intense prayer and love for Jesus was also gripping the campus.

Johnson knew that Samuel Buell, a Yale graduate, had preached in Jonathan Edwards' church in Northampton, Massachusetts, with the same peculiar manifestations occurring. The anointing was being passed on. Edwards described Buell's preaching in a letter to a friend, the Rev. Thomas Prince of Boston:

> There were some instances of persons lying in a sort of trance, remaining for perhaps a whole twenty-four hours motionless, and with their senses locked up but in the meantime under strong imaginations, as though they went to Heaven, and had there a vision of glorious and delightful objects. But when the people were raised to this height, Satan took the advantage, and his interposition in many instances soon became very apparent; and a great deal of caution and pains were found necessary to keep the people, many of them, from running wild.

Today we wonder if the accusation that the people's "strong imaginations, as though they went to Heaven," and their being "raised to this

253

height," which the clergy thought gave access to Satan, was not a tragic misjudgment by the ministry. Satan does not willfully glorify heaven. The "great deal of caution and pains necessary to keep the people from running wild" may have been another religious mistake. Records of Edwards' day tell that riotous laughter, jerking, loud shouting and groaning came upon the people. In all probability, their behavior was no different from the "drunken" actions on the day of Pentecost. We can be thankful that the apostle Peter seems to have made no effort to control those overcome with such manifestations.

197. What Was the Cane Ridge Revival?

From 1800–1802 the Holy Spirit fell on a Presbyterian church in rural Kentucky, and the "Second Awakening" shook America. Known as the "Cane Ridge Revival," it drew crowds of twenty to thirty thousand people who experienced signs and wonders identical to those of Jonathan Edwards' day. One spectator, James Finley, was overwhelmed by what he saw and wrote,

> I stepped on a log where I could have a better view. . . . The scene that then presented itself to my mind was indescribable. At one time I saw at least 500 swept down in a moment as if a battery of a thousand guns had opened upon them. . . . Many, very many, fell down as men slain in battle and continued together for hours in an apparently breathless and motionless state.

Another witness recounted that "while some lay as dead, 'slain in the spirit,' others shook uncontrollably, shouted, or staggered about in a drunken fashion. At times, roaring noises echoed through the forest." The howling racket and unusual bodily effects were accepted by those present because of the godly character changes that took place in the people.

At Cane Ridge, God violently smashed religious strongholds, cast out demons, and almost overnight rebuilt the moral structure of Kentucky. The Church in mid-America burst with new growth. Within two and a half years, Kentucky Baptists increased by ten thousand new members. Methodists added more than six thousand. The Presbyterian Synod reported "thousands." After visiting the scene in 1801, the president of what is now Washington and Lee University in Virginia said, "I found Kentucky the most moral place I had ever been in." This was a radical change from its previous condition of violence and depravity that typified much of the American frontier.

198. What Was the Welsh Revival?

Evan Roberts (1878–1951), a young Welshman, was God's chosen vessel to bring renewal to Wales and other parts of the British Isles. In 1904, when he was 26 years old, he began being awakened soon after midnight as the Holy Spirit challenged him to rise and pray. Roberts obeyed, anguishing before God until five in the morning and then through the day sensing the Holy Spirit's presence. Roberts had been praying for thirteen years for God to use him. A few months after the nighttime prayer sessions began, a young woman and new convert, Florrie Evans, rose in a prayer meeting packed with other young people and said, "I love Jesus with all my heart."

With that simple acknowledgment, the Holy Spirit suddenly flooded the room. Dozens of other young people began making confessions, seeking forgiveness, repenting, embracing each other in love. Everywhere in Wales, the Spirit seemed to be brooding over the churches. The following November, people packed into Moriah Chapel. Anguished prayer started rising from the congregation and quickly became a chorus of voices that lasted until three in the morning.

The Revival had begun and, before its end in less than a year, would bring more than a hundred thousand new believers to Christ. Roberts traveled throughout the area, leading prayer meetings and carrying the fire in his unassuming way. At some meetings he did not speak; he simply cupped his face in his hands and prayed. Eventually, the revival spread through England, Ireland and Scotland. In many services there was no preaching—only singing, praying and giving testimonies. Worship became an identifying mark of the Welsh Revival.

In time, Evan Roberts suffered a serious mental and physical collapse. Such an end to a ministry like his is disturbing. The explanation is important: When Jesus' disciples were suffering similar fatigue, He invited them to go with Him to a deserted place and rest awhile (see Mark 6:31). Evan Roberts did not do that. He drove himself until he collapsed. After a partial recovery, he spent most of his life in seclusion under the care of Jesse Penn-Lewis, dying in 1951. Thankfully, the revival did not end with Roberts' death. Other people of God came forward and carried it to great success.

199. What Is the Azusa Street/Pentecostal Revival?

William J. Seymour, a 34-year-old son of former slaves and interim pastor of a small holiness church in Houston, Texas, was a traveling evangelist speaking at meetings in Los Angeles, California. His teacher, Charles Parham, a well-known Pentecostal preacher, accompanied him. Returning to their rented building for meetings the second night, they found it locked with no explanation, and no one to let them in. Moving to a private home where Seymour spoke on the front porch, the large crowd caused the porch to collapse. Moving to another house, the foundation caved in.

On April 9, 1906, another building on Azusa Street, a former horse stable, was acquired. The first night the Holy Spirit fell. News of the revival spread, thousands attended and experienced the glory. Thus, the worldwide Pentecostal Movement was thrust onto the Christian scene.

Many who came as spectators at Azusa Street were radically converted and began preaching the message. By the turn of the century, more than five hundred million Christians worldwide had experienced the baptism with the Holy Spirit.

This number represents various Pentecostal denominations and thousands of unaffiliated churches. Pentecostals believe that baptism with the Holy Spirit is an event separate from receiving the Holy Spirit at conversion, and that the initial physical evidence is speaking in tongues.

200. What Is the Korean Revival?

On January 14, 1907, a group of Korean Christians and Western missionaries met in Pyongyang (now North Korea) for prayer and Bible study. Suddenly, the Holy Spirit fell upon them. Those present came under deep conviction and began confessing their sins to God and one another. Revival immediately hit the area and thousands were saved. Churches exploded in power and attendance. Prof. Samuel H. Moffett, son of a missionary to Korea, said "And out of that . . . came the work of the Spirit that finally broke out as at Pentecost."

This was the onset of revival in Korea, and within thirty years there were some three thousand churches operating in the nation. In 1950, the nation was attacked by the Communists and, following the war's end in 1953, Korea was divided into North and South.

The Holy Spirit was not finished. In May 1958, 22-year-old Paul (now David) Yonggi Cho, a former Buddhist, preached under a reject army tent with only a discarded mattress for the congregation to sit on. From that beginning came Seoul's Yoido Full Gospel Church with a membership today of one million active believers. The huge sanctuary seats more than ten thousand worshipers and holds repeated services throughout Sunday and many weekdays. Additionally, the church has spawned hundreds of other congregations across the nation, several being home to more than a hundred thousand members. South Korea has become the most Christian nation on earth. From its beginning, the Church emphasized the value of prayer and established a retreat know as "Prayer Mountain." The site contains ten thousand places for private prayer.

201. What Is the Latter Rain Movement?

In 1948, the Holy Spirit fell on a group of Pentecostal students, faculty and pastors at the Sharon Orphanage and Bible School in North Battleford, Saskatchewan, Canada, and gave birth to what became known as the Latter Rain movement. Those attending had come specifically to seek a fresh impartation of God's presence. Congregations with their leadership were radically changed; church services erupted into spontaneous periods of singing psalms and hymns or in tongues. This was very similar to the Spirit's fall in 1906 at Azusa Street and in 1994 at the Toronto Airport Vineyard Church.

In an overwhelming way, churches and congregations were radically awakened in this New Testament–style revival. The practice of "laying on of the hands" (1 Timothy 4:14), which had been reserved principally for pastoral ordinations, was powerfully restored to its full scriptural purposes. Its use in prayer for the sick, ministering the baptism with the Holy Spirit, restoration of spiritual gifts and other purposes was revived. The laity learned that ministry was not restricted to clergy; instead, Jesus said, "those who believe" would lay their hands on the sick to bring healing and other miraculous signs.

The movement came to the U.S. the following year primarily through "Mom" M. D. Beall (1894–1979), founder of Bethesda Missionary Temple, a three-thousand-seat auditorium in Detroit, Michigan. James Lee Beall (1924–2013), one of her sons, became and remained lead pastor of Bethesda for 67 years. Numerous Latter Rain pastors became significant in the U.S. and established prominent churches. In time, criticism came against the movement—some justified, some imaginary—but the benefit of the revival lives on.

202. What Is the Argentine Revival?

In 1954, a little-known American evangelist, Tommy Hicks, walked up to a guard at the palace of Juan Peron in Buenos Aires, Argentina, and asked to speak to the president. The purpose of his visit was to request use of the fifteen-thousand-seat Atlantic Stadium for an evangelistic and healing crusade.

At that moment, the soldier was in serious pain and interrupted Hicks to ask, "Can God heal me?"

Without hesitating, Hicks took the young man's hands and prayed. Immediately the power of God went through the guard. He was healed. Wide-eyed, he gasped in amazement, "Come back tomorrow!" he said. "You will see the president."

The next afternoon Hicks was escorted into the spacious presidential office and stood facing Mr. Peron. Hicks explained that God had sent him to Argentina to hold a salvation and healing crusade. He needed a large stadium with free radio and press coverage.

President Peron listened intently. Suddenly he said, "Can God heal me?" President Peron suffered from a dangerous eczema that was slowly disfiguring his body and causing a serious threat to his life.

As Hicks prayed, the power of the Holy Spirit went through the president's body. With everyone in the room watching, the president's skin suddenly became as soft and clear as a baby's.

"My God! I am healed!" he shouted.

Tommy Hicks had no difficulty getting the Atlantic Stadium, the free news coverage—or the people. The Holy Spirit began to move. Enormous crowds packed the stadium. Bleachers were filled half a day before services began. Peasants walked for miles from the surrounding countryside and camped under trees. Trains and buses were crowded.

Visitors flew in from other Latin American countries. In many cases, people stood for hours. Others slept all night on the metal walkways to be sure of getting a spot. The Holy Spirit fell in power and thousands upon thousands were healed; many of them were nationally known. When the crowds outgrew the Atlantic Stadium, they moved to another stadium that seats 180,000, and immediately overflowed it.

God turned Argentina upside down and planted the tree of the Gospel deeply into its soil. Starting at the bottom of South America, the Holy Spirit began an invasion that spread as far north as Mexico.

203. What Is the Charismatic Renewal?

In 1938, English evangelist Smith Wigglesworth, while preaching in South Africa, received a prophetic word that the Holy Spirit was going to invade modern, mainline churches with the power of God. "Signs and wonders" that occurred in the book of Acts, as well as in George Whitefield's, Jonathan Edwards' and Wigglesworth's own ministries, would take place in denominational churches. He quickly shared the word with his host-pastor, David du Plessis. The prophecy also said that Du Plessis would become a world traveler helping spread the news of renewal.

Both were astonished but waited expectantly. Instead of revival coming, Hitler invaded Poland and plunged the world into death and darkness. The war ended in 1945 and Wigglesworth died in 1948.

Nothing happened until Easter Sunday 1960; that day Fr. Dennis Bennett, rector at St. Mark's Episcopal Church in Van Nuys, California, testified that he had experienced the baptism with the Spirit and spoken in tongues. Within hours of his telling the congregation, he was asked to resign.

The news went nationwide. But exactly as Wigglesworth had prophesied, mainline churches began experiencing the Holy Spirit's miraculous presence. In addition, Du Plessis quickly became a world-renowned voice in the renewal. Few denominations have been left untouched. Ministers who formerly rejected all signs and wonders have found themselves experiencing them. In many instances where denominational leadership has rejected the Holy Spirit's presence and power, charismatic believers have left and organized themselves into very successful churches. The name *charismatic* comes from *charismata*, Greek for "a gift of grace." Like Pentecostals, charismatics view baptism with the Holy Spirit as a separate event from receiving the Holy Spirit at conversion, but differ from Pentecostals in that they believe tongues may or may not occur at the time.

204. What Is the Catholic Charismatic Renewal?

In August 1966, two Catholic professors from Duquesne University in Pittsburgh, Pennsylvania, Ralph Keifer and Patrick Bourgeois, attended the Congress of the Cursillo Movement in search of a deeper relationship with God. At that event they were given the book *The Cross and The Switchblade*, written by Pentecostal pastor David Wilkerson, which tells of the spiritual conversion of a street gang in New York City. Nicky Cruz, leader of the gang, was born again, filled with the Holy Spirit and radically changed. He became a Christian evangelist. The professors were deeply impacted by the book, which emphasized the Holy Spirit and His miraculous gifts.

The following year the two men, still in pursuit, attended a prayer meeting where they received the baptism with the Spirit and spoke in tongues. Keifer immediately began laying hands on faculty members, students and others at Duquesne, who were dramatically filled with the Spirit. In the next chapel service the Spirit fell and began an unstoppable fire. The news spread, quickly reaching Notre Dame University where a similar "falling" of the Spirit occurred with many of the faculty and students receiving the baptism. The movement spread worldwide and today—known as the Catholic charismatic renewal—it is established

261

in more than 230 countries with 160 million priests and people happily embracing the work of the Holy Spirit.

205. What Is the Third Wave?

The term *Third Wave*, which appeared in the early 1980s, is a new identification given to the ongoing work of the Holy Spirit. It presents a fresh new concept and challenge to the Pentecostal Movement (first wave), which originated in the early 1900s, and the charismatic renewal (second wave) of the 1960s. Early leaders John Wimber (1934–1997) and C. Peter Wagner (1930–2016) introduced slightly different interpretations and terminology regarding the baptismal work of the Holy Spirit.

While all three groups agree on the experience's spiritual reality, those in the Third Wave do not consider the baptism with the Holy Spirit as being a different experience from a person's new birth. It is not a "second blessing," as Pentecostals and charismatics consider it to be. Nor does the Third Wave consider tongues to be necessary. Rather it emphasizes power evangelism. The end result of all three "waves" is the same: Power for preaching, healing, other signs, wonders and various gifts of the Holy Spirit revealing His presence. The international impact has been strong in spiritual warfare, deliverance ministry, prophetic gifting and "Dominion authority."

206. What Is the Toronto Blessing/Catch the Fire?

In 1991, John and Carol Arnott became pastors of a young Vineyard fellowship located at the end of an airport runway in Toronto, Ontario.

Hungry for a greater work of God, they visited Argentina, where evangelist Claudio Freidzon laid hands on them. Back in the U.S., they learned that another Vineyard pastor, Randy Clark, was experiencing the Holy Spirit's power in phenomenal ways. He had received hands-on ministry from South African evangelist Rodney Howard-Browne, whose meetings were demonstrating amazing signs and wonders.

The Arnotts invited Clark to Toronto. He came, and on January 29, 1994, the Toronto Airport Vineyard Church experienced a Holy Spirit explosion of astonishing signs and wonders. Clark stayed for two months. The word spread worldwide quickly and, in the years following, millions of people from many nations crowded into the meetings at the church. Many carried the revival fire back to their homelands. After English churches were mightily benefited, a London newspaper labeled the phenomenon the "Toronto Blessing." Impact from the revival was so great that the Canadian board of tourism included the church on its list of major attractions.

In the mid-1990s, a conflict arose when Vineyard leaders criticized some of the manifestations at the Toronto fellowship—such as holy laughter—as excessive, even false. When the conflict could not be resolved, the Toronto congregation was dropped from the Vineyard constellation of fellowships. Renamed Toronto Airport Christian Fellowship, it experienced even greater power and international acclaim. Today, known internationally as Catch the Fire Toronto, the church continues its worldwide ministry with an ever-expanding impact.

207. What Is Holy Trinity, Brompton?

In 1994, the Toronto Blessing impacted Holy Trinity Anglican Church, Brompton, when its clergy visited Toronto and returned to London with the Holy Spirit's anointing upon them. The centuries-old building was suddenly invaded by the power of God and scores of sophisticated

Anglicans found themselves lying on the church floor, exploding into riotous laughter. Millions of Anglican believers around the world have since experienced renewal. One of HTB's greatest contributions has been its Alpha Course discipleship training program, which has impacted millions in many nations.

208. What Is the Brownsville Revival?

In 1995, Steve Hill, an American evangelist, had just returned to the U.S. from London, where he had received the Toronto Blessing from the vicar at Holy Trinity Anglican Church, Brompton. Invited as guest speaker at Brownsville Assembly in Pensacola, Florida, his ministry ignited revival. Signs, wonders and mighty deeds were present in every service. This revival, which lasted about four years, was attended by more than four million people and had an impact on churches around the world. More than a hundred thousand people were saved.

209. What Is the China Revival?

It is estimated that every day some thirty thousand people in Mainland China become Christian. Before understanding the significance of that conversion rate and China's "House Church" movement, it is important to know the spiritual background of its national leadership. Generalissimo Chiang Kai-shek (1887–1975) was the first Christian Premier of the Republic of China. Turning his back on centuries of Buddhism, he accepted Christ and was baptized in 1929. Chiang ruled from 1928 to 1949, his goal being the conversion of all Chinese and the nation's complete salvation.

In the Communist capture of Mainland China, he was forced to flee to Taiwan. Thousands of believers were executed or imprisoned. During that time, Chiang wrote in his diary that he feared it was his sins that brought such horrific suffering upon the people. For this he was deeply repentant, asking God's forgiveness for himself and grace upon the nation. His wife, Soong May-ling, a strong believer and prayer warrior, supported him in intercession for the nation's salvation. She had been educated at Wesleyan College in Macon, Georgia. Chiang Kai-shek and his wife lost the political war but won the spiritual victory. Scripture explains that when the Holy Spirit's anointing is on the head, it automatically flows down to the bottom of the garment (see Psalm 133:2).

The Chinese house church movement is very similar to the first-century spread of underground Christianity across the Roman Empire. There are no Bible schools, no political hierarchy, no communication system except word of mouth, and many congregations have no Bibles. This forces total reliance on the Holy Spirit. The result is that these churches are Spirit-filled, experiencing signs and wonders and possessing great converting power. When possible, their meetings last all night or hours on end. Purdue University's Chen Yang research center estimates that China could have a Christian population of 160 million by 2025 and 247 million by 2032. While the world watches, the Holy Spirit is doing a work in China that military weapons cannot stop.

210. What Is the Persecution of Christians?

Every year, 150,000 Christians are martyred for their faith. Many are beheaded, and some—including children—are crucified. Worldwide, an estimated one hundred million more are persecuted in equally horrific ways. Christian women and girls are raped, sold into slavery. Others disappear and are never seen again. Of the top fifty oppressing countries, 49 are in Africa, Asia and the Middle East. More than 65 countries are actively persecuting disciples of Jesus. Many believers have no protection from local authorities, and sharia law has no mercy for non-Muslims. The top ten countries noted for persecution are North Korea, Saudi Arabia, Afghanistan, Iraq, Somalia, Maldives, Mali, Iran, Yemen and Eritrea. Of these ten nations, eight are Islamic. Since May 2014, India's government has been controlled by a Hindu Party under the leadership of Prime Minister Narendra Modi. With his support radical Hinduism has increased and intolerance risen significantly. Hindu fundamentalists, for example, raided a church in central India during its Sunday worship, captured the pastor and his seven-month pregnant wife, threw gasoline on them and tried to set them ablaze. Even in America, intolerance for Christians is growing.

PART 15

Who Were Significant People in Church History?

211. Who Were the Early Church Fathers?

Beginning with the apostles, the early Church was blessed with numerous men and women who served the Kingdom of God bravely and suffered martyrdom for Jesus Christ. It was a saying in Rome that when one Christian died in the Coliseum, ten new ones left the grandstand. These early Church fathers and mothers sealed their testimony with their blood. Their ministry was not free from mistakes, but their noble example and love for Christ speak powerfully to us today. Some of these ancient individuals we salute are:

Clement (?–99), Bishop of Rome, was a preacher and Christian writer whose only surviving document is his letter to the Corinthians, which was read in churches for several centuries after his death.

Ignatius (c. 35–c. 108), Bishop of Antioch, was a student of the apostle John, writer of Christian theology, and a martyr in Rome where he was fed to wild beasts.

Polycarp (70–c. 155), Bishop of Smyrna, a writer famous for his holiness teachings, was a pupil of the apostle John and, thus, connected to the apostolic era and the period following their deaths.

Justin Martyr (100–165), a pagan reared in Jewish surroundings, became a disciple of Jesus in 132, and one of the most important Greek-Christian philosopher-theologians in the early Church.

Irenaeus (122–c. 202) heard the preaching of Polycarp, who as a young man followed the apostle John, and wrote the *Refutation of Heresies*, a defense of orthodox Christianity against Gnosticism.

Clement (150–215), Bishop of Alexandria, a Greek theologian, was born in Athens, traveled widely, converted to Christianity and taught Origen at the catechetical school in Alexandria, Egypt, until the persecution of 202 drove him out.

Tertullian (c. 160–c. 220) was a strong defender of the doctrine of the Holy Trinity and one of the most prodigious writers of early Christianity.

Origen (c. 185–c. 254), a controversial preacher, is famous today as one of the most important early Church fathers. He was an encourager of martyrs for whom he frequently risked his life. In his old age he was severely tortured by Emperor Decius; though set free upon the emperor's death, his health was broken and he died shortly thereafter.

Novatian (c. 200–258), assumed a martyr, was a scholar, pastor, noted theologian and writer in Rome who was excommunicated for opposing the papal-trend he saw developing and for allowing a movement of Novatian churches to develop under him.

Eusebius of Caesarea (263–339), earliest of Christian historians in the early fourth century, was contemporary with Emperor Constantine and present at the Council of Nicaea, where his confession became the basis for the Nicene Creed.

Hilary of Poitiers (c. 315–368), a resident of France, was raised a pagan, converted to Christ through the Scriptures, and became a champion defender of the doctrine of the Trinity and an opponent of Arianism, but came into disfavor with Emperor Constantine and was banished from France for a time.

Athanasius (298–373), Archbishop of Alexandria, and contemporary with Emperor Constantine, withstood the Arian controversy and became famous in AD 367 for canonizing the New Testament.

Ambrose (c. 339–397), Bishop of Milan, whose literary works are still regarded as masterpieces of Latin composition, is best remembered as the teacher who converted and baptized Augustine of Hippo.

Jerome (347–420) was born in Slovenia and educated in Rome, where he spent much time in the catacombs. He later translated the Hebrew and Greek Testaments into the Latin Bible—the Vulgate translation—and is acknowledged as one of the most important scholars of early Christianity.

Augustine (354–430), Bishop of Hippo in North Africa, philosopher-theologian, voluminous author (including *Confessions* and *The City of God*), and defender of doctrines of grace is one of the most significant Church fathers in Western Christianity.

Cyril (375–444), Bishop of Alexandria, was a positive influence in the doctrinal struggles in the fifth century when Nestorius, Archbishop of Constantinople, introduced controversial views about the nature of Christ.

212. Who Was Flavius Josephus?

Titus "Flavius" Josephus (37–100) was a Jew who led the Galilean troops against the Roman invasion of AD 63 and witnessed personally the burning of Jerusalem, destruction of the Temple and enslavement of his countrymen, which he recorded in great detail. He became a Roman citizen and friend of the Flavian dynasty. Moving to Rome, he wrote three outstanding works: *The First Jewish-Roman War*, which includes the siege of Masada, *The Jewish War* and *Antiquities of the Jews*. Later he was given a home in conquered Judea, and lived lavishly among the ashes of his people.

213. Who Was Constantine the Great?

Roman Emperor Constantine (272–337) was a strong administrator; some of his financial alterations influenced European banking for the next thousand years. With the "Edict of Milan" in 313, he (as leader of the West) along with Licinius (leader of the East) gave full legal recognition to Christianity, thus ending persecution of Christians throughout the Roman Empire. He won in battle the sole rulership of both East and West by 324. In 325, he called for a meeting of Christian bishops at Nicaea, in present-day Turkey, to quell heretical Arian teachings. It was from this council that the Nicene Creed was composed and became the standard for Christian Orthodoxy. Moving his residence from Rome to Byzantium, he renamed the city Constantinople and erected an image of himself holding a pagan goddess in his hand. His mother, Helena, converted to Christianity, visited the Holy Land and built shrines on historic sites. Constantine continued pagan practices, though he was baptized as a Christian shortly before his death.

214. Who Was Thomas Beckett?

Every tour group visiting Canterbury Cathedral in England today is taken to the spot where Thomas Beckett (1118–1170), Archbishop of Canterbury, was murdered on December 29, 1170. Beckett had refused to surrender Church principle to King Henry II. On order from Henry, four knights in armor rushed into the Cathedral, fell upon the defenseless man and cut him to the floor. Today Beckett is venerated as a saint and martyr by both Catholic and Anglican churches. One of Beckett's greatest gifts to humanity was his example of faith and courage. He would not sacrifice principle in return for the king's favors. Beckett proved his devotion to God by sealing it with his blood.

215. Who Was Thomas Aquinas?

Thomas Aquinas (1225–1274), who became one of the Catholic Church's greatest philosopher-theologians, was regarded in his youth to be mentally slow. Once when other students ridiculed him, Dominican scholar Albertus Magnus yelled at them: "You call him the dumb ox, but in his teaching he will one day produce such a bellowing that it will be heard around the world." That prophetic word came to pass. As Aquinas matured, the prowess of his mind seemed endless. Discovering Aristotle's philosophy, he absorbed the concepts, which became his own tools in communicating Bible truth. Aquinas proved himself a master theologian, teaching Old and New Testament principles in university classrooms and through his numerous books. His *Summa Theologica* is regarded as one of literature's greatest works. Today he is revered as both a doctor and saint.

216. Who Was John Wycliffe?

John Wycliffe (c. 1320–1384), English Catholic priest, University of Oxford professor, scholar and lover of Scripture, was an influential voice protesting abuses within the British Church during the fourteenth century. He is still remembered as England's "Morning Star" of the Reformation. Wycliffe became devoted to the grace teachings of Paul, embracing the same doctrines that later became prominent in the Protestant Reformation. His followers were known as Lollards. In 1382, Wycliffe, working with others, published his famous English language translation of the Bible.

217. Who Was Johannes Gutenberg?

In 1450, Johannes Gutenberg (c. 1395–1468), a German publisher and blacksmith who worked with gold and other metals, devised the world's first practical, moveable-type printing press. Five years later, he published 180 copies of the Bible, providing Renaissance Europe with copies of the book that fired the Protestant Reformation. Historians consider his press to be the greatest innovation of the millennium. Gutenberg provided for the wide dissemination of learning in every area of human concern—science, religion, economics, medicine, literature. Within a hundred years, his practical, economical press system that allowed mass production of books had revolutionized the world.

218. Who Was William Tyndale?

William Tyndale (1494–1536) was an English priest and scholar whose single influence changed the British Isles. Desiring to share the Good News of justification by faith, Tyndale gave England its first Bible translated directly from the Hebrew and Greek texts. Tyndale's success was followed by a death sentence. Only 42 years old, in 1536, he was convicted of heresy and executed by strangulation. His body was burned at the stake. Tyndale's dying prayer was, "God! Open the King of England's eyes!" Two years later, King Henry VIII authorized the Great Bible for the Church of England, which was primarily Tyndale's translation. God heard and answered.

219. Who Was Martin Luther?

Martin Luther (1483–1546), a professor of theology, was an Augustinian friar at the Castle Church in Wittenberg, Germany. In 1516, a papal commissioner arrived to raise money for St. Peter's Basilica in Rome by selling "indulgences for sin," offering to forgive transgressions and release loved ones from purgatory for the right amount of cash. This enraged Luther, who protested by nailing a list of 95 theological complaints to the church door. Among other objections, Luther insisted that salvation comes not through money or good deeds but only as a free gift of God's grace through faith in Jesus Christ. Word spread quickly and reactions grew violent. With that the Protestant Reformation was born.

220. Who Was John Calvin?

John Calvin (1509–1564), a former Catholic who joined the Reformation movement, was an influential French theologian, writer and pastor. Calvin was influenced by Augustinian theology, which emphasizes the doctrine of predestination and the absolute sovereignty of God. When a violent uprising surged against Protestants in France, Calvin fled to Geneva, Switzerland, where, ultimately, he introduced new forms of Church government and liturgy. Calvin's writing gave birth to the branch of theology that bears his name today: "Calvinism." Reformed, Congregational and Presbyterian churches regard him as the chief expositor of their doctrinal beliefs.

221. Who Was John Knox?

John Knox (1514–1572), a Scottish clergyman and leader in the Protestant Reformation, joined a movement to reform the Scottish Church. Unfortunately caught up in events surrounding the murder of Cardinal Beaton in 1546, Knox was arrested by French forces and exiled to England where he served in the Church of England. Forced to leave when Roman Catholic Mary Tudor ascended the throne, he traveled to Geneva where he met John Calvin, from whom he gained knowledge of Reformed theology. Knox's new liturgy of worship was adopted by the Reformed Church in Scotland. He is considered to be the founder of the Presbyterian denomination there.

222. Who Was King James?

King James I (1566–1625), a native Scot, came to the English throne in 1603 when the nation was in the midst of fiery dissension between Puritans and Anglicans, as well as between Catholics and Protestants. In January 1604, he ordered a meeting of English scholars and laid the groundwork for the publishing of a new Bible. The idea was opposed by the majority of Church of England clergymen. Even so, seven years later, as a result of the work of 54 of England's best biblical scholars, the King James Bible was presented to the world. More than one billion copies of this translation have been printed.

223. Who Was Count von Zinzendorf?

Nikolaus Ludwig (1700–1760), Count von Zinzendorf, offered asylum on his estate in Saxony, Germany, to a group of Moravian families and other non-conformists fleeing persecution. This Lutheran settlement would grow into the Moravian Church. Encouraging community living, the young von Zinzendorf encouraged covenant agreement to seek the Lord in travailing prayer. One morning, the Holy Spirit fell upon the worship in such shattering force that men in the fields ten miles away were stricken by it. Children began a prayer meeting that continued

SPIRIT-EMPOWERED THEOLOGY

nonstop, night and day, for more than one hundred years and supplied the world's mission field with tireless and devoted workers.

224. Who Was Jonathan Edwards?

Jonathan Edwards (1703–1758) was a New England pastor whose historic sermon, "Sinners in the Hands of an Angry God," swept a "signs and wonders" revival into Northampton, Massachusetts, and later the nation. The Holy Spirit fell in such power that wild shouting filled the building. Some collapsed to the church floor and remained motionless for hours, while others clung to trees in the churchyard groaning and weeping noisily. Edwards wrote, "I was forced to break off my sermon before done, the outcry was so great." The Great Awakening, of which the Northampton revival was an opening part, was one of the most important spiritual events in the history of North America.

225. Who Was George Whitefield?

George Whitefield (1714–1770) was an Anglican priest and evangelist instrumental in the Great Awakening in Britain and the American colonies. At Oxford University he met John and Charles Wesley, joined the "Holy Club" and became one of the founders of Methodism. Over a nine-year period he made seven trips to the Colonies and became one of the most widely recognized public figures in America. His ministry was accompanied with astonishing "signs and wonders." At Boston he refused to preach until people in the trees had come down. He knew many would drop to the ground like stones once the power of God came upon the congregation.

226. Who Were John and Charles Wesley?

John Wesley (1703–1791) and his brother Charles (1707–1788) were Anglican priests whose fiery ministry shook England and America. Through their labors with fellow cleric George Whitefield, the Methodist Church was born. These men were greatly anointed with the Holy Spirit's power and impacted the world with a fresh wind of evangelism. After a failed ministry to the Indians in the Georgia Colony, John returned to London and joined a religious society led by Moravian Christians. It was here he felt his heart "strangely warmed" and realized he had been truly born again. John, a prolific author, became famous for his preaching while Charles became one of the world's greatest hymn writers. Sadly, the United Methodist Church today expresses little interest in the miraculous ministry of these men.

227. Who Was William Wilberforce?

William Wilberforce (1759–1833) was a widely respected Englishman, member of Parliament, philanthropist and public figure. In 1787, Wilberforce joined the anti-slave movement and became a dominant figure for the abolition of the slave trade in Britain. By the late 1700s, 80 percent of Britain's foreign income was dependent on the practice. In some years British ships carried as many as forty thousand Africans across the Atlantic. In 1833, Parliament finally passed the Slavery Abolition Act, and three days later, after hearing the news, Wilberforce died. He was buried in Westminster Abbey.

228. Who Was Charles Spurgeon?

Charles H. Spurgeon (1834–1892) was a British Particular Baptist preacher who became known as the "Prince of Preachers." A prolific author, he served the Metropolitan Tabernacle in London for 38 years. Even today his messages are acknowledged as some of the best in Christian literature.

229. Who Was Dwight L. Moody?

Dwight L. Moody (1837–1899), connected with the Holiness Movement, was never ordained and had no schooling beyond the fifth grade. His best job was as a shoe salesman. But in 1855, in a spectacular work of God, he was not only born again but simultaneously called to the ministry and began witnessing to people on the street. When the Great Chicago Fire in 1871 destroyed Moody's mission church and home, he locked himself in a room to pray. Soon afterward he felt a "presence and power" come upon him. It is apparent that Moody was baptized with the Holy Spirit. It is estimated that in his lifetime he led as many as one million people to Christ.

230. Who Was William Booth?

God challenged an ordinary Englishman, William Booth (1829–1912), to walk away from religious tradition and experiment with an idea that was destined to bless people around the world. He obeyed and the result was The Salvation Army. Booth, a Methodist minister who was eventually banned from Methodism, took his message to the back streets of London. Even while feeding the homeless, he was stoned by people who distrusted him and hated his message of Jesus. In 1865 he established the "Army." Booth was the first general and served with his wife, Catherine, and nine children beside him. Today, his Army ministers to the homeless, refugees, addicts, prisoners, children, elderly and many more in nations around the world.

231. Who Was William J. Seymour?

William J. Seymour (1870–1922) was a 34-year-old minister, son of former slaves, who became God's spokesman for one of the greatest spiritual awakenings of all time. He arrived in Los Angeles on February 22, 1906, to preach with Charles Parham, but two days later was padlocked out of the building. He then preached from porches, finally being given a site on Azusa Street. It was at this Apostolic Faith Mission that the Holy Spirit fell in a manner reminiscent of the Upper Room and set afire the worldwide Pentecostal Movement, changing the course of Church history. Today one of every four Christians claims to have been filled with the Holy Spirit.

232. Who Was Charles Parham?

Charles F. Parham (1873–1929) is known affectionately today as the father of the Pentecostal Movement. As a teenager, Parham had been miraculously healed and called into ministry. It was he who accompanied William J. Seymour to Los Angeles, and was a principal part of the 1906 Azusa Street Revival. His understanding of glossolalia as evidence

SPIRIT-EMPOWERED THEOLOGY

of baptism with the Spirit had enormous impact on his ministry. Miraculous healing, tongues, signs and wonders were the hallmark of the revival that went around the world.

233. Who Was John G. Lake?

John G. Lake (1870–1935), a Canadian-American, was the first Pentecostal missionary in South Africa, where his labors are thriving today. Lake was born into a poor family of sixteen siblings and tried to hide his lack of formal education. He is best remembered as the 1914 founder of the Healing Rooms movement in Spokane, Washington. In 1999, the movement was reopened in that same city by Cal Pierce under a new organization. Today there are more than two thousand healing rooms across America and in 58 foreign nations. Several are in Israel. Lake's ministry was greatly influenced by the healing work of John Alexander Dowie and Charles Parham.

234. Who Was Aimee Semple McPherson?

Aimee Semple McPherson (1890–1944), whose "healing evangelist" ministry was characterized by wonders, was indeed a wonder in her own right, known for her dynamic platform presence and anointed preaching. In 1919, she held a series of meetings in Los Angeles and shot to national fame. Founding the International Church of the Foursquare Gospel, she preached that Jesus was the "Only Savior, the Great Physician, the Baptizer with the Holy Spirit and the Coming Bridegroom." She helped establish the Pentecostal Movement upon a clearer, more

280

effective foundation for its continued growth. Today there are some thirty thousand Foursquare churches worldwide.

235. Who Was Carrie Judd Montgomery?

Carrie Judd Montgomery (1858–1946) grew up in a family of Episcopalians in Buffalo, New York, and from early childhood suffered from severe illnesses, including a spinal disease that made the slightest touch on her body unbearable. Hearing the testimony of another woman who was healed through faith and prayer, she resolved to pray, get out of bed and walk. In a short time she was completely healed and had experienced the baptism with the Spirit. She opened a "healing home" in Buffalo, where she could receive people who desired prayer, which was a model throughout the country. A bridge between evangelicals and Pentecostals, her writing, teaching and preaching on the healing movement had great impact.

236. Who Was Smith Wigglesworth?

Smith Wigglesworth (1859–1947) was born into an impoverished though churchgoing English family. He was born again at age eight. In 1907, Smith fell under the power of God and received the baptism with the Holy Spirit. Referred to as "the Apostle of Faith," he was a pioneer within the Pentecostal revival. He began to see miracles as the glory of God fell upon his congregations. He received ministerial credentials with the Assemblies of God in the U.S. and had an international ministry. In 1938, while holding a revival for David du Plessis, he received a prophetic message that God was going to bring revival to mainline denominational churches.

237. Who Was Evan Roberts?

Evan John Roberts (1878–1951) was the primary voice in the Welsh Revival of 1904–1905. Roberts was widely known as a man of prayer. The first sign of revival began at Moriah Chapel and quickly spread across Wales, going into England, Ireland and Scotland. Within six months, one hundred thousand had been converted. A strong conviction of sin and deep yearning for the presence of God lay upon the meetings. The revival burned brightly for two years. Unfortunately, Evans allowed himself to be dominated by others, including his friend and confidant, Jessie Penn-Lewis, who convinced him to step down and allow others to exercise leadership. The power of God lifted and the revival faded away.

238. Who Was Pope John XXIII?

Pope John XXIII, born Angelo Giuseppe Roncalli (1881–1963), was a man beloved by Catholics, Protestants, Jews and people of other faiths worldwide. When the First World War began, he left his religious studies to become a medical orderly and care for the wounded. During the Second World War, then an archbishop, he rescued thousands of Jews fleeing the Nazi Holocaust by forging visas and other paperwork. For this, the International Raoul Wallenberg Foundation nominated him as one of the "Righteous Among Nations." During the Cuban Missile Crisis between the U.S. and Russia (October 16–28, 1962), it is believed that Pope John's appeal to Nikita Khrushchev over Vatican Radio helped rescue mankind from disaster.

239. Who Was A.W. Tozer?

Aiden Wilson Tozer (1897–1963) was an American pastor in the Christian and Missionary Alliance who was chiefly known for the revelation depth of his writing, reaching a reader's inner self with just a few lines of print. Seemingly, Tozer could pull back the veil and allow the person to recognize truths he had never seen before. Aiden grew up in poverty in Akron, Ohio. Five years after his conversion and without theological schooling he became pastor of a C&MA congregation. His pastoral ministry lasted 44 years during which time he lived simply, shunning public applause.

240. Who Was William Branham?

William Branham (1909–1965) was born in a log cabin in Cumberland County, Kentucky, the oldest of ten siblings in an impoverished family. Branham claimed that from early childhood he had visions and prophetic dreams. Ordained as an Independent Baptist minister, he became aware of Pentecostalism, opened tent revivals and gained acclaim as a faith healer, initiating the modern healing revival. Branham would frequently identify a person's illness before being told what the problem was.

241. Who Was Gordon Lindsay?

James Gordon Lindsay (1906–1973), born in Zion, Illinois, is best remembered as founder of Christ for the Nations Institute in Dallas,

Texas, and publisher of the *Voice of Healing* magazine. The school has been a significant training site and launching pad for numerous Full Gospel ministries around the world. As a child, Lindsay was converted under the preaching of Charles Parham, one of the evangelists involved in the 1906 Azusa Street revival. John G. Lake and William Branham were also strong influences in Lindsay's life.

242. Who Was Kathryn Kuhlman?

Kathryn Kuhlman (1907–1976) began her ministry at age fourteen, telling Idaho farmers about her experience of being born again in the local Methodist church. In her twenties, Kuhlman began traveling as an evangelist. While she was preaching about the Holy Spirit in the old Billy Sunday Tabernacle in Franklin, Pennsylvania, a woman exclaimed that a tumor in her body had disappeared. That first healing was quickly followed by others. In time, many thousands more healings occurred, and Kathryn was catapulted into international fame. Criticism of her theatrical style and her private crises were unable to stop her. Television and radio carried her broadcasts across all of North America, and she left a legacy of anointed teaching.

243. Who Was Corrie ten Boom?

Cornelia "Corrie" ten Boom (1892–1983) was a Spirit-filled Dutch Christian whose family helped Jews escape the Nazi Holocaust during World War II. On the top floor of their house behind a false wall, the Ten Boom family built a secret room. The "hiding place" was about thirty inches deep. When Nazis raided the house in 1944, six Jews were in hiding.

They and the Ten Boom family were arrested and sent to concentration camps. Though Corrie survived Ravensbruck, her father and one sister died there. When the war ended, Corrie traveled the world, telling her story of forgiveness. It is estimated the Ten Boom family and others in the Dutch Underground helped rescue eight hundred Jews.

244. Who Was David du Plessis?

David du Plessis (1905–1987) was born to missionary parents in South Africa and ordained by the Apostolic Faith Mission. While hosting a revival in 1938 with Smith Wigglesworth as evangelist, Wigglesworth prophesied to him that God was going to visit the mainline denominational churches with Holy Spirit renewal. Further, Du Plessis would become a main spokesman for the movement. Though shocked, both believed the word and waited for its fulfillment. Du Plessis became an active supporter of ecumenism, beginning in the 1950s to share the Pentecostal experience with Christians in the historic denominations, chiefly Roman Catholicism. In 1960, renewal hit the mainline churches. The ministry of "Mr. Pentecost" had worldwide impact.

245. Who Was Dennis Bennett?

Dennis Bennett (1917–1991) was rector at St. Mark's Episcopal Church, Van Nuys, California. On April 3, 1960, he told his congregation that he had been baptized with the Holy Spirit and spoken in tongues. Immediately, angry shouting broke out. Members began yelling, "Throw the damned tongue-talker out!" Being forced to resign, he did so shortly after. Strangely, the news went nationwide. In a short time every denomination seemed pulled into the clash as pastors and laymen alike experienced baptism with the Spirit: charismatic congregants were told to leave; ordinations were cancelled; ministers were barred from their pulpits; church bulletins carried announcements that members who believed in the Holy Spirit's miraculous gifts or spoke in tongues should go elsewhere. Dennis Bennett soon became a key leader among charismatic believers internationally.

246. Who Was Lester Sumrall?

Lester Frank Sumrall (1913–1996) was an American Pentecostal pastor and evangelist who began preaching at the age of seventeen after God miraculously healed him of tuberculosis. Two years later, he founded a church in Green Forest, Arkansas, and was ordained by the Assemblies of God, from which he later withdrew. He began traveling abroad, established churches and a Bible college (later Indiana Christian University) and raised up a humanitarian aid organization to feed the hungry. Sumrall became known as the "father of Christian television."

247. Who Was John Wimber?

John Wimber (1934–1997) grew up in a non-Christian family. At age 34, as a well-known secular musician, he had a dramatic conversion to Christ. The Holy Spirit began an immediate work of transformation in him, imparting revelation, empowerment and an amazing ability to communicate biblical concepts. Wimber helped to mainstream the charismatic renewal and, with C. Peter Wagner, to identify a "Third Wave" of spiritual restoration. Wimber had joined the Vineyard Christian

Fellowship, a young charismatic denomination, and by the time of his death had become its international director. He also joined the staff at Fuller Theological Seminary as founding director of the Department of Church Growth. Wimber became a popular conference speaker with healing, signs and wonders done publicly before astonished congregations.

248. Who Was Derek Prince?

Derek Prince (1915–2003) was born in Bangalore, India, to British military parents. At age five, he was sent home to England to be educated, and at age thirteen was elected a King's Scholar at Eton, King's College, Cambridge, where he excelled in Greek and Latin. Here he later taught Platonian philosophy from the original Greek. After entering military service in World War II, he was saved in a Pentecostal church, and two weeks later in his army barrack experienced a dramatic filling of the Holy Spirit. After the war his ministry grew phenomenally. Through his astute scholarship and the Holy Spirit's anointing, he became a world-renowned Bible teacher. Foremost in the field of deliverance ministry, he helped introduce the concept into evangelical and charismatic churches.

249. Who Is Billy Graham?

Billy Graham (1918–), a Southern Baptist minister born near Charlotte, North Carolina, became an evangelist loved the world over. He stepped into national prominence in 1947 when he began holding evangelistic crusades across America. These crusades, many of them telecast, filled stadiums and brought thousands of new converts to Christ. Graham was welcomed to the White House, and several presidents became his close friends. Graham also hosted a popular radio broadcast called *The Hour of Decision*. It is estimated that he preached the Gospel to more than 2.2 billion people—more people than anyone else in Christian history. He is now in retirement in North Carolina.

PART 16

What about Scientists and Scripture?

250. Is Evolution a Valid Explanation for the Origin of Life?

The biggest conflict today between modern science and the Bible swirls about the origin of life. The theory of evolution claims that a single bacteria-like water-borne organism descended by chance over millions of years into the life-forms on earth today. That the elephant and the gnat buzzing around its eye both evolved from the same source. The Bible explains that God simply spoke and all life (except humans) came into being. God took a few extra steps with humans, but He still worked in instantaneous fashion.

These are vastly different accounts. Those who believe that science is the only trustworthy authority conclude that the Bible account is fable—it is simply an interesting myth that early peoples used to explain what they could not understand. They feel justified in knocking the Bible from its platform of inerrancy because of the "overwhelming evidence" in favor of evolution. After all, the vast majority of scientists in many disciplines believe it; fossils and bones give us glimpses of marvelous creatures that existed in the past; and nearly every public school biology textbook presents the fundamental concepts of evolution as fact. Then again, scientists once believed that blood was stationary in the body and that the sun revolved around the earth—that is to say, scientists have been known to be wrong.

Is evolution really supported by enough scientific evidence to make it more credible than the Bible's account of Creation?

Creationists offer a compelling answer to that question by considering evolution in conjunction with the scientific method of study. The scientific method of study, which is used in all scientific disciplines, is simply the gathering of data with the least bias possible. A researcher asks a question and then conducts experiments in hopes of answering it. If the same results come from the same experiments over and over again, then the researcher has confidence that those results are sound and can draw certain conclusions. The more experiments, the more conclusions. The more conclusions, the more we know about our world.

The significant problem with evolution is that it is impossible to run any experiments on the origins of life. Our beginnings are historical; they happened before people were around to observe them.

Since scientists cannot observe evolution in a lab—impossible for something they believe took millions of years—they lose the great safeguard of the scientific method: its protection against bias. Remove the experiment from the scientific method and you no longer have the scientific method. Instead, one runs the risk of coming to conclusions that align with one's own beliefs. And if, as a Cornell University survey shows, 87 percent of evolutionary biologists do not believe in God, what conclusions are they likely to draw?

But if we cannot use the scientific method to determine how life began, where do we turn? We look to the biblical record as a historical document—the same way we look to Homer's *Iliad* for information about what happened in the ancient city of Troy. We trust the Bible's authors the same way we trust any historian. And if we do, we will find many clues about our beginnings.

As Christians we are grateful for scientific study, appreciating the many benefits it provides us. But science changes; the Word does not. We do not need to try to reconcile claims that conflict with Scripture. We can trust the Bible's unerring explanations.

Be assured: The Bible stands!

251. What Is Intelligent Design?

Perhaps the most robust opponent of the theory of evolution is the concept known as intelligent design, which says, simply, that biological life is too wonderfully constructed to have developed accidentally. By contrast, evolution suggests that organisms develop new structures by random (accidental) mutations in their DNA; some of these structures are harmful to the organism, while other structures are beneficial and make the organism more likely to survive and reproduce. Over millions of years, the theory goes, enough new structures accumulate in a species to allow it to evolve into a new species.

But think, for a moment, about the many interdependent parts that make up the structure of just a single cell. If evolution were true, each one of the parts of a cell would have to evolve into being purely by accident from its own gene. And yet unless all the parts evolved together in perfectly synchronized fashion, the structure would fail.

In the book *Darwin's Black Box*, author Michael Behe uses the mousetrap to explain why this random mutation of parts all developing along together is not possible. A mousetrap is a simple machine with only a few parts. It is simpler in construction than a single human brain cell. As simple as the mousetrap is, (1) it is still *complex* in that it requires the working together of multiple parts in order to function, and (2) its complexity is *irreducible*—the mousetrap is the *least* complex it can possibly be. It cannot be made any more simple. Without a trigger, for instance, the mousetrap would never release the spring. Without the platform, none of the parts would hold together.

Organisms are full of structures that are "irreducibly complex" (a term that Behe coined). And this is the nail in evolution's coffin. Evolution depends on random genetic mutations to work. More than that, evolution depends on many such random genetic mutations to happen *all at once*; the structures cannot be built piece by piece, because a partially built structure (like a mousetrap without the spring), according to evolution itself, would likely die before the organism could pass that partially built structure to its offspring for remodeling.

The theory of intelligent design is a way of explaining irreducible complexity. It presupposes that a designer who was intelligent specially created life structures to function and produce offspring like themselves. While science is not able to shed light on who the intelligent designer is, life—even at the bacterial level—requires that there be an intelligent designer, which is fully compatible with Christian belief in a creator God who designed the entire universe.

252. How Does the Human Body's Design Challenge the Evolutionist?

The human body functions like a well-oiled machine. Consider the brain. Scientists have yet to decipher it. The brain is composed of approximately 86 billion nerve cells, each with branches that connect to other nerve cells, creating a vast web of cells that can communicate with the body. When a person senses danger, for instance, the brain coordinates a number of responses, including an increased heart rate and respiratory rate, and the movement of more oxygenated blood to the larger muscles that might need to move quickly. All of these responses happen almost instantly and without the person's conscious participation.

The entire human body could be reconstructed from the genetic information stored in just one cell. The DNA in that cell, if stretched in one unbroken length, would be almost six and a half feet long. The human body contains an estimated 37 *trillion* cells, producing enough DNA to reach from earth to Pluto more than seventeen times. Every time the body forms a new cell, it makes a copy of its DNA, and to do so it must precisely copy the DNA's "code," which is made up of three billion base pairs. The cell also produces proteins that "proofread" the DNA after it has been copied—and repair incorrect base pairs! The random genetic mutations that drive evolution are insufficient for producing systems with this many interworking parts.

This is but a tiny fraction of the wonderful mechanisms in the human body. While these do not disprove evolution per se, their amazing complexity and massive number do cause a reasonable person to question how the human body could possibly have evolved by chance when it so obviously has been designed. And humanity is only part of the picture, as there are millions of species of living things on earth, each with its own distinctive genetic code. In the presence of such overwhelming evidence of life's miraculous design, the claim of accidental evolution reaches into the realm of absurdity.

253. What Are the Odds That Evolution Could Produce Life?

Among the hurdles the theory of evolution must leap is the probability that the molecules necessary for life formed randomly. Take a simple protein. Science tells us that a typical size for that protein is about three hundred amino acids. For the protein to work properly, all three hundred amino acids need to be assembled in the proper order. The odds for this happening are about 1 in 10^{300}, a number so small as to be inconceivable.

Evolutionists' response to this is twofold. First, they argue that it is impossible to calculate this kind of probability because we do not know all of the environmental factors that went into assembling the first proteins. This is certainly true, but it also sounds like a refusal to answer the question. If evolutionists are so certain of the random origin of life as to claim that it is overwhelmingly proved by scientific evidence, then it is fair to expect that they be similarly certain of that early evidence.

Second, they argue that, in laboratory experiments, simple life-essential molecules have been synthesized and shown to act in ways that represent basic molecular functions. This attempt to answer the question has problems of its own. For one thing, in the laboratory, *these molecules did not appear randomly.* They were formed by scientists investigating their theories under ideal conditions for producing these molecules—and, frankly, nobody knows if these conditions actually existed in the early earth. An evolutionist might argue that the scientists were simulating natural selection, that their actions in the laboratory "selected for" the molecules that could support life. This was hardly random, however; it was intentional.

For another thing, the creation of life-essential molecules in a laboratory does not solve the problem presented by "irreducible complexity" (see "What Is Intelligent Design?"), for even the simplest life-form has multiple parts that must function together. This makes the odds much lower. And they conclude further that many millions of combinations were being formed constantly over a very long period of time. And add to that the lack of evidence that these life-essential molecules ever existed. They do not exist today, and we have no proof that they ever did.

Once again, evolution cannot be observed according to the scientific method, and scientists are reduced to drawing conclusions that are almost certainly governed by their opinions on the matter before they started.

The emergence of life through natural selection depends on a series of coincidences that are mathematically impossible. The odds of random development of life run against all sensible claims.

254. What Is the Big Bang Theory?

Christians who believe in the biblical account of Creation have always acknowledged that the universe had a beginning, a single point in time: In the beginning, God created the heavens and the earth. Scientists, influenced by the "age of reason" and who were not disposed to trust the Bible, contended for several hundred years that the universe had always existed and was essentially static.

In the first third of the twentieth century, new research indicated that this view of a static universe, the "steady state" theory, was incorrect. A Belgian priest with a doctorate in physics, Georges Lemâitre, applied Einstein's equations of general relativity to his research, and discovered that the universe could not be static; rather it must be either stretching or shrinking. In 1929, astronomer Edwin Hubble confirmed Lemâitre's conclusions by observing that the universe is, in fact, expanding, and at such a rate as to give rise to the likelihood that it "exploded" into being from a very small, fixed point in the past.

This distressed scientists who wanted to believe that the universe had "always been." That it had a sudden birth and fixed age sounded much like the Bible's account of Creation. Einstein himself thought Lemâitre had gone too far and resisted Lemâitre's conclusions until Hubble's observations confirmed them. In the middle of the century, astrophysicist Fred Hoyle, a proponent of the steady state idea, gave the new theory the (derogatory, he thought) name "Big Bang." Evidence for the Big Bang grew, however, and now it is considered to be the most likely explanation.

In more recent times, Christians have been the ones to discount the Big Bang theory, because it indicates that the universe formed over billions of years, an apparent conflict with the six-day biblical account. This need not be of great concern for Christians, however. Astronomers believe the universe is billions of years old because it *looks* billions of years old. Certain stars are hundreds of thousands of light years away from us, for example, yet we can see their light from earth. Because that light required hundreds of thousands of years to reach earth, it is easy to conclude that the universe must be at minimum hundreds of thousands of years old. But just as Adam and Eve appeared to be of childbearing age when they were just one day old, neither can we say with certainty how old the universe actually *is*, just how old it *appears* to be.

What is significant is that most physicists believe that the universe had a distinct beginning, that time itself had a distinct beginning. How did it come to have a beginning, and who was the prime mover behind the Big Bang? Science cannot answer these questions. British astrophysicist Edward Milne ventured this reply: "As to the first cause of the Universe . . . that is left for the reader to insert, but our picture is incomplete without Him."

255. What Is the Anthropic Principle?

In the last century, as tools for observing and measuring the universe have improved, a number of facts show it to be wonderfully tailor-made for life to exist. The strength of gravitation right after the Big Bang, for example, had to fall within a very narrow range. Too strong, and the new, expanding universe would come to a halt and collapse in on itself; too weak, and matter would have dispersed too fast for stars and galaxies to form. A strong force that helps hold an atom's nucleus together has a tiny window of opportunity, outside of which carbon could not form and carbon-based life could not exist. Similar "coincidences," such as the distance of the earth from the sun, have led to the observation that a very large number of details had to turn out just so (and, in fact, *did*) in order for intelligent life to form.

This extraordinary order within the universe has caused various reactions from its inhabitants. Some see it as obvious evidence that God purposefully designed the universe to support life. Others argue that these coincidences are nothing but coincidences. Still others have embraced the anthropic principle.

The anthropic principle suggests that intelligent life is an automatic, unavoidable result of the universe's predisposition to order and symmetry. The organizational perfection in the universe demanded intelligent life capable of observing and appreciating it. In other words, intelligent, living humanity was formed by powers that were non-intelligent and nonliving. There is further speculation that many different universes exist, and ours happens to be one that can support life—even though it is impossible to observe these other hypothetical universes.

Promoted by Stephen Hawking, John D. Barrow, Frank Tipler and others, the anthropic principle is a way of assigning a non-intelligent and nonliving foundation to the presence of intelligent life, so as to avoid the conclusion that it was created by an intelligent designer—God.

This claim is atheism's best scientific attempt to deny Him.

It fails!

PART 17

What Is the Covenant Basis of Our Faith?

256. Why Were Historical Covenants Made?

Historically, a covenant (*briyth* in Hebrew, *diatheke* in Greek) was an agreement between two parties who wanted to provide for themselves and their families, and to protect their future generations. In the ancient day, covenants ended wars, restored peace, united tribes and tied nonrelatives together by an indivisible bond. Children were taught the meaning of covenant from infancy, and cultures honored its strength and durability. The most binding of all covenants was the blood covenant, in which men bound themselves, their kingdoms and their families together. The ceremony, called "cutting a covenant," was this: An animal was sacrificed, and the covenant makers stood in its blood to declare their devotion to each other and their determination to keep the vow. To Christians the concept is important because God has chosen covenant as His way of uniting believers to Himself.

257. What Was the Ancient Process of a Blood Covenant?

In making a covenant, two men would agree on time and place, and invite others to be their witnesses. An animal was killed—usually a bull, goat, lamb—and its body divided equally down the middle. The two parts were then separated and a pool of blood caught between them. Standing in the pool, the men first exchanged coats, each giving his to the other; these garments usually carried tribal insignias, identifying their ancestry and authority. In this act each declared, "In giving you my coat, I also give you everything I own; all my possessions are now yours." They then exchanged weapon belts, which held each man's sword and bow. The act declared, "I now give you responsibility to protect me; my enemies are now your enemies. You will use my weapons to defend me, as I accept responsibility to defend you with yours. We will defend each other to death; fighting as we would defend ourselves." Finally, they exchanged names; frequently, the new name was inserted into the middle of the man's original name.

Each had now surrendered his individuality to the other. They were no longer two; they were one. At this point each one walked between, and then around, the two halves of the sacrifice in the form of a figure eight. Stopping in the middle, each recited the blessings and curses of the covenant that would come upon the one who kept or violated the agreement. The guilty one who broke the covenant would die as the sacrifice had died with his blood being trampled into the ground.

After walking through blood, the two making the covenant took a knife and each made an incision in his hand or wrist. They then gripped hands, wounds touching, so that each man's blood joined the other. The wounds were then treated with a substance that increased permanent scarring. In some cultures the blood was also caught in a cup of wine from which each man drank. Note that this wine in the cup helps us understand what Jesus meant when He said, "Most assuredly, I say to you, unless you eat the flesh of the Son of Man and drink His blood, you have no life in you. Whoever eats My flesh and drinks My blood has eternal life, and I will raise him up at the last day" (John 6:53–54). The conclusion of the ceremony was a covenant meal, which the two ate together. Usually, this was simply bread and wine such as Jesus prescribed for commemorative use at the Last Supper.

You can see that covenants were fiercely binding. It is vital, therefore, that we understand the New Testament warning about covenant abuse as it regards Jesus and the New Testament:

Anyone who has rejected Moses' law dies without mercy on the testimony of two or three witnesses. Of how much worse punishment, do you suppose, will he be thought worthy who has trampled the Son of God underfoot, counted the blood of the covenant by which he was sanctified a common thing, and insulted the Spirit of grace? For we know Him who said, "Vengeance is Mine, I will repay," says the Lord. And again, "The LORD will judge His people." It is a fearful thing to fall into the hands of the living God.

Hebrews 10:28–31

This is a frightful warning. Moses ratified the Old Covenant by sprinkling it with the blood of bulls and goats. Jesus ratified the New Covenant by sprinkling it with His own blood. If the Old is unchangeable, how much more is the New unchangeable? Those who claim that any part of it has lost its truth are in dangerous territory.

258. What Is the Covenant Nature of the Bible?

Covenant is an extremely powerful commitment through which God has given His promise to mankind. What we call "Old Testament" and "New Testament" can equally be called "Old Covenant" and "New Covenant." Both were sprinkled with blood: the first by Moses with the blood of bulls and goats; the second by Jesus with His own blood. Both are inalterable (see Hebrews 9:11–27). We see God's commitment to keeping His Covenants in the words He spoke to David, promising him an everlasting throne. God said, "My covenant I will not break, nor alter the word that has gone out of My lips. Once I have sworn by My holiness; I will not lie to David: His seed shall endure forever, and his throne as the sun before Me" (Psalm 89:34–36).

259. What Is the Covenant of Grace?

The covenant of grace provides for the salvation of mankind from sin and eternal death. Adam's failure in the Garden plunged him—with all his posterity—into sin and stripped us of our relationship with God. Spiritually, Adam died and could not bring himself back to life. His only hope was to be forgiven, restored and raised by One greater than himself. Scripture explains, "In Adam all die, even so in Christ all shall be made alive" (1 Corinthians 15:22). "'The first man Adam became a living being.' The last Adam [Jesus] became a life-giving spirit" (1 Corinthians 15:45).

The shout of Christ from the cross, "It is finished!," was the announcement to earth, heaven, hell and all other realms and dimensions that covenant atonement for mankind's sin and redemption to heaven had been achieved. This ultimate covenant of grace, made by God for the benefit of humankind, involved His Trinitarian being: The Father made the choice by grace to save mankind; the Son became the price of redemption; and the Holy Spirit became the agent by which that grace was applied. "He saved us, through the washing of regeneration and renewing of the Holy Spirit, whom He poured out on us abundantly through Jesus Christ our Savior" (Titus 3:5–6).

The New Testament word *grace* translates from the Greek *charis* and means "favor, blessing, kindness." We are not saved by our own works of righteousness, but by His mercy. "It is the gift of God, not of works, lest anyone should boast" (Ephesians 2:8–9).

260. What Are Five Principal Bible Covenants?

Theologians differ over the number of covenants in the Bible but the following five are significant:

The Adamic Covenant was made by God between Himself and Adam. By it, Adam was assured of everlasting life in the Garden. The condition was his obedience to God (see Genesis 1:28–30; 2:15). Adam failed, broke the covenant and was driven from the Garden. The word *covenant*, which means "agreement," was not used in this instance, but it is represented in the structure of the agreement.

The Noahic Covenant was confirmed by God to Noah after the flood when He promised never again to destroy the earth by water (see Genesis 9:11). The sign of that covenant is the rainbow (see Genesis 9:13). Noah's obedience in believing God, building and entering the Ark was his act of confirmation.

The Abrahamic Covenant is progressive in its revelation and continues over several chapters in the book of Genesis, beginning at chapter 12. The elements of the covenant are threefold: Abraham's seed would become a great nation; Abraham would be blessed personally; and through Abraham's seed all nations of the earth would be blessed. This final promise is still being fulfilled through Jesus, the Son of Abraham, and His Kingdom's reign worldwide. The terms of the Abrahamic covenant were unconditional. Abraham's obedience in circumcising himself and his sons was his act of covenant confirmation.

The Mosaic Covenant was made by God between Himself and the Israelites. In it, they became "a kingdom of priests and a holy nation" (Exodus 19:6). The sign of the covenant was the two tablets on which were written the Ten Commandments (see Exodus 24:12). This covenant was predicated upon the Law of Moses and the Hebrews willingness to keep it. Moses' act of sprinkling both the people and the book of the Law with blood was Israel's act of covenant confirmation.

The New Covenant, of which the New Testament is the written document, is between Christ and His Bride, the Church. The covenant sign is baptism (see Colossians 2:11–12) with continued participation in the covenant via the Lord's Supper (see 1 Corinthians 11:25). Our act of covenant confirmation is this: "If you confess with your mouth the Lord Jesus and believe in your heart that God has raised Him from the dead, you will be saved" (Romans 10:9).

261. Why Is the Rainbow God's Sign of Covenant?

After the flood God said to Noah: "This is the sign of the covenant which I make between Me and you, and every living creature that is with you, for perpetual generations: I set My rainbow in the cloud, and it shall be for the sign of the covenant between Me and the earth" (Genesis 9:12–13).

When seen from ground level, the rainbow is a half circle. When seen from above—God's view—it is a complete ring, like a wedding band. That is not accidental; in our earthly limitation we see only half of God's provision in our lives. Not until we are with God will we be able to look back and understand His total work on our behalf. Events that now seem tragic, unfair, painful will then be viewed through the complete ring of His providence and grace. Only then will we know as we are known and experience God's wiping all tears from our eyes (see 1 Corinthians 13:12; Revelation 7:17; 21:4). In spite of the hazards and crises we experience, God makes "all things work together for good" (Romans 8:28).

Believers who grasp this holy truth now find that it releases incredible reconciliation within them. The covenant sign of the rainbow that appears first in Genesis does not reappear in Scripture until the book of the Revelation. There, the bow reveals its complete circle, horizontally encircling the throne of God and the 24 elders within it (see Revelation 4:3). Only then is the final purpose of God with the bow fulfilled. The number of 24 elders is significant: Twelve represent the twelve tribes of Israel, and twelve represent the Apostles of the Lamb. This means that both covenants or dispensations are encased in one great, eternal plan of grace.

262. What Is the Covenant Meaning of Hebrew Circumcision?

Beginning with Abraham, every Hebrew male bore in his body a circular scar, the physical mark of circumcision—"circular cutting." It was the sign of Hebrew covenant. The spiritual meaning of the mile-wide rainbow and the few inches of circumcision are identical. Each contains all the majesty of the other. The rainbow, the greatest visible covenant sign in creation, was replicated on the body of covenant-man. God willed that the conception of every Hebrew child taking place in the mother's womb would be in the presence of his father's covenant sign. Half of the genes of every future generation passed through his father's covenant-ring. God wanted that mysterious, creative act of conception in which children are made in His "image" and in His "likeness" (Genesis 1:26) to take place within the sign of the covenant.

263. How Should Christians View Circumcision?

As Christians, we regard circumcision as an Old Testament, physical example of a New Testament nonphysical truth. Circumcision is no longer a cutting away of the physical body but a spiritual cutting away of the heart. Paul explains that this circumcision is enacted in water baptism: "In Him you were also circumcised with the circumcision made without hands, by putting off the body of the sins of the flesh, by the circumcision of Christ, buried with Him in baptism, in which you also were raised with Him" (Colossians 2:11–12). Peter, however, cautions us to know that baptism does not remove "the filth of the flesh, but [is] the answer of a good conscience toward God" (see 1 Peter 3:21). For both Jews and Christians, circumcision is a sign of covenant. What the Jews practiced in a tangible example, we experience in a spiritual reality.

Circumcision is permissible among Christians provided it is not done for religious reasons. As a religious observance, no, it should not be practiced. Those who accept responsibility for any part of the Jewish Law make themselves responsible to keep the whole Law. Paul states this clearly: "I testify again to every man who becomes circumcised that he is a debtor to keep the whole law" (Galatians 5:3). Jesus, through His sacrificial death, has "redeemed us from the curse of the law, having become a curse for us" (Galatians 3:13). He is "the end of the law" for everyone who believes in His atoning work (Romans 10:4). There are more than six hundred Jewish regulations from which we have been delivered. Returning to any of them with an eye to self-justification is a foolish mistake.

PART 18

What Do These Terms Mean?

264. How Does Faith Differ in the Old and New Testaments?

In spite of its obvious theological importance, the word *faith* appears only two times in the Old Testament; significantly, these two instances illustrate the extremes of faith: (1) "children in whom is no faith" and (2) "the just shall live by his faith." Between these contrasting points, the just and the unjust, the entirety of God's dealing with His covenanted people is revealed.

Also of importance is the fact that the familiar quotation, "The just shall live by faith," from the prophet Habakkuk, is the most frequently quoted Old Testament passage appearing in the New. The Protestant Reformation was born out of the impact this verse had in converting Martin Luther; he realized his self-efforts for salvation brought only failure. Salvation is not a work of the flesh but an acceptance of "justification by faith."

Here are the two Old Testament references to faith: "And he said: 'I will hide my face from them, I will see what their end will be, for they are a perverse generation, children in whom is no faith'" (Deuteronomy 32:20); "Behold the proud, his soul is not upright in him; but the just shall live by his faith" (Habakkuk 2:4). Equally significant is the fact that, in the New Testament, Hebrews 11 is devoted in its entirety to the "heroes of faith" in the Old Testament. This reveals an important truth: It is not using the word *faith* that brings a person into its blessing; it is the exercising of faith that wins the attention and favor of God.

265. What Is Meant by Opening the Door of Faith?

That there is a distinct, identifiable moment in which the "door of faith" is sometimes opened in a new believer is illustrated in John Wesley's experience. While listening to a message by Peter Böhler, a Moravian bishop and missionary, Wesley suddenly felt his heart "strangely warmed." That simple moment changed his life and ministry forever. Scripture explains how this "opening" also happened in Iconium in the ministry of Paul and Barnabas: "Now when they had come and gathered the church together, they reported all that God had done with them, and that He had opened the door of faith to the Gentiles" (Acts 14:27).

The day of the resurrection when Jesus (unrecognized) joined the disciples on the Emmaus Road we read: "Then their eyes were opened and they knew Him; and He vanished from their sight. And they said to one another, 'Did not our heart burn within us while He talked with us on the road, and while He opened the Scriptures to us?'" (Luke 24:31–32). A short time later, after they had returned to Jerusalem, Jesus appeared to them along with the Eleven and other disciples gathered with them and said, "'These are the words which I spoke to you while I was still with you, that all things must be fulfilled which were written in the Law of Moses and the Prophets and the Psalms concerning Me.' And he opened their understanding, that they might comprehend the Scriptures" (Luke 24:44–45).

266. How Does God Open the Door of Faith?

We are not left to guess how God opens the door of faith. God's method, then and now, is the same. Paul explained that "in mighty signs and wonders, by the power of the Spirit of God . . . I have fully preached the gospel of Christ" (Romans 15:19). He told the Corinthians that he did not come to them as a great orator, but simply as one who preached "Jesus Christ and Him crucified," doing so "in demonstration of the Spirit and of power" (1 Corinthians 2:2, 4). Luke wrote that as Paul and Barnabas preached boldly and gave witness to the grace of God through Jesus Christ, He granted that signs and wonders be done by them (see Acts 14:3).

As it was then, so it should be now!

267. What Does the Word *Christian* Mean?

The identifier *Christian* was applied to early believers because of the anointing of the Holy Spirit that was on them. *Christianos* means "anointed ones" and recalls the title given to Christ—the "Anointed One." It was a reference to the power early believers carried rather than a religious community name. It was a personal identification of the Holy Spirit's presence on them.

268. What Does the Word *Disciple* Mean?

A disciple is a disciplined believer. *Disciple* and *discipline* are synonymous. One does not exist without the other. As regards Christianity, such a person is baptized, is systematically taught, is deliberate in his or her walk with God, bears spiritual fruit and seeks it in the lives of others. A disciple is a "good tree" (see Luke 6:44). Many are admirers of Christ but not all are disciples. The Holy Spirit never produces inept, ineffective, unqualified results either in a church or an individual. An undisciplined, disorganized church cannot produce true disciples. A disciple is a disciplined, committed follower of Jesus.

269. What Is Renewing of the Mind?

Tragically, many Christians go through life repeating failures and never achieving their full potential because they have not experienced the Holy Spirit's work of mental restoration. Paul exhorted the Roman Christians to avoid conformation to this world but to be transformed by the "renewing" of their minds that they might experience the "good and acceptable and perfect" will of God" (Romans 12:1–3). The word for *renewal* in New Testament Greek is *anakainosis* and means "renovation, restoration and redevelopment." This is an ongoing process.

Renewal, first of all, is to be set free from internal demonic habitation. Secondly, it is the surrender of negative belief systems about God. In reality, holding on to negativity is a deliberate refusal to trust God and keeps many born-again people in captivity. Jesus could not have been more direct than when He said, "I have come that they may have life, and that they may have it more abundantly" (John 10:10). Mental restoration can be built only on the absolute assurance that God has made us "accepted in the beloved" (Ephesians 1:6). The end result is a renewed, energized and confident personality.

270. Why Does the Intellect Fail in Matters of the Spirit?

Jesus had a specific reason for telling the disciples not to leave Jerusalem until they had been endued with power from "on high." He did not want them to attempt ministry in their own strength or intellect.

In various ways Jesus had already shown them the difference between ministering in their own strength and in the strength of God. This happened the stormy night He came walking to them on the water (see Matthew 14:25–31). They stared at Him from the boat in fearful shock and unbelief. More so, they were incredulous when He told Peter to come to Him. Peter climbed out of the boat onto the turbulent sea and for one awesome moment stood solidly on the rolling waves. Then he took a few steps without sinking. The next moment, when his gaze went from Jesus to the water, he plunged downward.

Peter's failing attempt speaks to everyone today who is trying to approach Jesus from the realm of intellect and reasoning. That will not work. While we thank God for the mind and its wonderful abilities, "the world through wisdom did not know God" (1 Corinthians 1:21). Human wisdom and effort cannot take us into the spiritual realm. Personal Christianity must not be based on the fact that we read the Bible and believe it, but because we personally experience what the Bible says we will. Apart from spiritual encounters with Him we have no more "life" than did the Pharisees whose intellect kept them locked in their spiritual darkness. The equipping God wants for all Christian ministry is that we, like Peter in those astonishing moments on the sea, taste the "powers of the age to come" (Hebrews 6:5).

271. What Is the Great Falling Away?

Paul wrote,

> Now the Spirit expressly says that in latter times some will depart from the faith, giving heed to deceiving spirits and doctrines of demons, speaking lies in hypocrisy, having their own conscience seared with a hot iron, forbidding to marry, and commanding to abstain from foods which God created to be received with thanksgiving by those who believe and know the truth.
>
> 1 Timothy 4:1–3

Speaking prophetically, Paul identified seven marks of apostasy within the Church in the end times. It is apparent that we are there. Sexual sins that Paul identifies in Romans 1, for instance, are not only accepted by parts of the Western Church today, but are defended as normal and desirable.

Paul continued to explain that in the end times, people will pursue a "form of godliness" but will have no authentic power. These will be "perilous times" when boastful, headstrong people seek their own pleasure more than pleasing God (2 Timothy 3:1–5). To the informed, empowered Christian, this distressing picture is not a cause for panic. Instead, even in death we overcome Satan "by the blood of the Lamb and by the word of [our] testimony" (Revelation 12:11). When Satan's sword is laid on the neck of the Church, there will be many who deny Christ to save their own lives. True believers in such cases will accept martyrdom. Even in death these are "more than conquerors" through Him who loved them" (Romans 8:37). In the end, the apostate church will perish in the fire.

272. What Are Three Methods of Prayer?

Three general methods of prayer are these.

Praying according to human understanding. This is praying about information we know intellectually through our five senses. This prayer is important but dependent upon knowledge gained primarily through hearing and seeing. Information for such a prayer is therefore limited to sensory knowledge; it is sometimes erroneous, marred by misunderstanding and failure (see James 4:3). The perfect prayer is the one Jesus taught the disciples and recorded for us: "Our Father in heaven. . . . "

Praying "in the Spirit" (1 Corinthians 14:15; Jude 20). This prayer originates from the specific direction of the Holy Spirit. Through the gift of tongues, we speak mysteries far beyond human comprehension or human language (see 1 Corinthians 14:2–3). Paul said of it, "If I pray in a tongue, my spirit prays" (1 Corinthians 14:14). The mind's confusion is bypassed as the spirit communicates directly with the all-knowing Holy Spirit.

Praying as "the Spirit Himself makes intercession for us with groanings which cannot be uttered" (Romans 8:26). This groaning prayer (which is not to be confused with the gift of tongues) originates with Jesus' intercession at the right hand of the Father (see Romans 8:34). In response to His prayer, all creation is now in a state of travailing birth pangs, waiting for its own deliverance from the bondage of corruption, and the simultaneous manifestation of the children of God (see Romans 8:19–23). On the day of His triumphal entry into Jerusalem, Jesus revealed the capacity of even the stones to cry out (see Luke 19:40). Some individuals find themselves drawn involuntarily into this groaning prayer. While in such intercession, they encounter an overwhelming intimacy with creation's deepest cry for deliverance. Such intercessors frequently find themselves in a birthing position, such as Elijah experienced on Mount Carmel when he was bent down with his face between his knees (see 1 Kings 18:42). The prayer Jesus began at the throne is now permeating the entire universe, causing it to yearn mightily for His return and its own deliverance from the bondage of corruption.

273. What Is Repentance to Life?

The word *repentance* is thought to prescribe a life of denial, deprivation and sacrifice. In reality, the exact opposite is true. *Repentance*, which means to "turn around and go the other way," is the entrance point into a lifestyle blessed beyond the ordinary. The transition is from a planetary life on the order of animals to one directed by the Holy Spirit, in communication with heaven, and experiencing heightened spirituality, angelic visitations and empowerment by God Almighty. All this and more is in the potential of repentance.

When Peter returned to Jerusalem and described his visit to the home of Cornelius, the Gentile Centurion, he told how the Holy Spirit had come upon the Gentiles just as He had "at the beginning." The Jewish believers "became silent; and they glorified God, saying, 'Then God has also granted to the Gentiles repentance to life'" (Acts 11:15–18). The expression *repentance to life* is apocalyptic. Repentance—"turning to God"—is the doorway to God-empowered living. Paul identified the amazing potential that comes with repentance. He wrote Timothy about those whose repentance opened the door for them to "know the truth," "come to their senses" and "escape the snare of the devil" (2 Timothy 2:25–26). Apart from repentance, Christians cannot know the truth, come to their senses or escape the snare of Satan. Repentance cleans the mind, energizes the psyche, refreshes brainpower. Many believers go through life never discovering wonderful truths about themselves, developing their hidden talents or escaping crises that could have easily been avoided. Examine these benefits of repentance:

Repentance provides a greater encounter with Christ (see Matthew 3:11).

Repentance opens us to the baptism with the Holy Spirit! (see Matthew 3:11; Acts 2:38).

Repentance convicts us and rescues us from sin (see Acts 3:19).

Repentance brings times of refreshing from the Lord (see Acts 3:19).

Repentance delivers us from the poison of sin and rebellion (see Acts 8:23).

Repentance brings cleansing to unclean thoughts in our hearts and minds (see Acts 8:22).

Repentance equips us for a fruitful life (see Acts 11:19).

Repentance leads us to salvation (see 2 Corinthians 7:10).

Repentance opens us to greater truth (see 2 Timothy 2:25).

Repentance cleanses our senses (see 2 Timothy 2:26).

Repentance gives us an escape from the snare of the devil (see 2 Timothy 2:26).

274. What Is the Sin Leading to Death?

The apostle John tells us there is a sin that leads to death but does not identify what the sin is or the kind of death it causes: "There is sin leading to death. . . . All unrighteousness is sin, and there is sin not leading to death" (1 John 5:16–17). It may be the wisdom of God in not telling us what the sin is—that we will be more cautious about all sin.

Paul warned the Corinthians of the danger of sin in regard to the sacrament of Communion. He said, "Whoever eats this bread or drinks this cup of the Lord in an unworthy manner will be guilty of the body and blood of the Lord." He enjoined his readers to examine their lives so that they would not take Communion "in an unworthy manner" and so bring judgment on themselves (1 Corinthians 11:27, 29). We are safe in believing that the "sin leading to death" is a willful, unrepentant, deliberate sin from which the person refuses to turn away.

In the Old Testament we have the example of King Saul whose unforgiven sin stayed with him until he died. Though he did not fall dead from its impact, he was never restored to acceptance with God. In the New Testament, Ananias and Sapphira lied about a gift to the Church and fell dead literally. Peter explained they had "not lied to men but to God" (Acts 5:4).

In 1756 there was a similar experience when George Whitefield—whose ministry was confirmed by astonishing signs, wonders and manifestations of the Holy Spirit—preached in Haworth, England. He was standing on an outdoor platform at St. Michael's Anglican Church facing a congregation of several thousand. In a loud, commanding voice, he announced his text: "It is appointed unto men once to die, but after this the judgment" (Hebrews 9:27 KJV). A shriek followed. A man in the congregation had dropped dead. His body was carried out. Whitefield waited, then repeated the Scripture loudly again. A second shriek followed. Another person had dropped dead. This body also was carried away. Whitefield resumed preaching. We know nothing of those who died or their state before God, but these deaths were an alarming signal that God was in their midst.

275. What Is the Unpardonable Sin?

The unpardonable sin is a specific, identifiable sin that Jesus distinguished carefully from all others. It is important for us to know that. People who have not committed this sin sometimes fear they have and bring great—and unnecessary—grief upon themselves. The unpardonable sin is to accuse Jesus of being conceived by the devil (see Matthew 12:31–32; Luke 12:10).

Hear the Scripture carefully. Certain scribes from Jerusalem were saying this about Jesus: "This fellow does not cast out demons except by Beelzebub, the ruler of the demons." Jesus' response was to speak to them in parables: "Every city or house divided against itself will not stand. If Satan casts out Satan, he is divided against himself. How then will his kingdom stand?" Then He said, "Anyone who speaks a word against the Son of Man, it will be forgiven him; but whoever speaks against the Holy Spirit, it will not be forgiven him, either in this age or in the age to come." Scripture tells us that He gave this warning because they were saying "He has an unclean spirit." (Matthew 12:24–26, 32; Mark 3:30).

You might think this was blasphemy against Jesus and not the Holy Spirit. Not so. Jesus was conceived by the Holy Spirit. To say, therefore, that His conception was the work of Satan is blasphemy in the worst form—against the Holy Spirit. There are many blasphemies against the Holy Spirit that are forgivable; this specific sin is not.

276. Why Is Worship Important?

It is the intent of God that when we worship, we detach from the world and its noisy surroundings, and escape into His Presence. When that wonderful contact takes place between God and His people, we experience consciously a Fatherly bonding with Him and He with us. Faith is reassured, hope restored and our love swells with greater devotion for Him. That joyful moment calms anxieties and restores peacefulness as nothing else can. It is from the God-encounter of true worship that our spiritual person steps into renewed strength and power.

Worship for Christians is both private and public. After the Reformation there was a subtle—but strong—shift from a church service that was centered on the sacraments and singing to one that was sermon centered. Sermons, though important, are not the center-point of worship. Congregations today who welcome the Holy Spirit's tangible presence know well the awesome blessing that comes when they "sing with the spirit" (1 Corinthians 14:15). There is no worship so transcendent as this. True worship goes beyond the senses and takes the worshiper into the realm of the Spirit.

In typology, the pattern for Christian worship was fully displayed in Israel's ancient Tabernacle: the Outer Court, the Holy Place and the Holy of Holies. It was only in the inmost Holy of Holies chamber that the Shekinah glory could be seen. Those who remained in the Outer Court never witnessed it. Nor did priests in the Holy Place. Scripture explains the process for us. We "enter into His gates with thanksgiving." With singing, we make our approach. When accepted we "enter into His courts with praise" (Psalm 100:4). The court is site of the King's throne (see Esther 5:1).

Many participate in singing who, unfortunately, never enter the King's presence. High praise is wonderful; sermons can be transporting. But deep, profound worship is necessary for us to go "under the veil" and behold His Glory. Our aim in worship is to encounter God, honor Him and go forth to serve Him in the renewed power of the Holy Spirit.

277. How Do We Enter Worship?

In true worship, we rise beyond the limits of earth and time and commune with our Creator God. Worship is much more than listening to music, singing, praying, expressing words of devotion, etc. These are mere aids or tools to help us enter worship.

In worship, private or congregational, we make actual contact with the Creator and momentarily escape the restraints of this present dimension. This state is achieved when we enter His gates with thanksgiving in our hearts and His courts with praise (see Psalm 100:4). The basic Hebrew word for worship, *shachah*, means "to bow down in reverence, to acknowledge God in obeisance." The most frequently used of three Greek words in the New Testament, *proskuneo*, means "to kiss the hand of God or kiss the ground before Him in deep devotion and reverence." The concept is to flatten oneself before God. As in the case of Queen Esther, who stood humbly in the presence of her kingly husband and to whom he extended the scepter, we, too, come before God with reverence. We bow in His presence, trusting He will hold out the scepter and welcome us into His royal court.

278. What Is an Out-of-Body Experience?

The term *out-of-body experience* probably comes from Paul's words about being caught up to the third heaven. The man whom Paul describes might or might not have traveled in his body—Paul seems unsure—but his mind was alert as he entered Paradise and heard inexpressible words (see 2 Corinthians 12:2–5).

The Greek word here for "caught up" is *harpazo*, meaning "snatched, seized, by force pulled away." Paul used the same word to describe the rapture—or catching away—of the Church: "Then we who are alive and remain shall be caught up together with them in the clouds to meet the Lord in the air" (1 Thessalonians 4:17). We see it again when Philip baptized the Ethiopian and afterward was "caught away," that is, he was instantly transported to Azotus (see Acts 8:40). Philip was—and the Church will be—caught up in the fullness of spirit, soul and body. But in some instances, more literally "out of the body," an aspect of the soul can apparently travel away from the body and return. If the person's spirit leaves the body, that person is dead (see James 2:26); individuals have been known to return to their bodies after having died.

Current examples include these actual events: A teenager pinned to the kitchen floor being beaten severely by his stepfather who suddenly finds himself on the ceiling looking down on the scene and feeling no pain; a woman in a hospital bed, gravely injured from an automobile accident, who leaves her body and travels throughout the hospital seeing other rooms and people; an old man in a hospital bed who discovers he can swing his legs down through the mattress, then realizes he has become detached from his body, visits heaven and returns to the body a changed man; a teenage girl, a paralyzed bed patient, whose mother finds her unconscious, comes to and tells about being with the Lord in a different dimension of such incredible beauty she cannot describe it; a woman undergoing surgery whose heart stops is resuscitated, but in her absence from the body sees heaven, is astonished by its indescribable beauty, recognizes deceased loved ones she knew on earth, wants to stay but feels herself being pulled away, returns to the body, wakes up, and is disappointed that she did not stay dead; a young man returning home from a revival is in deep worship while driving his car when he is suddenly "caught away" into the glorious presence of God, receives an astonishing—life changing—revelation of the love of God, and finds upon his return that in his absence his car continued to be driven safely.

279. What Is a Theophany?

A theophany is a manifestation of God that is recognizable to the human senses—though it is not an actual display of God Himself. Probably, the most beautiful theophany in Scripture is the "dove" of the Holy Spirit lighting upon Jesus at His baptism (see Matthew 3:16). A theophany is found in Daniel 5:5 when "the fingers of a man's hand appeared and wrote . . . on the plaster of the wall of the king's palace."

God always appears incognito to mankind. He explained it this way to Moses: "No man shall see Me, and live" (Exodus 33:20). God Almighty often revealed Himself to Old Testament people in a way that was easily recognizable to them.

Genesis 18:1–33: God appeared to Abraham as three men and gave him the promise of Isaac's birth.

Genesis 32:22–30: Jacob wrestled all night with an angelic "Man" who blessed him.

Exodus 3:2–4:17: God appeared to Moses in the form of a burning bush.

Exodus 24:9–11: God appeared to Moses, Aaron, his sons and Israel's seventy elders in a thunderous cloud on Mt. Sinai.

Deuteronomy 31:14–15: God appeared to Moses and Joshua in a pillar of cloud.

All Old Testament theophanies are prophetic forecasts of the coming incarnation of Jesus. Interestingly, Jesus said to Philip, "Have I been with you so long, and yet you have not known Me, Philip? He who has seen Me has seen the Father" (John 14:9). Jesus was the ultimate theophany.

280. What Is an Epiphany?

Epiphanies may be spiritual or secular. To Christians, an epiphany is a miraculous and extraordinary encounter with God that takes the form of a vision, personal revelation or sudden consciousness of His presence and love. Such moments usually come unexpectedly and with great spiritual revelation; the effects are usually permanent and life changing.

The moment of conversion, when a person comes to faith in Christ and is born again, can be a glorious epiphany. The disciples' experience with the Holy Spirit in the Upper Room was one of the greatest epiphanies in history. Saul of Tarsus' encounter with Jesus on the Damascus Road was an epiphany. That was followed by another when Ananias laid hands on Saul and he was filled with the Holy Spirit. The epiphany was not Ananias' physical action of touching Saul; rather it was the effect of Saul's being touched. Epiphanies frequently produce authentic, lasting conversion. Every Christian should pray earnestly to be enlarged through such God-given experiences.

In the secular sense, anyone can experience an epiphany. We call this a breakthrough. In the working world, for instance, people of every profession can experience epiphanies as sudden revelations in their labors. This apparently occurred with Albert Einstein. As a young child he was given a compass and was enthralled with the realization that an invisible force was making the needle move. This encouraged his mind toward the unseen world of gravitational science. Did he have an epiphany? God only knows. Christians should pray for such blessings in their lives and work.

281. What Is Anointing Oil?

"So they went out and preached that people should repent. And they cast out many demons, and anointed with oil many who were sick, and healed them" (Mark 6:12–13). James said, "Is anyone among you sick? Let him call for the elders of the church, and let them pray over him, anointing him with oil in the name of the Lord. And the prayer of faith will save the sick, and the Lord will raise him up" (James 5:14–15).

There is no mystical power in oil for anointing—or in water for baptism or in bread and wine for Communion. Of themselves, they are only physical properties. All, however, may become channels for great power as a result of a believer's obedience to God. "To obey is better than sacrifice" (1 Samuel 15:22). Obedience releases faith. Power comes when faith is released. Great changes result from that power.

282. What Is Positive Confession?

The topic of confession involves a number of important scriptural truths. First, confession is a vital part of the act of being saved. Jesus said that anyone who acknowledges Him in front of other people, He will acknowledge before the Father; likewise, anyone who denies Him will be denied before the Father (see Matthew 10:32–34). Paul reaffirmed this when he wrote that "if you confess with your mouth the Lord Jesus and believe in your heart that God has raised Him from the dead, you will be saved" (see Romans 10:9). Notice, Paul said *believe in your heart.* Believing in the mind is not sufficient. The same applies to confession. The heart must be in command and the mouth be in obedience.

For the person who is born again, renewal of his mind and compliance with Scripture-truth will proceed only at the rate of his confession. If he still believes in his heart and says with his mouth that he is defeated, crushed, vanquished, he will be. His challenge becomes one of overcoming doubt, unbelief, fear and negative habits by declaring vocally the greater authority of Jesus Christ. The moment he comes to true belief, saying he is "more than a conqueror in Christ," and believing it, he will become that person. "Out of the abundance of the heart the mouth speaks" (Matthew 12:34). It is at this point that a "positive confession" reveals its purpose and power.

By his own choice a newly saved believer can come to full maturity in Christ or continue in his sin-dominated consciousness of defeat and hopelessness. His confessing Christ that initially brought him to salvation must continue to assure his future growth. Confession plays a very important role. Without it, there will be no spiritual growth or outward change. If the person continues thinking he is defeated, overwhelmed by Satan and imprisoned by his own circumstances, that is what he will be.

283. What Are Tithes and Offerings?

In the Old Covenant, Jews were commanded to tithe a tenth of their income to the Temple priests. Ordinarily in the Church today, tithes are given where one worships and receives ministry. Money is called "currency." When we give to another, we put ourselves into the current or "flow" of blessing, and what we receive in return is potentially without limit. The greatest reward is in gaining the favor and blessing of God. It is, therefore, more blessed to give than to receive. Scripture encourages us to get into the current of giving and receiving (see Philippians 4:15).

Jesus broadened the concept of giving. He taught that one should "lay down one's life for his friends" (John 15:13). Christians are to be more loving, more giving, more self-sacrificing than anyone else. In lifestyle we are to go beyond requirements of the Law. Jesus told the disciples, "Freely you have received, freely give" (Matthew 10:8). Our guiding principle is not Law but love. Ten percent should be a starting point.

Offerings or alms are gifts we give voluntarily to those in need or those who serve us. They are expressions of our desire to bless them. When we tip parking attendants, restaurant servers, strangers in need, etc. we are giving alms. Scripture says, "Give alms of such things as you have" (Luke 11:41). This can be in the form of cash, food, gifts, clothing or items that are helpful. The importance of offerings, as with tithes, is that we be generous. "God loves a cheerful giver" (2 Corinthians 9:7).

284. What Is the Law of Reciprocity?

The ancient concept of reciprocity, which the New Testament identifies simply as "sowing and reaping," existed both in the Code of Hammurabi,

King of Babylon (c. 1754 BC), and some three hundred years later in the Law of Moses. Anciently it was a system for punishing crime; in the New Covenant, it is a system of receiving and giving grace. The ancient Laws, Babylonian and Hebrew, demanded an "eye for an eye" and a "tooth for a tooth." If you blinded someone, you, too, would be blinded. If you caused someone to lose a tooth, then your corresponding tooth had to be broken out. (See Exodus 21:23–24.) In both cases, the law was reciprocal with no provision for grace and forgiveness.

Jesus totally recast the system into one of doing good—and then receiving good in return. Elevating the subject far above the crime and punishment level, Jesus said to the disciples, "Give, and it will be given to you: good measure, pressed down, shaken together, and running over will be put into your bosom" (Luke 6:38). Instead of causing someone pain, He taught that we should bless—and then watch blessing return into our own lives. It is the same principle of "casting your bread upon the water," and seeing it come back (see Ecclesiastes 11:1).

Paul recaptured Jesus' concept more than any other New Testament writer and explained it this way: "He who sows sparingly will also reap sparingly, and he who sows bountifully will also reap bountifully. So let each one give as he purposes in his heart, not grudgingly or of necessity; for God loves a cheerful giver" (2 Corinthians 9:6–7; see Galatians 6:7). The one who does this, said Paul, will find that God "is able to make all grace abound toward you" and provide "an abundance for every good work" (verse 8).

We can benefit immeasurably by this principle today: The law of reciprocity is still in operation. If there is no flow of blessings into a believer's life, that person has the power to reset the motion, reverse the curse and attract blessings. Christians who are in dire need should begin providing for others. History records times when believers who had no money to give, no food to share, donated their time in free labor for others. In this way, they set the flow in motion and began receiving.

The promise of Jesus is for all: "Whatever you want men to do to you, do also to them, for this is the Law and the Prophets" (Matthew 7:12). Modern society, in recognizing the validity of Jesus' teaching, has restated the axiom in the Golden Rule: "Do unto others as you would have them do unto you." In part, this is the law of reciprocity.

285. What about God's Silence?

We all face crises when God is silent and does not respond to the urgency of our prayers. While we cannot know His reasons, we do know that such times provide opportunities for us to "walk by faith and not by sight." Joseph, when betrothed to Mary, faced such a crisis. When he realized that the woman he loved and to whom he was engaged was pregnant—and not by him—he made plans to "put her away secretly" (Matthew 1:19). His heart was broken. Apparently, Mary was not at liberty to explain, and God let him endure the silence.

Why? We do not know. God could have spoken much sooner than He did. Several years after that crisis had passed, when they were living in Egypt, God told Joseph that Herod was dead and for the family to return to Israel. Arriving there he learned that Herod's son Archelaus was on the throne. Joseph again was gripped with fear: This man was as dangerous as his father.

Why had God not told him? Why did God not tell him the whole story? We know only that in that moment of fear Joseph went to Nazareth to avoid Jerusalem. Did he realize that choice was foreordained of God—for Matthew tells us that prophets of old knew the Messiah would be called a Nazarene? (See Matthew 2:23.) Again, we know only that God was silent about important information.

We also have the example of Paul and his team traveling slowly across hundreds of miles in western Turkey, attempting "to preach the word in Asia," but being "forbidden by the Holy Spirit" (Acts 16:6). The wasted time and effort was frustrating. It was only after they reached Troas that Paul, falling into troubled sleep, was given a vision in the night. A Macedonian stood before him saying, "Come over to Macedonia and help us" (Acts 16:9).

Secret things belong to God (Deuteronomy 29:29). So it is with other believers; so it is with us.

286. What Are Soul Ties?

Soul ties are spiritual bonds between people. These may be good or bad. Unless they are cancelled intentionally, soul ties remain even if the relationship has ended. Death does not necessarily end a soul tie, nor does divorce. The influence of the deceased spouse or former partner may continue.

While the New Testament does not use the term *soul tie*, the principle—good and bad—is present in significant ways. Ephesians 5:31 explains that in marriage, a couple develops a good tie in spirit, body and soul. A virtuous soul tie between friends developed between David and Jonathan, Saul's son. Paul speaks of a good soul tie when he says of the Laodicean believers "that their hearts may be encouraged, being knit together in love" (Colossians 2:2). Believers and unbelievers both experience a "knitting together" in good and bad relationships.

Illicit sexual relationships are the most frequent cause of injurious soul ties. Oaths and vows of hatred bond people in darkened soul ties. Some organizations require oaths that dominate their victims by soul ties in very powerful ways. A person can be years removed from a bad soul-connection but still be influenced negatively by it.

In ridding oneself of bad soul ties the process is similar to experiencing exorcism. The receiving party should identify the relationship, repent of the personal involvement, speak forgiveness to the offender, be anointed with oil in the name of Jesus Christ and yield to the Holy Spirit. The one ministering "lays hands" on the receiving party, then commands the soul tie to be broken and every related spirit contrary to God to be banished in the name of Jesus Christ. If the source of the tie is unknown, it can still be effectually cast out in the same way. Follow-up ministry is always important.

287. Are Secret Societies Ever Dangerous?

Many secret orders require initiation oaths of new members that are evil and damning. The motive behind them is to desensitize the victim spiritually and psychologically and render the victim unable to recognize the deception he or she is entering. One of the most common is an oath in Freemasonry in which the initiate vows to have "my throat cut across, my tongue torn out, and with my body buried in the sands of the sea at low-water mark" should he betray the organization. In another ceremonial Masonic oath, the individual places a goat's head over his own, drinks wine from a human skull and asks that all the sins of the dead person be charged to him if he ever betrays the Order.

Under no circumstance can a Christian participate in such demonic oaths and ceremonies. Without full repentance and internal cleansing such individuals bring a spiritual darkness into the Church that resists the presence and grace of the Holy Spirit. Scripture declares that Christians have "renounced the hidden things of shame" (2 Corinthians 4:2). James tells us: "Above all, my brethren, do not swear, either by heaven or by earth or with any other oath" (James 5:12). Jesus said: "I say to you, do not swear at all" (Matthew 5:34). Joshua said to Israel, "Choose for yourselves this day whom you will serve. . . . As for me and my house, we will serve the LORD" (Joshua 24:15).

So be it with Christians! People who have debased themselves with ungodly oaths will find the Lord eager to forgive and restore. They need deep repentance, confession of sin and exorcism from these bondages. Unclean spirits eagerly grab all who make such vows and leave only when they are forced to go.

288. What Is a Cult?

A cult is an organization of people who embrace doctrinal ideas that deny one or more cardinal principles of the true Christian faith. They might claim to be Christian or might revel in being non-Christian, such as satanic cults. Such groups are usually dominated by a powerful leader. An identifying mark of a cult is the demand that, to be "right," one must belong only to them; they alone possess truth and members must not listen to any other opinion. Family relationships are frequently sacrificed. Broken homes are usual results. Cults focus on themselves. Once a person has come under their powerful control, escape is difficult. Their effect is hypnotic and mesmerizing, and possesses the power to blind individuals to family love, healthy relationships and the truth of Scripture. "Christianized" cults are extremely dangerous.

289. How Do Eternal Life, Immortality and Endless Life Differ?

The word *eternal* refers to a state that has neither beginning nor end. It is a condition of timelessness. *Immortal* means "not subject to death." The word *endless* means a state that has a point of beginning but continues without interruption. These latter two words do not describe *eternal*. Eternity has no beginning and no end.

Albert Einstein had an excellent grasp of this truth when he said, "People like us who believe in physics know that the distinction between past, present, and future, is only a stubbornly persistent illusion." The Greek word *aionios*, "eternal," speaks of a state of perpetuity and is used to identify the most basic nature of God. He has always been—is always being—and always will be. He is the unchanging, constant great I Aм, and "Endless Now." Ultimate salvation is when eternal life, which has been infused into us with God's eternal nature, coalesces in a way that makes time, space, past, present, future disappear.

We calculate time by the passing of days, weeks, months and years. Our day is 24 hours long because the earth is 25,000 miles around and is spinning approximately at the rate of a thousand miles per hour. Time, in our present element, is determined by the physical rotation of the earth. What would happen to time if we got off the earth and moved beyond its rotation into outer space? The answer is simple: Time as we know it would cease to exist. For that reason, science relies on methods other than our clock to compute time in outer space. Eternal life and time coexist in us now.

290. What Is the Symbol IHS?

IHS is an abbreviated religious monogram that predates Christian history but was adapted for Christian use. It is an acronym corresponding to the first three letters of the Greek word Jesus: *iota* = I; *eta* = H; *sigma* = S. Another explanation is that the letters stand for *Iesus Hominum Salvator*, Latin for "Jesus Savior of Men."

The symbol appeared in early Catholic churches and was later adopted by many Protestants. It is found on paraments, candelabras, vases, etc. Unfortunately, before the Christian era the letters were used in Babylon and represented Isis, Horus and Seb, three pagan deities—father, mother and child of the gods. Constantine is accused of encouraging the use of this father-mother-child IHS symbol so that his Christian and pagan troops could all worship at the same banner. In modern times *IHS* has been assigned a new meaning: "I Have Suffered" or "In His Service."

291. What Was the Shepherding/Discipleship Movement?

The shepherding or discipleship movement began in the early 1970s when five of America's most trusted Christian teachers, Derek Prince, Don Basham, Bob Mumford, Charles Simpson and Ern Baxter, mutually bound themselves to each other in a covenant relationship. Each man submitted to the others, giving them authority over vital decisions of his personal life. Using their own example, they encouraged other Christian leaders and groups to follow the same pattern of trust and subjugation.

Soon a nationwide pyramid of cell groups organized under them and spread across America with some in England. The project began with godly intentions but, tragically, the control that developed under many local "shepherds" (as cell leaders were called) became obsessive and dangerous. Not every shepherd was worthy or qualified for the trust he commanded over his flock. Excesses developed quickly. In an almost imperceptible way, control moved from spiritual trust to psychological domination.

Some shepherds, at their height of power, told those under them which jobs they could take, when they were allowed vacations, whom they could—or could not—marry, and in some cases demanded divorce when a member's spouse offended the cell's leadership. If individuals left the group, the remaining family members were forbidden to speak to them. The psychological domination was so great that, at its extreme, parents and children were separated and not allowed contact. The shepherding movement became a primary example of Paul's warning to Christians that men from their own ranks would arise and draw away disciples after themselves (see Acts 20:30–31).

Derek Prince was the first of the five to acknowledge their error and break away. In leaving he said they had committed the "Galatian error"—having begun in the Spirit they had implemented their actions in the flesh (see Galatians 3:3). Charles Simpson and Bob Mumford later joined him in a public acknowledgment of their error. Remnants of the movement can still be found today where good people remain trapped in the mind-control tragedy (see 2 Timothy 2:26).

292. What Is the Age of Accountability?

The age of accountability refers to the period in a child's life when he or she passes from innocence to being fully accountable for sin. The New Testament provides no scriptural teaching about the age of accountability. Our scriptural support for believing that all children who die are saved is 2 Samuel 12:22–23. David's infant son by Bathsheba did not live. David said, "While the child was yet alive, I fasted and wept; for I said, 'Who can tell whether the LORD will be gracious to me, that the child may live?' But now he is dead; why should I fast? Can I bring him back again? I shall go to him, but he shall not return to me." David knew with perfect faith that he would someday join his infant son in heaven.

Children die, sometimes tragically, because Adam sinned; yet they live again because Jesus died for them! The Jewish practices of bar mitzvah for boys and bat mitzvah for girls acknowledge the age of thirteen as the point when they become responsible for their own sins. The Talmud says this is the age when a young person's vows become legally binding.

293. What Are *Kronos* and *Kairos* Time?

The Greek language uses two separate words meaning "time," *kronos* and *kairos*, which in most English Bibles are translated the same. This is unfortunate as there is a subtle—but important—difference in the meaning of the two. *Kronos*, from which we get the word *chronological*, implies time as the passing of days. Since the length of our day is determined by rotation of the earth on its axis, time in the *kronos* concept is sequential.

Kairos has nothing to do with the calendar. It means time in the sense of an opportunity. A scriptural example would be the time that Jesus drew near to Jerusalem and wept when He saw the city. He grieved because the city was blind to the day of visitation of its Messiah and was opening itself to destruction because of it. He said, "[Your enemies] will not leave in you one stone upon another, because you did not know the time of your visitation" (Luke 19:44). Great blessings are lost because people fail to discern the signs of the times. In other words, a *kairos* moment may bring an opportunity that never returns. It can be a moment of destiny that never comes again. Someone described *kairos* this way: "The opportunity of a lifetime must be seized in the lifetime of the opportunity." *Kairos* is a time of heightened anticipation, expectation, exhilaration. Like the baseball player who watches for the ball to leave the pitcher's hand and prepares his swing, so is the alert Christian who seizes the *kairos* opportunity and obtains the blessing.

294. What Is Truth?

When Jesus stood condemned before Pontius Pilate, the Roman governor stared at Him and said, "What is truth?" (John 18:38). Jesus gave no answer, and we do not know if Pilate spoke in anger, with a sneer or out of depression. In many ways Pilate's question is still unanswered. Even now *truth* is a beautiful concept that is more easily identified by what it does than by what it is. Its apex is the statement of Jesus, "I am the way, the truth, and the life" (John 14:6). There is a power in truth that goes beyond our ability to identify. Truth liberates, instructs, protects, sustains.

As a precept, truth is a universal, cosmic principle balanced against falsehood in the same way that good is antithetical to evil or light to darkness. Like gravity or thermodynamics, truth has but one origin: God Almighty. It is a revelation of His character, creative power and being. Regardless of its particular topic, all truth comes from God the Creator. In other words, truth is "oneness" from which many other aspects may be seen.

In New Testament Greek the word for "truth" is *aletheia*; the Old Testament Hebrew word for "truth" is *emeth*. Both convey the same concepts as our English *reliability, firmness, constancy, durability*, etc. Whether Greek or Hebrew, Jesus is the physical display of ultimate, invisible truth. Jesus Christ is not only "full of grace and truth" but is "the truth" (John 1:14; 14:6). The Holy Spirit is "the Spirit of truth" (John 14:17; 15:26). God the Father is "the God of truth" (Psalm 31:5; Isaiah 65:16).

295. What Is Purgatory?

Purgatory is an imaginary place of pain and suffering believed by ancient pagans to be awaiting all who die. After sufficient purging (hence, the name), sinners can be released to heaven. Others who cannot be adequately purged descend to hell. The idea has no support from either ancient Jewish or New Testament writers. The idea of purgatory was introduced as a dogma of faith in the Roman Catholic Church by the Council of Florence (1431–1449) and was officially made part of Catholic doctrine at the Council of Trent (1545–1563). The doctrine offers "a final cleansing of human imperfections before one is able to enter the joy of heaven." Prayers and masses said for the dead help with one's early release. The doctrine insinuates that human suffering can be a just substitute for the atoning work of Jesus Christ. Early Catholics knew nothing about it. The idea is a leftover from pre-Christian days and should be ignored.

296. What about Angels?

Angels are spiritual, created beings identified as holy and unholy. Scripture indicates that originally there were three archangels: Michael, Gabriel and Lucifer. Michael was a warrior, Gabriel a messenger and Lucifer a worshiper. Under these three, there appear to be three series of ranks and responsibilities of other angels. With Lucifer's fall, his third of the angels transgressed with him: "The great dragon was cast out, that serpent of old, called the Devil and Satan, who deceives the whole world; he was cast to the earth, and his angels were cast out with him" (Revelation 12:9). Scripture tells us nothing about how sin gained access to them.

The Bible gives accounts of the Lord Himself appearing to individuals as an angel. This is the case with the first use of the word *angel* in the Bible. In Genesis 16:7 we read that the "angel of the LORD" rescued Sarah's maid, Hagar, from death in the desert. "[Hagar] called the name of the LORD who spoke to her, You-Are-the-God-Who-Sees" (verse 13). In other instances, God uses His servant angels to rescue as well as send messages. The Bible calls them "ministering spirits," as the Hebrew letter explains: "Are they not all ministering spirits sent forth to minister for those who will inherit salvation?" (Hebrews 1:14).

Employing His holy angels, God stopped Abraham from killing Isaac; commanded Balaam, the false prophet, to bless Israel; brought food to Elijah; killed seventy thousand Israelites; gave the prophet Zechariah foreknowledge of the future; told the elderly father of John the Baptist that his wife would conceive; opened the prison to let Peter escape; instructed Cornelius, the centurion, to send for Peter; appeared at the resurrection. We each have a guardian angel. They are to be acknowledged and appreciated but never to be worshiped (see Revelation 19:10).

297. Who Is the Antichrist?

According to Scripture, the Antichrist—who is a man possessed by a powerful evil spirit—will appear during a time of worldwide chaos, rescue humanity from its pain, and establish a reign of universal peace. In the beginning he will pose as a man of compassion and power but internally be an instrument of Satan. The Antichrist will mimic the true Messiah and be accepted by a world eager for calm and safety.

It is significant that this same concept also appears in Islam in great detail where he is called the "Mahdi." During his reign, Islam will be established as the only world power. There are many other parallels between the New Testament's description of the Antichrist and the Muslim Mahdi. The term *Antichrist* occurs five times in 1 and 2 John, once in plural form and four times in the singular. This is typical of the demonic realm in which individual spirits are both singular and plural (see Luke 4:34), and is a copy of God Almighty who is both One and triune (see Genesis 1:26).

According to Christian understanding, Jesus the Messiah will appear in glory at His Second Coming, face the Antichrist and defeat him. Islam teaches that Jesus will appear and submit to the Mahdi. "Every spirit that does not confess that Jesus Christ has come in the flesh is not of God. And this is the spirit of the Antichrist, which you have heard was coming, and is now already in the world" (1 John 4:3; see 1 John 2:18, 22; 2 John 7). Will the Antichrist rise from Islam? Many believe that he will.

298. What Is the Great Tribulation?

In Matthew 24, Jesus tells of a time of violence, hatred and persecution of believers coming on the earth when numerous false prophets and false Christs will deceive many. Parallel to this, Revelation 13 tells about the reign of the Antichrist and his persecution of the saints who refuse to worship him or receive his mark. Jesus describes worldwide conditions at that time: "For then there will be great tribulation, such as has not been since the beginning of the world until this time, no, nor ever shall be. And unless those days were shortened, no flesh would be saved; but for the elect's sake those days will be shortened" (Matthew 24:21–22). Thankfully, this period of the Tribulation will be cut short for the sake of the elect. The Greek word is *koloboo*, which means literally "to amputate."

But Jesus said this will also happen: "Immediately after the tribulation of those days" the very "powers of the heavens will be shaken." At that point, the Son of Man will come "on the clouds of heaven with power and great glory. And He will send His angels with a great sound of a trumpet, and they will gather together His elect from the four winds, from one end of heaven to the other" (Matthew 24:29–31), an event known as the Rapture. Still, much debate surrounds the topic of whether or not the Church will be present on earth during the Tribulation.

299. What Is the Rapture of the Church?

The concept of the "carrying away" or rapture of the Church is a debated topic and several conflicting theories have developed around it—principally concerning its timing as related to the Tribulation. The term *rapture* comes from a Latin word meaning "a carrying off, a transport or a snatching away." Paul explained that the Lord Himself will descend from heaven "with a shout, with the voice of the archangel, and with the trumpet of God. And the dead in Christ will rise first. Then we who are alive and remain shall be caught up together with them in the clouds to meet the Lord in the air. And thus we shall always be with the Lord" (1 Thessalonians 4:16–17).

The Rapture will involve an instantaneous transformation of our bodies to qualify them for life in the eternal realm: "The trumpet will sound, and the dead will be raised incorruptible, and we shall be changed. For this corruptible must put on incorruption, and this mortal must put on immortality" (1 Corinthians 15:52–53). John explained that when Christ appears we will be like him and see Him in His glory (see 1 John 3:2).

There are few—if any—prophetic teachings in the Old Testament about the Rapture, and this is probably the reason Paul referred to it as a "mystery." The reality of the Rapture should be a comforting doctrine full of hope; God wants us to "comfort one another with these words" (1 Thessalonians 4:18).

300. What Is Jesus' Second Coming and Thousand-Year Reign?

Three prominent opinions exist regarding the theology of Jesus' Second Coming and His thousand-year reign (see Ezekiel 38–39; Revelation 20:1–7). These are premillennial, postmillennial and amillennial. Each view presents a very different picture of world conditions during that period of time.

The *premillennialist* regards the Millennium as a literal event related to Jesus' Second Coming. Though Jesus' return is referred to some three hundred times in Scripture, the passages leave much room for discussion. The Second Coming or *Parousia*, which refers broadly to the grand scope of His presence or appearing, includes events in which Christ will be visibly present in His resurrected body.

Whereas His initial coming was quiet and lowly, Jesus said that His next coming will be a startling revelation of "power and great glory." He will first be witnessed "coming on the clouds of heaven" and sending His angels to gather His people (Matthew 24:30–31) to meet Him in the air (1 Thessalonians 4:17). At a subsequent event He will come from heaven riding "a white horse" with His armies as described in Revelation 19, after which believers in their glorified resurrection bodies will reign on the earth with Him for one thousand years.

When this thousand-year reign ends, Satan, who had been cast into the bottomless pit, will be loosed for a season to wage war against Christ and His saints. Satan will be defeated. Christ will raise all the unbelievers from the dead, consigning them, Satan and all his cohorts to eternal condemnation. At some juncture—either at the commencement of the Millennium or after Satan's defeat and condemnation—the heavens and the earth will be renewed.

The *postmillennialist* sees a continuous increase in the growth and progress of the Gospel throughout the whole earth, resulting in the conversion of multitudes to Jesus Christ. The Gospel impacts society in such measure that Christian standards become the world's norm, leading to peace and righteousness everywhere. At the end of this "millennial age" (more of a period of time and not an actual thousand years), Christ comes back to earth, both believers and unbelievers are raised, the final judgment takes place. This pleasant state becomes the new heaven and new earth, and the saved enter into a state of eternal happiness.

The *amillennialist* regards the biblical phrase *a thousand years* as a mere figure of speech and not necessarily a specific period of time. In this viewpoint, the Millennium is being fulfilled now in this present Church age and ends with Christ's return. At that time He will resurrect both believers and unbelievers—the first to eternal glory and the rest to eternal condemnation.

The grace of our Lord Jesus Christ be with you all. Amen.

Revelation 22:21

Index

Charles Carrin, D.D., was ordained in 1949 and devoted more than 65 years to consistent study of Scripture and Christian ministry. He received his education at the Atlanta Division, University of Georgia, Columbia Theological Seminary, and enhanced his knowledge by traveling much of the world. He made a dozen trips to the Middle East studying Old and New Testament history, visiting sites of the seven churches of Asia, and retracing the missionary journeys of the apostle Paul. As a young pastor he was taught that all miraculous gifts of the Spirit had been withdrawn; those parts of Scripture endorsing them were to be ignored. In his mature years he recognized the fallacy in that claim, accepted the full message of the New Testament, and received a powerful, life-changing baptism with the Spirit. This came through the "laying on of hands" by a Spirit-anointed prisoner in the Atlanta Federal Penitentiary. That event changed Dr. Carrin's life, and he has since ministered to the Body of Christ preaching Jesus' Ascension message: "You shall receive power when the Holy Spirit has come upon you."